T0275106

The Root Cause is a uniquely powerful, intelligent, and insight-filled book on the nature of leadership and the concepts, mindset, and willingness to change and adapt that great leaders need to be truly successful. Drawing on significant intellectual, artistic, and philosophical sources—from W. Edwards Deming to Colonel John R. Boyd, from Mark Twain to Roald Dahl and Albert Toffler—Norden surgically unpacks, builds, and supports a leadership mentality and practice that is a stunning wake-up call. Norden makes it clear that if leaders wish to make a positive difference in the world and leave a legacy, then they must learn to operate authentically and ethically, with integrity and compassion, to analyze dysfunctional systems dispassionately, determine root causes courageously, and adapt to changing realities as a matter of course, not necessity. Highly informative, practical, and far-reaching, *The Root Cause* is filled with invaluable and unforgettable leadership lessons.

> **—Gregg Ward**
> author of *The Respectful Leader*

The Root Cause is not another book about best practices or some new set of formulas to be plugged into an organization. Instead, it offers a different level of thinking and a rich source of unique ideas and metaphors to guide executives with an adventuresome mind and a clear sense of purpose. I enjoyed the reading, and I intend to read more of Norden's sources as well.

> **—Barry J. Schwartz, PhD**
> applied neuroscience consultant

The Root Cause is a phenomenal book that provides managers, directors, and especially C-suite executives a road map, context, and step-by-step instructions for optimizing business systems. Every professional needs to read this book. I can see a need for consultants trained in the application of these concepts helping companies to implement them, especially in alignment with major enterprise system development projects, like Enterprise Resource Planning, customer-facing Software-as-a-Service products, and other strategic initiatives. This book is essential reading for all ambitious leaders.

> **—Gabor Fulop**
> Director of IT Applications at a major US auto
> parts company

You get John Boyd and his ideas. You have put them down in such a way that a layman can understand how to utilize the information. I love the analogies; it makes it easier for some who may not be as technically proficient in theory. I like the interweaving of different schools of thought put together to gain a full picture. As you know, my dad used many references from many fields when he was putting his theories together. You are doing the same, which speaks well to your time and effort in this book. Too many people focus in one area and do not look to other areas to increase their ability to synthesize information. I am enjoying the reading but notice I keep going back and re-reading areas as I go through. To me a good book is one where you go back and start re-reading areas what you have already read.

—Mary Ellen Boyd
executrix of the Colonel John R. Boyd (USAF) estate

Hans Norden had an epiphany when, as a bank project manager, he consulted on situations where everyone agrees they have a big problem but no one admits to making a mistake because everyone is just doing their job. Norden saw up close the costly damage done by such systemic (and seemingly insoluble) interdepartmental challenges.

The Root Cause, the distillation of the author's years of consulting, study, and observation, is part field guide, part poetic inspiration, and part exhortation based on the polarity of persistent challenges and accessible opportunities in the modern organization.

Norden's clarion call to leaders is to recognize the limiting factors (what he calls "business gremlins"—the imaginary creatures that sabotage aircraft), overcome the gravitational pull of the Peter Principle, and embark on a journey of mind-bending adventure that fully embraces one's free will (in other words, seek to do something rather than simply be someone). *The Root Cause* takes the reader on a journey of meaning and substance, addressing the journey, vehicle, and destination in a comprehensive yet navigable way.

It spans the domains of philosophy, economics, behavioral science, sociology, military theory, physics, aviation, and literature and fuses all these disciplines with stories that define effective governance, making it a worthwhile read. Hans Norden challenges leaders to greatness with *The Root Cause*.

—Doug Kirkpatrick
partner at NuFocus Strategic Group and author of
Beyond Empowerment

The Root Cause is like a deep learning exercise on how the world works—people, business, and organizations. I greatly appreciate the focus on business as a system, the fundamental principles that drive and guide the system, and notable historic bodies of thought. They are woven together to give a deeper and more powerful foundation for the building of mental models to help understand business behavior and the itinerary planning for success that follows. It is a substantial read that can transform someone's way of being and doing in the world. Remarkable and valuable for anyone who wants to lead an epic journey.

—Brett Hoffstadt
Project Management Professional (PMP),
inventor of multiple aviation devices, and author
of *Success with Drones in Civil Engineering* and
How to Be a Rocket Scientist

THE ROOT CAUSE

RETHINK YOUR APPROACH TO SOLVING STUBBORN ENTERPRISE-WIDE PROBLEMS

HANS NORDEN

New York Chicago San Francisco Athens London Madrid
Mexico City Milan New Delhi Singapore Sydney Toronto

1 2 3 4 5 6 7 8 9   LCR   27 26 25 24 23 22

ISBN   978-1-264-27017-0
MHID   1-264-27017-8

e-ISBN   978-1-264-27460-4
e-MHID   1-264-27460-2

CEO Effectiveness™, CEO Dilemma™, The Missing Link in the Value Chain™, Mind Shift™, Business Gremlins™, Business Mechanics™, Business Governance™, Management Integration™, and Creating Authentic Solutions™ are trademarks of Johannes Norden.

Illustrations by Hans Norden

Library of Congress Cataloging-in-Publication Data

Names: Norden, Hans (Business consultant), author.
Title: The root cause : rethink your approach to solving stubborn enterprise-wide
    problems / Hans Norden.
Description: New York : McGraw Hill, [2022] | Includes bibliographical references
    and index.
Identifiers: LCCN 2021052640 (print) | LCCN 2021052641 (ebook) |
    ISBN 9781264270170 (hardback) | ISBN 9781264274604 (ebook)
Subjects: LCSH: Organizational change | Corporate turnarounds. |
    Executive coaching.
Classification: LCC HD58.8 .N67 2022 (print) | LCC HD58.8 (ebook) |
    DDC 658.4/06—dc23/eng/20211129
LC record available at https://lccn.loc.gov/2021052640
LC ebook record available at https://lccn.loc.gov/2021052641

To Cristina

Je ne sais où va mon chemin,
mais je marche mieux quand ma
main serre la tienne.[1]

—Alfred de Musset
French dramatist, poet, and novelist

CONTENTS

Acknowledgments   vii

Introduction   1

PART I
CEO EFFECTIVENESS

CHAPTER 1   **The Peter Principle at Work**   15

CHAPTER 2   **Top Three Business Gremlins That Sabotage CEO Effectiveness**   59

CHAPTER 3   **Four More Business Gremlins That Handicap Executive Performance**   93

CHAPTER 4   **Mind Shift: The Antidote to the Peter Principle**   127

PART II
BUSINESS MECHANICS

CHAPTER 5   **Stewardship and Craftsmanship**   161

CHAPTER 6   **The Journey—Function**   189

CHAPTER 7   **The Vehicle—Form**   205

CHAPTER 8   **The Destination—Itinerary for Arrival**   239

CHAPTER 9   **Business Governance**   269

CHAPTER 10   **Role of the Chief Executive**   319

Bibliography   341

Notes   345

Index   357

ACKNOWLEDGMENTS

would like to express my sincere appreciation to the following people for granting their permission to quote from their copyrighted material:

- Mary Ellen Boyd, executrix of the John R. Boyd estate, for permission to quote from her father's presentations
- The Joseph Campbell Foundation (jsf.org) for the use of quotations from Joseph Campbell's book *The Hero with a Thousand Faces*
- Robert Coram for the use of his description of Colonel John R. Boyd's so-called "To Be or to Do" speech from his book *Boyd: The Fighter Pilot Who Changed the Art of War*
- Professor Michael Porter for the use of the Value Chain Model as presented in his book *Competitive Advantage: Creating and Sustaining Superior Performance*
- Messrs. Doug Wiegmann and Scott Shappell to reproduce the HFACS model, Unsafe Acts Model and Swiss Cheese model from their book *A Human Error Approach to Aviation Accident Analysis: The Human Factors Analysis and Classification System*
- Donald J. Wheeler, PhD, to reproduce a section from his book *Understanding Variation, The Key to Managing Chaos*; Copyright © 2000 by SPC Press, Knoxville, Tennessee
- GOAL/QPC—courtesy Elaine Curtis—to quote from the article "On Learning and Systems that Facilitate It" by Russell L. Ackoff that was published in the 1996 Fall edition of *The Center for Quality of Management Journal* Vol. 5, No. 2

You give leaders a best practice solution, and you help them solve ONE symptom ONE time only. You teach them to eliminate the root cause of a systemic problem, and they will solve ALL its symptoms for the rest of their careers.

—Hans Norden

INTRODUCTION

Arm me with audacity.
—William Shakespeare
English Renaissance poet, playwright, and actor

*Nothing truly valuable arises from ambition
or from a mere sense of duty.*
—Dr. Albert Einstein
German-born theoretical physicist who
developed the theory of relativity

T *he Root Cause* is about change because nothing is more constant than change. Change is about decisions and events that disrupt a business system's integrity, but it is also about implementing solutions to restore system integrity and making course corrections in order to pursue a new strategic direction. Hence, change is the opposite of routine—business as usual.

Routine operations are the hallmark of a system. Therefore, maintaining, renovating, and innovating those processes is key to operational effectiveness and efficiency. Yet, over time, these initiatives tend to increase system complexity—making processes more interdependent and increasingly reliant on key resources they share for the fulfilment of their individual functions.

Complexity, in combination with unfolding new and unforeseen circumstances, produce systemic problems that manifest themselves throughout the enterprise. Fixing these problems is a unique executive responsibility because every lower ranking hierarchical leader will experience a conflict of interest with their peers when they try to solve the issues on their own. The main source of conflict lies in people's fear that the burden of change will not be shared equally among all departments involved—a state of affairs that higher level leaders must acknowledge and address.

Systemic problems tend to be stubborn because their root cause(s) are not obvious; it takes a deliberate and concerted effort to diagnose them and to create authentic solutions. Unfortunately, only a few CEOs deliberately choose to initiate and sustain such an effort. The majority of CEOs tend to favor investing in the same familiar solutions that caused the systemic problems in the first place—because they find them prudent, safer, and easily defensible because others have already opted for the same solution. This is precisely why systemic problems are so costly and why they can linger in the system for such a long period of time. Nothing changes until someone intervenes with innovative and effective solutions, or until these problems unleash a destructive chain reaction—whichever comes first.

WHO SHOULD READ
THE ROOT CAUSE AND WHY?

It is often said than anyone can become a leader—whether they are born or made. But not every leader can change the business system. Only those who are authorized to approve such initiatives can. Therefore, people without authority to make changes to the system cannot be held responsible when the system produces unintended and unwanted results. Without authority, there can be no responsibility!

The Root Cause is intended for current and future chief executives. After all, the CEO position confers the right to exercise ultimate authority and thus the duty to assume ultimate responsibility for the business's success and failure. Because systemic problems are difficult to solve without a CEO's active involvement, these kinds of problems are not just business problems, they are a CEO's personal problems. Failing to solve systemic problems adequately and in a timely fashion negatively affects a CEO's performance review, and can possibly lead to his or her dismissal. Indeed, studies show that board members have grown increasingly intolerant of underperforming chief executives.[2]

Instead of promoting a new tool, more advanced technology, or a best practice, *The Root Cause* advocates that leaders adopt a new level of thinking. The rationale behind this approach is found in the universal law of cause and effect, in which thought represents the level of cause, and real-life experiences represent the level of effect. If all you get are unintended and unwanted outcomes, you'll have to change your level of thinking. There is no other way.

The Root Cause is also intended for other C-suite executives, consultants, coaches, advisors, counselors, and board members who assist CEOs in their decision-making processes. In order for them to be effective, they will have to rise to the chief executive's new level of thinking. Their thinking must be aligned, because opposing thoughts combined with a conviction of their validity will inevitably lead to unnecessary friction and conflict with little chance of reconciliation or compromise.

The Root Cause is also intended for educators of the aforementioned categories of people, because they are instrumental in shaping their students' minds and thus their perception of good business practices and how they should go about creating authentic solutions for stubborn systemic problems.

Last but not least, *The Root Cause* is also intended for venture capitalists and angel investors. After all, their understanding of the importance of motivating executives responsible for the businesses in which they invest to rethink their approach to solving stubborn enterprise-wide problems, improves these financiers' influence on increasing the return on their investment.

Willingness to Make a Difference

In addition to possessing the necessary enterprise-wide authority, organizational change requires a personal sense of purpose, as well as a vision for developing the best possible system. If you're a CEO, this implies that you'll have to decide what you want your legacy to be. You'll have to make a conscious decision on who you want to be, the values you espouse, behaviors you'll display, and how you will inspire others as their chief executive.

To my knowledge, nobody explained this critical decision better than the late Colonel John R. Boyd, USAF, who was known for his "To Be or to Do" speech:

Tiger, one day you will come to a fork in the road, and you're going to have to make a decision about which direction you want to go. If you go that way you can Be somebody. You will have to make compromises and you will have to turn your back on your friends. But you will be a member of the club, and you will get promoted and you will get good assignments.

Or you can go that way and you can Do something—something for your country and for your organization and for yourself. If you decide you want to Do something, you may not get promoted and you may not get the good assignments and you certainly will not be a favorite of your superiors. But you won't have to compromise yourself. You will be true to your friends and to yourself. And your work might make a difference. To Be somebody or to Do something. In life there is often a roll call. That's when you will need to make a decision. To Be or to Do. Which way will You go?[3]

The Root Cause is intended for anyone in a position of authority, intellectually curious about systemic problems, and inspired to make a laudable difference in creating authentic solutions for their organization, their country, the planet, their fellow man, and ultimately for themselves. And, in the end, by choosing to Do something you will create a legacy worth remembering.

THE QUESTIONS THAT MUST BE ANSWERED

Dr. W. Edwards Deming, America's eminent scholar on quality management, said: "There is an excuse for ignorance, but there is no way to avoid the consequences." To avoid the consequences of ignorance, it's important to answer the following questions:

- Why do executives feel threatened by complexity?
- Why is promotion in rank causing occupational incompetence (the Peter Principle)? (See Chapter 1.)
- What does it take to improve business performance sustainably?

- Which prerequisites and critical success factors need to be satisfied first in order to raise bottom-line results consistently and sustainably, while being respectful of humanity?
- Why do unfolding new and unforeseen circumstances erode CEO effectiveness?
- How can we experience gigantic problems when everyone is just doing their job?
- Why are authentic solutions for systemic problems so hard to pursue, get adopted, and be implemented?

I think the answers to these questions, and many more, should be found in this well-known quotation attributed to Dr. Albert Einstein: *"The problems that exist in the world today cannot be solved by the level of thinking that created them."*

In other words, our current level of thinking is ill-equipped to successfully explain a business system's actual state in terms of its many cause-and-effect relationships. Consequently, we need to embrace a new or up-to-date level of thinking because, as Eckhart Tolle explained in his book *The Power of Now*, "Once you understand the root of the dysfunction, you do not need to explore its countless manifestations."[4]

RECURRING AND PERSISTING PROBLEMS

The root of the dysfunction manifests itself as a chain of effects, such as disappointing top-line results, poor bottom-line results, low employee engagement, the war for talent, a lack of creativity and innovation for self-renewal and reinvention, insufficient differentiation and sustainability, eroding profit margins and an ensuing attrition price war with competitors, a disregard for generating long-term value, loss of integrity (which reduces credibility), erosion of leaders' trustworthiness, inadequate social responsibility, absence of environmental consciousness, disrespect for humanity, ethics violations, fraud, executive burnout, and a high CEO turnover rate.

Executives who describe their work experience as "putting out fires" and "up to their elbows in alligators" are, in fact, expressing frustration with these stubborn symptoms of a failing system. Whenever they think they solved one symptom, another one pops up somewhere else, or the same one is so persistent that it keeps coming back. It feels similar to playing the arcade game Whac-A-Mole.

As if being preoccupied with the countless manifestations of unknown root causes is not enough, executive performance is measured by the person's ability to improve financial performance year over year. Executives are thus faced with two challenges. First, solve the current level of underperformance. Second, work even harder to reach new targets. I would posit that there's a third challenge that's even more important: changing one's current level of thinking about business in order to solve systemic problems.

The truth is that the lead time for showing some initial results from a business system reorganization is close to a chief executive officer's average tenure. In other words, there is little time left for making adjustments and changes when the reorganization is not 100 percent successful the first time around. In addition, board members' and shareholders' tolerance for underperformance has dropped. Consequently, the incentive for being creative and innovative is, to say the least, not overwhelming, and yet there seems to be consensus among business leaders worldwide[5] that creativity is the answer to solving system complexity. Now, ask yourself, how can creativity be successfully applied when the situation is not fully understood? Be that as it may, the gauntlet has been thrown down for every current and future CEO.

Are you up for the challenge?

MENTAL PROGRAMMING

Scientists have proven that we can only "see" what our brain is capable of accepting as valid and true—yet our eyes see more than the brain registers. That means our perception of the world depends on our beliefs, assumptions, ideas, concepts, theories, principles, values, or techniques we use to explain our experience. Therefore, we should be able to solve stubborn systemic problems by opening our minds to any previously unknown or rejected beliefs, assumptions, ideas, concepts, theories, principles, values, or techniques. These mental constructs contain the potential for unlocking the appropriate cause-and-effect relationships that—eventually—allow us to solve stubborn systemic problems.

Reality is what it is and as it is. We can only change ourselves—our orientation and with that our perception of reality. Because not everything we perceive is true, perception is just a belief, which is subject to change.

Therefore, although we often cannot change the reality of a situation or condition, we can change our experience, perception, or orientation toward a specific situation or condition. The ability to change one's orientation is the source of ingenuity, resourcefulness, originality, and authenticity, which is instrumental in finding solutions where we couldn't possibly see any before. This is also an interesting explanation for the biblical dictum of turning the other cheek[6]—to change one's perspective and look at it from a different angle or with a different mindset. And that is how effective executives distinguish themselves from others with the same know-how.

Our mental programming or orientation informs us about phenomena that we believe to be possible, valid, and true. Rather than progressing in a linear and continuous way through education and life experience, our curiosity needs to open up our minds toward the possibility of new approaches to understanding the nature and character of a complex business system. For example, although the common dominant level of thinking informs us that *making money* is the purpose of a business, you might become compelled to adopt a new level of thinking that believes the purpose of a business is to become the *obvious choice supplier* to members of an intended target audience.

Please stop and think: From which people or businesses do you think the money you intend to make will originate? And with whom would those decision makers prefer doing business—someone who enters the relationship just for the money or someone who takes pride in solving real human needs? Which relationship promises to be more cost-effective and sustainable in the long run? Is your answer at odds or aligned with the common dominant level of thinking?

Many in the scientific community consider the transformation of how we now regard consciousness—and its dramatic consequences for our understanding of reality—a paradigm shift in their thinking. The challenge posed by these paradigm shifts in the way we think is that they do not allow for a cafeteria menu from which to pick and choose according to one's mood or liking; there is no middle ground. Is that why we are so resistant to change?

DESCRIBING VERSUS PRESCRIBING

Most forms of instruction and advice on business practices, and on leadership specifically, *prescribe* how specific symptoms or effects should be addressed. In simplest terms, if this is your pain, then here is your medicine. Consequently, there is an endless supply of out-of-the-box solutions, off-the-shelf technology, universal tools, expert opinions, and best practices that claim instant success. If one solution does not work, you just try harder or try something else.

This rather simplistic trial-and-error perspective on solving symptoms stands in stark contrast with the medical field that admonishes its practitioners with the expression *"Prescription without diagnosis is malpractice."*

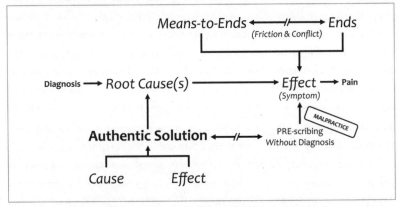

Figure I.1: Need for Diagnosis of Root Cause(s)

Misalignment between means-to-ends and ends causes friction and conflict, which become painfully manifest in various specific effects or symptoms of a systemic problem. Effects can only be treated successfully after diagnosis of its root cause(s). Treatment of symptoms—without knowing their root cause(s)—is malpractice. Root causes can only be solved with solutions which efficacy is grounded in proven cause-and-effect relationships, thus predicting to restore integrity to the system. That is what distinguishes them as authentic solutions.

The purpose of this book is to help executive decision makers diagnose systemic problems by *describing* cause-and-effect relationships between their decisions regarding the design, organization or structure, implementation or operation, maintenance, and management of a business system and its performance. After all, without recognizing the many symptoms or effects as manifestations of one and the same systemic problem, and without awareness of its root cause(s) that are undermining a system's capability and capacity, there is no guarantee for creating authentic solutions for systemic problems. That is why systemic problems persist and recur, which undermine business performance.

Consequently, executives who fail to recognize the cause-and-effect relationship between their decisions and the occurrence of systemic problems will also fail to recognize the cause-and-effect relationship between a root cause and its authentic solution. The challenge to a decision maker is not in finding a solution—and in assessing its efficacy, elegance, simplicity, complexity, or the eloquence with which it is proposed—but identifying the right principle, method, theory, or premise that sustains and facilitates the cause-and-effect relationship.

Decision makers tend to settle conclusively on either principles or methods, and/or on specific outcomes. Applying the same method as before is very likely to produce the same outcome as before. In addition, a single method cannot realize two mutually exclusive outcomes—for example, achieving maximum operational efficiency and achieving maximum customer need satisfaction. Each outcome requires its own specific method to instigate the appropriate cause-and-effect relationship.

MAKING A DIFFERENCE

In order to explain why trade-off decisions between efficiency measures and effectiveness measures are necessary, this book provides a methodology—*business mechanics*—for understanding how a business functions as a singular, unique, integrated, and open system.

This approach is distinctively different from the methods promoted by mainstream business education institutions, including centers for executive development. Their approach to understanding how a business functions is to study each of the nine constituting links of the value chain separately and in isolation of each other (see Figure 1.1 in Chapter 1), and the purpose of the business system as an organic whole. Their aim is to create material experts for every silo of specialized knowledge within the value chain in order to optimize the efficiency of their silo of specialized knowledge separately and in isolation of every other silo of specialized knowledge.

The conflict between these two approaches is explained by Colonel Boyd, who wrote: "According to Gödel's Incompleteness Theorems, Heisenberg's Uncertainty Principle, and the Second Law of Thermodynamics one cannot determine the character or nature of a system within itself. Moreover, attempts to do so lead to confusion and disorder."[7] In other words, the principles or methods that explain cause-and-effect relationships within a separate part of the system cannot explain cause-and-effect relationships within the system as an organic whole. More specifically, the fact that a course of action is successful for the part does not imply that it will be equally beneficial for the system as an integrated whole as well.

Interestingly, executive decision makers from around the world expressed their experience of confusion and disorder because of system complexity in an IBM report called "Capitalizing on Complexity: Insights from the 2010 IBM Global CEO Study." The obstacle standing between a CEO's experience of confusion and disorder and solving systemic problems is the individual's own mental programming—in other words, the principles and methods she or he accepts because of a belief that they are valid and true and those she or he rejects because of a belief that they are invalid and untrue.

Furthermore, there are no better sales techniques, nor are there superior methods for presenting, explaining, demonstrating, or convincing a CEO of the validity of an authentic solution when the deciding CEO rejects the validity of its organizing principle. I can explain it to them, but I cannot understand it for them. Consequently, the curse and the redemption are one and the same; the decision makers' (un)willingness to change their minds!

Exercising Free Will

Deming said that 94 percent[8-9] of all results are systemic in nature, which means they are inherent to the value chain's design, organization or structure, implementation or operation, maintenance, and management. The CEO must assume ultimate responsibility for the success and failure of the entire value chain because she or he has the right to exercise ultimate authority with his or her decisions to change the value chain. Ultimately, CEOs cannot insulate themselves from the consequences of their actions or inactions.

Executives who use their free will in order to change their mental programming distinguish themselves from others with the same know-how. They are the ones who make a positive difference in the lives of many people and leave behind a great legacy.

Historically, such dramatic changes in one's personal beliefs have typically been the result of a hero's journey (as described in Joseph Campbell's well-known book *The Hero with a Thousand Faces*), which provides the familiar framework for a wide range of stories about human maturation. The hero goes on an adventure and—in a crucial watershed moment—wins a victory, which transforms forever his or her perception of life and the three-dimensional world in which we live.

The Root Cause is intended to provide such a watershed moment for its readers. Expect to do battle with new and unfamiliar principles that—when you allow them—will transform your level of thinking about business. At times, you may feel confused and irritated when challenged to learn, unlearn, and relearn the simple relationships between cause and effect and means and ends. But you can take solace in knowing that only a new level of thinking can help you create authentic solutions for stubborn systemic problems.

NOTE TO THE READER

The following legends are used for the illustrations in *The Root Cause*.

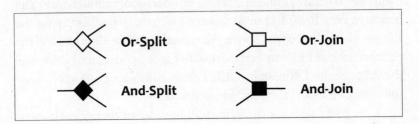

Or-Split   Or-Join

And-Split   And-Join

PART I

CEO Effectiveness

*The person who knows how will always have a job;
the person who knows why will always be the boss.*

–John C. Maxwell
American pastor and *New York Times*
bestselling business author

CHAPTER 1

The Peter Principle at Work

A problem cannot be solved if you don't know what it is! Even if it was already solved, you'd still have the problem because you wouldn't recognize that it has been solved. Who can see that a problem has been solved if he thinks the problem is something else?

—Lesson 79
from *A Course in Miracles,*
The Foundation for Inner Peace

Chief executive officers differentiate themselves from their peers by their capability to disprove Dr. Laurence J. Peter's Principle, which states, "In a hierarchy every employee tends to rise to his level of incompetence."[1] In other words, the Peter Principle suggests there is a cause-and-effect relationship between promotion and occupational incompetence.

Business leaders seem obsessed with growing their business, which is generally understood to mean increasing the physical size of the business, by expanding its modes of doing business, enlarging its geographical reach, and above all increasing its bottom-line results. Because leading a larger business typically coincides with the insertion of additional hierarchical levels of management, the distance between executive decision makers and frontline operators increases in size too. Unfortunately, this growing divide blurs the cause-and-effect relationships between executive decisions and underperformance, which manifests as bureaucratic ineffectiveness, internal friction and conflict, waste, mistakes, accidents, violations, erosion of profit margins, and ultimately business system collapse.

Studies[2] show that executive decisions can create latent conditions that in combination with relatively insignificant active failures can unleash a chain reaction that inflicts serious harm on the business system. Despite the existence of a time lag between a cause and the manifestation of its effect—which makes this relationship less obvious—business problems pose immediate personal challenges to the occupational competence of a CEO, or, more accurately, the soundness of his or her judgment and decision-making skills.

THE ACHILLES' HEEL OF EXECUTIVE LEADERSHIP

Occupational competence refers to an individual being adequately able, suitable, or well qualified physically, morally, intellectually, and legally for the successful execution of a specific task. This includes a personal character trait of "intellectual integrity,"[3] which refers to one's willingness to stand up for what one thinks is right and wrong. This trait reveals itself by:

- Refusing to defend whatever view is popular or expedient.
- Pursuing the truth by figuring things out for oneself and forming one's own opinion.
- Standing up for what one thinks is true precisely because one thinks it's true. (Legality does not equate to morality; something illegal is not by definition morally wrong, whereas what is morally right might not always be legal.)
- Being open to the truth just because it is the truth. This requires a willingness to admit that one is wrong; intellectual integrity is not simply a matter of being consistent or steadfast.

Occupational competence is important for both routine operations and change initiatives that are aimed at developing a business's operational processes and adapting those processes to accommodate demands from new and unforeseen circumstances when operating in fluid and dynamic environments.

The need for occupational competence within a competitive environment is well expressed by Colonel John R. Boyd, who said, "He who can handle the quickest rate of change survives."[4] Failure to compel a business system to become the best possible fit for the challenges ahead, to shape and adapt its character and nature with flexibility and speed—agility—is the Achilles' heel of executive leadership.

Business as Usual versus Change

During its life cycle, every business experiences periods of relative calm, when everything functions like clockwork. Managing a business under normal operating conditions is then similar to flying an aircraft on autopilot. Note that the autopilot computer is only capable of maintaining heading, altitude, and airspeed by adjusting the flight controls in order to counteract disturbances in the aircraft's center of gravity caused by people walking up and down the aisle and to compensate for disturbances caused by air turbulence, and cross- or head- and tailwinds.[5] Whenever routine or normal operating conditions are disrupted by new and unforeseen events, the executive in command needs to disengage the autopilot and take manual control. From that point forward, the business functions under special operating conditions, which is called change. Change is thus the opposite of routine.

Therefore, performing more and better of the same routine operations cannot make a business system behave differently, produce different outcomes, accommodate demands from new and unforeseen circumstances, or pursue a new strategic direction. Real change requires that a business system possess new and different capabilities to achieve the purpose for which the system was originally intended—its raison d'être. This requires adjustments, additions, upgrades, updates, replacements, removal, renewal, renovation, or innovation of the system's current processes, their capability, and capacity.

VALUE CHAIN AND ORGANIZATIONAL CHART

Whenever we talk about routine operations (or working under normal operating conditions) and the object of change initiatives (or working under special operating conditions), we refer to functions that a business system is intended to perform day after day.

Professor Michael Porter[6] identified nine generic business functions, which he illustrated succinctly with his creation of the Value Chain model, shown in Figure 1.1.

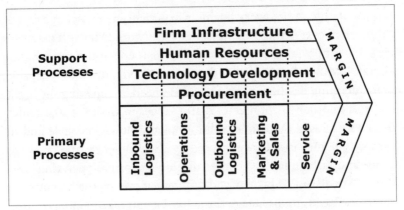

Figure 1.1: The Value Chain Model by Michael Porter

The value chain separates a business system into its component parts for the purpose of studying activities that each part performs individually and in interaction with each other.

These nine functions need to work in concert in order for the value chain as an integrated whole to generate a profit margin.[7] Porter has shown that a superior value chain will generate a superior profit margin. Let's have a closer look at the functions of a value chain:

1. **Inbound Logistics.** Relationships with suppliers, including all activities necessary to receive, store, and disseminate inputs
2. **Operations.** All activities necessary to transform inputs into outputs (products and services)
3. **Outbound Logistics.** All activities necessary to collect, store, and distribute the output from operations

4. **Marketing and Sales.** Activities that inform buyers about products and services, induce buyers to purchase them, and facilitate their purchase

5. **Service.** All activities necessary to keep the product or service working effectively for the buyer or user after it is sold and delivered

6. **Procurement.** The acquisition of inputs, or resources, for the firm

7. **Technology Development.** Equipment, hardware, software, procedures, and technical knowledge brought to bear in the firm's transformation of inputs into outputs

8. **Human Resources.** All activities involved in recruiting, hiring, training, developing, compensating, and (if necessary) dismissing or laying off personnel

9. **Firm Infrastructure.** All activities that serve the company's needs and tie its various parts together; consists of functions or departments such as accounting, legal, finance, planning, public affairs, government relations, quality assurance, and general management

Primary versus Support Processes

It's easy to understand how the first five functions contribute directly to the realization of the purpose for which the system was intended. They are the ones that, so to speak, bring home the bacon. Therefore, they are called "primary business functions."

Originally, management theorists identified labor, raw materials, and capital as the only requisite organizational facilities for the proper functioning of core or primary business functions. However, globalization, liberalization, deregulation, computerization, the advent of the information age, advances in science, and developments in many other diverse aspects of life have caused business environments to become more dynamic and complex. As a result, the list of requisite organizational facilities now includes:

- **Organization.** Administering tasks and responsibilities to business units
- **Personnel.** Recruitment, deployment, and training of employees (previously called labor)

- **Administrative Organization.** Procedures, guidelines, rules, and regulations
- **Finance.** Financing and budgeting
- **Information.** Data, data processing, and information systems
- **Legal Issues.** Providing a legal framework for entering into contractual obligations and the protection of assets, including intellectual property and taxes, and directors and officers (D&O) liability insurance and indemnity arrangements
- **Technology and Tools.** Equipment or means of production (previously part of capital)
- **Housing.** Location and selection of sites, buildings, and facilities

Because all business functions are dependent on timely delivery of an adequate amount of these organizational facilities, responsibility for supplying these facilities is centralized within dedicated business functions numbers six to nine. Subsequently, they are called "secondary" or "support business functions" because their contribution to the realization of the value chain's purpose is indirect.

The Value Chain as an Input → Process → Output (IPO) Model

The value chain can be understood as an input–process–output model, which is depicted in Figure 1.2. Generating specific output variables—products and services—requires specific input variables, such as capital, raw materials, data, knowledge, material expertise, moral guidance, and skills. And transforming these input variables into the intended output variables requires a specific transformation process. This process tends to be proprietary because it determines to a large extent the utility that buyers and users obtain from their relationship with a business. In other words, differences in the transformation of identical or similar input variables are reflected in a business's brand identity, which account for differences in a user's brand experience.

Within the value chain, each business function has its own objective that contributes to and supports the realization of the overall purpose of the value chain. Consequently, every process within each business function, and every business function in its own right, is

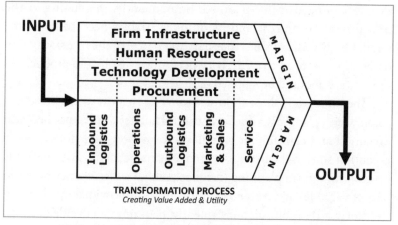

Figure 1.2: The Input → Process → Output Model

The value chain is a representation of the process by which input variables are transformed into output variables. Therefore, the value chain's design, organization or structure, implementation or operation, maintenance, and management are a function of its competitive advantage.

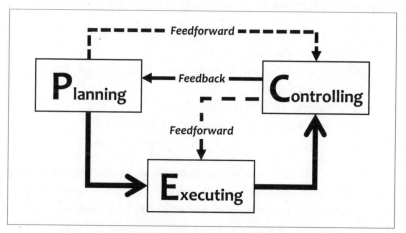

Figure 1.3: The Cybernetic Process or Governance

The cybernetic process of a business system is a methodology for humans and some machines to respond to or make adjustments to the value chain's design, organization or structure, implementation or operation, maintenance, and management , based upon input from their internal and external environment.

subjected to the **P**(lanning) **E**(xecuting) **C**(ontrolling) cycle for their proper governance (see Figure 1.3).

In order to ensure an effective and efficient transformation of input variables into output variables, this transformation process—

execution—needs to be planned. Subsequently, the quality of the transformation process and its output variables need to be monitored. Quality assurance is thus part and parcel of the transformation process, as opposed to an activity performed just before products or services are about to be shipped or delivered.

Therefore, the role of control is to verify that execution behaviors comply with planning. Whenever control notices a difference between execution and planning, it provides information—feedforward—to execution so that it can adjust or change its behavior. Alternatively, control can inform planning (feedback) about a discrepancy between output variables and a standard measurement provided by planning (feedforward) to control. Subsequently, planning can decide to adjust or change the information they provide to execution, or control for the next PEC-cycle. That's how continual improvement takes place.

Control Variables

Moreover, each transformation process has the same control variables:

- **M**oney (for developing process capability and capacity, which includes people)
- **O**rganization (for structuring the component parts into an organic whole)
- **T**ime (duration of throughput)
- **I**nformation (quantitative and qualitative data)
- **Q**uality (of processes and products and services)

Of these MOTIQ variables, money, time, and quality form the so-called Devil's Triangle, because a problem with one can be resolved with either one of the other two. For example, when you are short on time, you can either ask for more money to hire more resources or lower the quality standard. Alternatively, when quality is below par, you can either ask for more money to hire better expertise or ask for more time to get it right. And, when money is running out, you can either lower quality standards or spread out the project over a longer time period.

Good business governance requires that planning and control are performed on a higher hierarchical level than execution, and that planning and control are separated from each other in order to avoid conflicts of interest. We have now entered into the realm of the organizational chart.

Translation of a Value Chain into an Organizational Chart

The purpose of an organizational chart is to provide a visual representation of the delegation of authority, and thereby the assignment of responsibility, to hierarchical leaders by their chief executive. Note that planning and controlling processes must be conducted on a higher hierarchical level than any executing processes in order to avoid conflict regarding authority and responsibility. Hierarchical levels reflect the authority and responsibility of individual managers within the business system. The chart displays several principles:

- **Unity of Command.** Every employee is only responsible to one superior.
- **Span of Control.** The number of people reporting to a hierarchical leader.
- **Unbroken Line of Command.** The line of command from shop floor to executive suite is unbroken.

Remember that processes determine the behavior of a business and thus how customers experience their relationship with that business. There is a simple methodology for assigning authority to individual leaders and thus responsibility for the proper execution of a specific process or function—in other words, the translation of the value chain into an organizational chart. Note that authority can be delegated, but responsibility cannot! Without authority to make changes to a process, no one can be held responsible for the actual performance of that process, except for mistakes and errors due to personal negligence.

When we take inventory of all tasks that need to be performed within the value chain—creating a work breakdown structure—we can identify tasks that are similar in nature and combine them into an activity, as shown in Figure 1.4. For example, the tasks of answering the phone, looking up tracking numbers in the computer, and informing clients about the status of their orders can be combined into a single activity called *order tracking*.

Next, when we identify similar activities such as order fulfillment and warranty claims, we can combine those into a job with the title customer service manager.

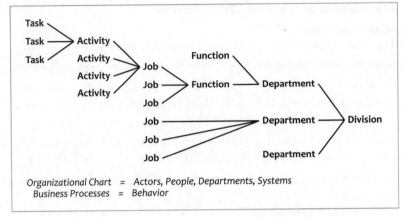

Figure 1.4: Translating Processes into an Organizational Chart

A system is a network of *functions* or *activities* within an organization that work together for the *aim* of the organization. Formal organizational charts are derived from process maps. Identifying business processes and translating them into an organizational chart belongs to the realm of information analysis.

Next, by combining similar jobs such as sales manager and branch network support manager, we can create the sales department.

Finally, similar departments such as marketing and PR and advertising can be combined into the business function of sales and marketing. Note that in small organizations some jobs are combined directly into a business function, such as human resources, without the formation of a separate department.

BUSINESS AS AN ORGANISM INSTEAD OF A MECHANISM

Note the difference in perception of a business, and therefore its value chain, as an organism or as a mechanism. The specifications and design of individual component parts that constitute a value chain are less important than their intricately interdependent and synergistic relationships, which determine a business's character and nature as an organic whole.

Consequently, performance, systemic problems, change, and authentic solutions refer to a business's behavior—the interaction among the system's component parts, or brand identity—rather than any of its separate component parts. Therefore, the significance of change is the ability to influence the behavior of one or more individual processes or functions by either:

1. **Disrupting the integrity of normal operating conditions.**
   The root cause consists of new and unforeseen circumstances that challenge the value chain's capability and or capacity—the complexity and interdependency of its processes—to adjust or adapt. These challenges are systemic in nature because they are not directly attributable to the action or inaction of a single individual or a group of people. Alternatively, implementing a new strategic direction also disrupts the integrity of normal operating conditions.
2. **Restoring integrity to normal operating conditions.**
   The root cause consists, in this case, of an initiative to solve systemic problems within the value chain.

Within the context of solving systemic problems, the word "change" takes on a specific connotation. Change is not used for replacement of a broken resource for a new one of the same kind and type, such as replacing a printer or exchanging its empty toner cartridge for a full one.

However, replacing an old-fashioned photocopy machine for a multifunctional one constitutes real change. Once manufacturers realized that a photocopier is actually three separate machines in one—a scanner, a printer, and a copier—they unlocked those facilities and made each accessible separately by attaching the multifunctional copier to the information technology (IT) network. While this sounds logical and hardly consequential, for businesses with a facilities management department, it is a big deal. After all, no self-respecting IT department will allow a third party to attach an unfamiliar piece of hardware to their network without their explicit approval. They will cite concerns for security, fear of incompatibility, and undermining management of hardware and software (ITIL).[8] In addition, users will perceive the multifunctional copier as IT equipment and thus call the IT helpdesk for all their problems and inquiries. With this change, facilities management will have to relinquish their responsibilities for photocopiers to the IT department. For the facilities management department of a large corporation, that impacts their annual budget and the jobs of many of its employees.

A centrally located, high-capacity printer provides users with additional functionalities, and utilizes more of the overall available printing and copying capacity within the office. Because most "copiers" are leased on the basis of a prorated number of prints per year, this change reduces the overall cost per page. In addition, the multifunctional copier makes regular scanners and printers redundant, which cuts annual expenses for their maintenance, service-level agreements, and the ordering and stocking of many different sizes of toner and ink cartridges.

Thus, change affects the flow of information through the individual links of a value chain, which in turn influences the behavior of their processes and people. Good flow, or operator-friendly processes, contributes to employees' job satisfaction, whereas poor flow, or operator-unfriendly processes, detracts from employees' job satisfaction.

IDENTIFYING SYSTEMIC PROBLEMS

Throughout this book I'll compare a business to a vehicle, especially an aircraft. Earlier we saw how an executive needs to disengage the autopilot when an event disrupts normal operating conditions. What does this mean?

Under normal operating conditions, the outcome of a formal business process should be predictable. After all, the idea behind formulating (standardized) work processes is to systematize necessary activities so they can be repeated time and again with the same level of effectiveness and efficiency. Today, many business processes have been automated and function without the intervention of a human being.

Whenever normal operating conditions are disrupted, we experience a discrepancy between either the execution of an activity or the results generated by that activity and the norms for which management is aiming. This discrepancy between results and aim is called *the problem*. We recognize two categories of problems:

1. **Effectiveness problems.** Problems related to the outcome of a process, product, or service. Shortcomings in product quality affect customers directly and therefore deserve priority over other problems. After all, adverse customer experiences translate into bad publicity, which undermines brand identity, brand loyalty, and hence unit sales and income.

2. **Efficiency problems.** Problems related to the execution of a process or business function. Shortcomings in process quality concern the amount of resources—time, money, raw materials, equipment utilization or capacity, and labor used within a process. Efficiency problems are an internal matter that should not affect the customer. Unfortunately, the obsession with operational efficiency among many executives often leads to predatory cultivation cost-cutting that undermines product quality and is detrimental to brand loyalty when noticed by buyers and users.

    For example, loyal shoppers at a health food store buy fresh-made and locally sourced soups because they do not contain any preservatives. The corporate office of this chain store can decide to cut cost by centralizing the production of these soups and transporting them to its stores. Because the soups can no longer be sold and consumed right away, they must add preservatives, which makes some loyal customers decide to stop buying them. Predatory cultivation can be this simple.

The first challenge that needs to be overcome in identifying the problem is to establish the standard or norm for measuring a process's execution or its desired outcome (see Figure 1.5).

This norm must be expressed unequivocally by management and accepted by the manager responsible for the execution of that particular process. After all, a norm must be realistic and achievable in order for anyone to accept responsibility for its realization. Alas, norms are not always defined clearly or specifically enough.

Without a norm and recognition of that norm, the extent of a problem cannot be established. The first line of action is then to establish a norm and to get buy-in from the manager responsible for executing that process.

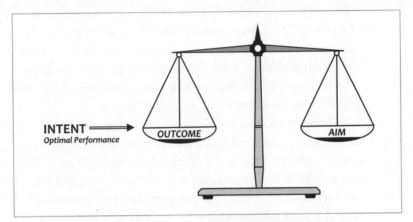

Figure 1.5: The Desired State of the Value Chain

The desired state describes the business's benchmark for
success—when the business will have succeeded at aligning
performance outcomes with its aim or forecast.

Problems are measured in equivalents that are easily compared among other problems and from period to period. Think of time, units per minute, out-of-pocket cost, cost per unit, units per dollar, and number of people, among other factors.

Defining the Problem

Contrary to popular belief, unintended and unwanted results are hardly ever caused by a single employee. Dr. W. Edwards Deming said that only 6 percent of all results,[9] both intended and unintended, are directly attributable to a single person or a group of people, who either excelled at their jobs, ignored orders, or violated rules and regulations.

The remaining 94 percent of all results are systemic in nature. This means that how a business system behaves, or how it performs, is largely determined by its design, organization or structure, implementation or operation, maintenance, and management.

Therefore, it is unrealistic to expect a system—including any of its employees—to deliver results for which it is not properly equipped. However, people will do their utmost to realize the impossible, but there are limits to their abilities and to the amount of unrealistic—and sometimes immoral—demands they are willing to accept from their supervisors and leaders. Deming has written about this phenomenon extensively in his books on continual improvement of quality.

Because a problem is defined as a discrepancy between the outcome of an activity and its aim, we must recognize the possibility that change did not occur within the activity but in the aim—the expected outcome. We tend to think that change happens outside of us, but what happens when we change our beliefs about what is right and wrong, valid and false, moral and amoral, or even immoral? Change is change, regardless of which scale tipped the balance. Different causes can result in similar effects, which underscores the importance of analyzing cause-and-effect relationships to understand change (see Figures 1.6 and 1.7).

Management changes the aim of an activity or process in three ways:

- **Product or service quality.** Changing the features and or specifications of a product or service, which are also known as their *critical success factors.*
- **Process quality.** Changing the control factors MOTIQ, which are also known as a process's *prerequisites.* Control factors are normally changed in an effort to increase operational efficiency. In addition, process quality is also changed when removing, replacing, upgrading, renovating, or innovating the production process.
- **Strategic direction.** Changing product–market combinations; outsourcing specific parts of the value chain; backward integration; divestment of a business unit; merger and acquisition; joint venture; strategic alliances; or changing ownership or management structures all together.

People often mistake effects or symptoms for problems. Hence, poor quality is not a problem but a symptom or effect. An effect or symptom just describes the altered state of a business, whether this new state was intended or unintended. Every effect has a cause, which is not always immediately apparent. Effects are more easily detected in the form of change in a financial amount or ratio simply because we happen to measure performance in monetary or numerical equivalents.

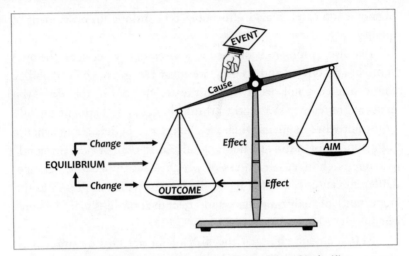

Figure 1.6: The Current State of the Value Chain (1)

It makes sense to distinguish between the desired state and the current state when they are misaligned—when the value chain experiences change. The root cause can originate from outperforming the aim or by easing up on the aim, or by changing the benchmark for success.

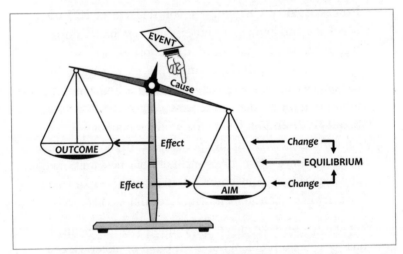

Figure 1.7: The Current State of the Value Chain (2)

The root cause originates from underperforming the aim or by raising the aim a notch, or by changing the benchmark for success.

Measuring a Problem

Beware of managers with a finance background who are prone to perceive this altered state as a financial problem in need of a financial solution, which usually means increasing operational efficiency. The unfortunate effect of treating symptoms is ignorance about the magnitude of the problem, jumping to conclusions that might even aggravate the problem, and allowing the problem to linger and fester. As a result, problems will persist, recur, or become a latent condition that can wreak havoc when least expected and tend to arrive at a critical moment in the business's future.

I realize that we are getting a little ahead of ourselves by discussing possible causes when we're still trying to determine what the actual problem is and assessing its gravity. But the reason that I bring this up now is for you to become aware that what we call "the problem" often turns out to be the experience of a collection of diverse symptoms originating from multiple sources. This should hardly be surprising considering the intricately interconnected nature of processes in combination with tight coupling of resources, that is, executing processes from the same or different business functions on the same machines, such as a computer platform, to contain the cost of investment and operations.

Having found evidence of one or more processes displaying behavior or results that deviate from its aim or norm, we want to assess the magnitude by measuring its:

- **Severity.** Difference between the current state and the norm or aim. (See Figure 1.8.)
- **Growth.** Trend by which severity develops over time (stable or linear progression). See Figure 1.9.)
- **Urgency.** Instance upon which the problem changes in nature. In fact, at that point in time, a new and different problem arises with its own severity. (See Figure 1.10.)

The best example of an incidence of urgency and its severity that I have experienced was the introduction of a new single currency—the euro—within all countries that qualified for admission to the European Monetary Union (EMU). From January 3, 1999, forward, all financial instruments issued within the EMU were to be traded in euros.

That date was the urgency for every financial services company within the eurozone, no exceptions, and the severity was the risk of finding oneself out of business on that fatal date due to non-compliance. This urgency was equally felt outside the EMU by stock exchanges trading financial instruments issued by countries and corporations from within the EMU.

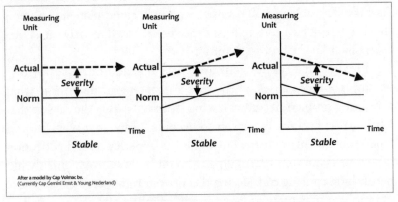

Figure 1.8: Measuring Severity of a Problem

Although severity is stable percentage-wise, it can change
in actual numbers—units, time, or money.

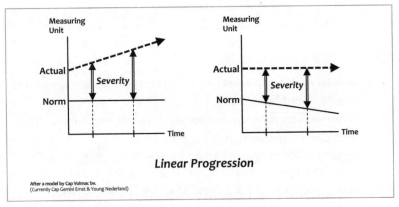

Figure 1.9: Measuring the Severity's Growth Trend

Over time problems can increase or decrease in severity
both percentage-wise and in actual numbers.

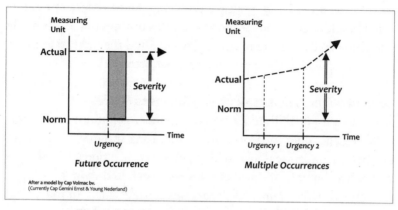

Figure 1.10: Measuring Urgency of a Problem

Severity does not only manifest itself in the present, it can also
be anticipated at a foreseeable point of time in the future.

Problem and Root Cause Are Not the Same

Just as symptoms or effects are often mistaken for problems, in turn,
problems are often mistaken for root causes. In order for you to avoid
making this mistake, know that a problem is defined by:

- A discrepancy between the value chain's actual behavior
  (current state) and a specific standard or norm (desired state)
- A person, called the "problem owner," who is responsible
  for the affected area(s) within the value chain because the
  individual is justified and authorized to make changes to that
  part of the value chain
- A specific standard or norm that is realistic and accepted by
  the problem owner

A root cause is an initiating event, action, or decision that manifests itself within the value chain's performance when it displays an
imbalance or misalignment between its current and desired state.
This discrepancy is called a problem. Beware of the fact that a single problem is more likely than not to have multiple root causes.
However, the disruptive effect of individual root causes varies significantly. Some root causes are of minor consequence and their effect
can be considered acceptable, so you can decide not to address them.

On the other hand, multiple problems can be reduced or eliminated by addressing a single root cause. This testifies to the intricately interconnected nature of business processes and the tight coupling of resources on which these processes are performed.

Organizational Hierarchy versus Business Processes

Mark Twain said, "Thunder is good, thunder is impressive; but it is lightning that does the work." In paraphrasing this quote, I'd like to say that organizational hierarchy is good, organizational hierarchy is impressive; but it is the business processes that do the work.

Job titles and names of departments over which an individual can exercise full authority can be impressive indeed and carry a lot of weight in decision-making processes. However, all activities that need to be fulfilled in order to successfully complete a specific process from end to end often extend far beyond the scope of the department that initiated that process. In fact, the process may involve multiple departments, each with its own responsible hierarchical leader. Likewise, building, maintaining, and developing a successful brand identity requires the cooperation and interaction of all processes and all people in every department.

When identifying and mapping a process, you'll recognize that it runs from end to end. In other words, a process does not end where the responsibility of a department ends. For example, when examining the process that generates the monthly profit and loss statement, you'll recognize that it starts at the old general ledger and it ends at a new general ledger. Similarly, the sales process starts with a customer with an unsatisfied need and ends with a customer whose need is satisfied. To be more precise, if the customer pays cash, the process ends after receiving the money and recording the transaction in the cash register. If the customer pays by credit card, the process ends with the receipt of the money from the credit card company, a week or a month later. Imagine which and how many departments are involved in the sales process from end to end in order to get an idea about complexity and interdependencies within a process. Actually, you don't have to imagine that when making the process visible through process mapping.

Whenever an event disrupts normal operating conditions, and certain processes start behaving differently from usual, most people will notice the symptoms or effects on their day-to-day work. When these symptoms persist or recur, people will start to complain among themselves and to their supervisors. In the absence of a timely and adequate response from management, people will start pointing fingers at each other and passing blame on other departments for messing up. (For example, finance or accounting may blame the IT department for mistakes, omissions, or delays in the production of their financial statements.) The risk involved is that relationships between departments and individuals within those departments will become polarized, which reduces the chance of their future cooperation in sorting out problems and finding solutions.

Identifying the Problem Owner

Even though making mistakes and then learning from those mistakes is the path of progress, making mistakes is generally frowned upon. (I once saw a humorous sign that read: To err is human but to forgive is not company policy.) Nonetheless, the fact that someone accepts responsibility for a problem is not a confession of culpability, but a sign of true leadership. After all, real change is only possible when someone in a leadership position assumes 100 percent responsibility for solving that problem. (See Figure 1.11.)

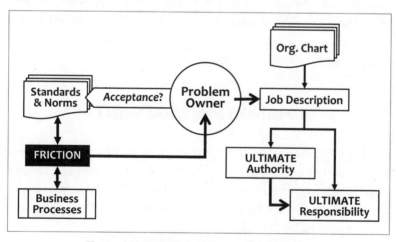

Figure 1.11: Identifying the Problem Owner

Every problem has a problem owner—a person who is responsible for correcting the situation because she or he was bestowed with the necessary authority to change the situation.

Given the fact that most problems are systemic in nature, not every employee can be held accountable for solving problems, because they simply lack authority to make any changes to the system. However, because there is no real responsibility without authority, imagine the frustration felt by employees who, nonetheless, experience a sense of responsibility for the outcome of the processes they perform. All they can do is bring it to the attention of the problem owner and explain the consequences of indecision and inaction.

Identifying the person who is authorized to make changes to the affected parts on the process map—the problem owner—requires overlaying the organizational chart with the process map. A process map visualizes the behavior of processes within the business system and the organizational chart identifies individual managers—process owners—who are authorized to change, and thus are responsible for, those processes or business functions within the business system.

Note that some end-to-end processes, such as producing financial statements, can have two or more contributing subprocesses, each with their own process owner. Consequently, there is a fair chance that a proposed solution will result in a conflict of interest among the contributing process owners. No process owner wants to be told by another process owner how to do his or her job. Therefore, the ultimate problem owner must be found on the next higher hierarchical level where conflicts of interest no longer exist. In many instances, that problem owner will be the person with ultimate authority and thus ultimate responsibility, and that is the chief executive.

CHANGE MANAGEMENT

Solving systemic problems is a discipline in its own right, generally known as change management. While writing a treatise on change management is beyond the scope of this book, I want you to be aware of some major change management principles, which are an executive's responsibility to implement.

Allocating Resources to Implement Change

Because the concept of problem ownership is based on top management authorizing a single individual to make changes to certain processes of the value chain, this individual is a hierarchical leader. Solving systemic problems is outside the realm of routine business operations, which makes it doubtful that any hierarchical leader's annual budget has provisions to absorb the unexpected expense. Therefore, successful completion of change management initiatives requires the allocation of all necessary resources. This is part and parcel of executive sponsorship for change.

Identifying the Problem Owner

Because of the interdependent nature of processes and the need for tight coupling (sharing of expensive resources), problems have ample opportunities to migrate throughout the value chain, indiscriminate of departmental boundaries. And, whenever the affected end-to-end process encroaches on more than one department, there is a potential conflict of interest among hierarchical leaders on the same echelon. In that case, as we saw before, the designated problem owner will need to be the hierarchical leader on the next highest echelon where there is no longer a conflict of interest among peers.

Appointing and Supporting a Project Manager

Change management initiatives are most successful when they are executed in the format of a formal project. These change projects need to be assigned to an independent project manager who is accountable to a single principal—the problem owner within the standing organization. The project manager creates and structures a dedicated project organization parallel to the standing organization, which will be operational only for the duration of the project—which can vary between a couple of months to a maximum of two years. Longer lasting projects will be more successful when they are broken up into multiple short-term projects.

The problem owner and the project manager have joint accountability for successful execution of a specific change management initiative (see Figure 1.12). The problem owner provides executive sponsorship for change, which entails the allocation of resources and delegation of authority to the project manager. Without executive sponsorship, hardly any change management initiative will be completed at all, let alone finished on time and within budget. The project manager is responsible for defining, creating, and implementing the project's deliverables and migrating the new processes from the project environment to the existing value chain of the standing organization.

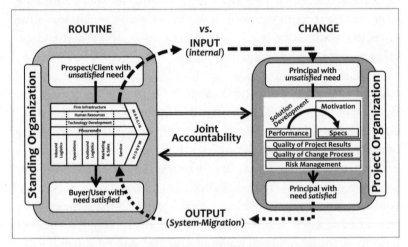

Figure 1.12: Dedicated Project Organization

A project organization is created to function parallel to the standing organization for the duration of the project. It receives its mandate for conducting the change initiative from the problem owner. Both parties have joint accountability for the success and failure of the project.

Please note that change management and project management are two separate disciplines, and their practices are distinctly different from conducting routine operations under normal operating conditions. Consequently, having a hierarchical leader conduct the project is ill-advised because that leader will need to assume responsibility for the project in addition to their present full-time job. And employees who are allocated to the project are exposed to the "two-boss problem." This means that one-and-the-same person is both their functional boss when working on the project and their hierarchical boss—the one who writes their annual performance reviews—when doing their regular job. This is problematic since it is inevitable that a conflict will arise between the mission of the project and the hierarchical leader's department(s) day-to-day operations. In other words, employees cannot be expected to always favor decisions that are in the best interest of the project and ultimately for the organization as an integrated whole. After all, "Whose bread I eat, his song I sing."

Identify Root Causes

Most change projects that fail do so because of the absence of a dedicated project organization at the outset. Additional causes of failure are (1) a lack of clarity from executive management regarding the value chain's intended purpose and (2) the project manager's failure to clearly identify the root cause(s), which includes measurement of the magnitude of the systemic problem. How else can anyone be expected to succeed at restoring the value chain's integrity?

Simply because similar effects can originate from different root causes, which may require different solutions, no solution should be chosen based on the fact that it helped someone else who was plagued by similar symptoms. Unfortunately, that seems to be the claim of most best-practice solutions—if it worked for XYZ, Inc., then it will work for you. This argument makes for a rather lame excuse when the decision maker is held accountable when a chosen best-practice solution fails to deliver on its promise.

Trust the Problem-Solving Process

Solving a systemic problem is analogous to solving a mathematical equation. Finding the value for X is not immediately obvious and can only be found by executing a series of intermediary computations. No systemic problem can be solved without defining the problem and identifying the root cause(s) first. Failure to do so may cause many executives to procrastinate and eventually decline a request for their sponsorship of an urgently needed change management initiative. Resistance to change is their Achilles' heel, and their failure to provide leadership in solving systemic problems results in underperformance and ultimately may derail promising executive careers.

Solutions show up when we stop obsessing about the "solution" and start trusting the problem-solving process. The Problem-Gravity chart (see Figure 1.13) helps to rank the priority of each problem.

Starting with the problem with the highest priority, one lists every possible root cause. Then, for each possible root cause, we identify all possible solutions. Of all possible solutions, we choose the most likely or probable solutions to create three or no more than five solution alternatives. From these solution alternatives, we choose the one that is most authentic for the particular purpose and needs of the value chain (see Figure 1.14).

	Problem	Problem Owner	Severity	Growth	Urgency
I.					
II.					
III.					
IV.					
n.					

Figure 1.13: Problem-Gravity Chart

A systemic problem is often a collection of multiple smaller problems. A Problem-Gravity chart organizes these problems according to their need of attention.

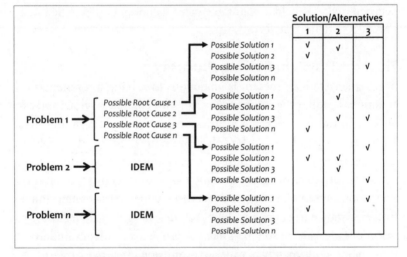

Figure 1.14: Creating Solution Alternatives

For each individual problem, one or more possible root causes are identified. This exercise reveals that multiple problems can be caused by the same root cause, and solved with the same possible solution. From all possible solutions three to five solution alternatives are created and presented to the problem owner for a decision.

This shows that the sequential application of the rules for each successive step will eventually unlock an authentic solution. Failure happens whenever one violates the rules of change management and mistakenly believes to know a shortcut. You just cannot shortcut your way to success!

CHECKLIST

Albert Einstein is reputed to have said, "If I had 60 minutes to save the world, I'd spend 55 minutes defining the problem and 5 minutes finding a solution." Therefore, let me share with you my proven checklist for defining the problem to boost confident sponsorship of any change management initiative:

- **Symptoms.** Take inventory of the symptoms that the business is experiencing; these are the different manifestations of a root cause that are disrupting routine operations of one or more departments.
- **Current state.** Gain insight into the current state of the business system. What is the business system actually doing as opposed to what it is expected or assumed to do?
- **Desired state.** Establish consensus among senior management team members regarding the desired state of the business system. How is the business system intended and expected to behave in order to realize its intended purpose?
- **Problem(s).** Measure the discrepancy between the current and the desired state of the business system. Do not confuse problems with symptoms.
- **Root cause(s).** Perform a proper diagnosis of the root dysfunction that disrupted the business system's integrity. This step is of critical importance to recovery because a single root cause can manifest itself in many different guises, creating active failures and latent conditions. Complexity and tight coupling only facilitate a root cause's ability to infect the system more invasively and destructively. Do not confuse problems with root causes.
- **Critical success factors.** Describe in detail the end result you expect a viable solution to create and deliver in terms of its efficacy to restore integrity to the business system, its look and feel, its ease of operation or maintenance, and its management.
- **Prerequisites.** Describe in detail the restraints, conditions, and requirements for the process by which the approved solution must be implemented. This refers to the process's efficiency such as its cost, duration, quality, and acceptable disruption of day-to-day operations.

- **Risk(s).** Foresee potential risk(s) and develop possible mitigating solutions that are congruent with the intent of the change initiative's critical success factors and prerequisites.
- **Authentic solution.** Create a solution that addresses the root cause(s), supports the realization of the business system's intended purpose, aligns with strategy, and reflects the beliefs, values, and moral standing to which a leader professes to adhere. These are the qualities that make a solution authentic to the system, which integrity it is intended to restore.
- **Strategy.** Define a plan of action by which to sustain and improve your ability to communicate or interact with your environment on three levels: moral, mental, and physical. In this case, the plan of action refers to executing the change management initiative from beginning to end, which includes milestones and deliverables.

Interestingly, the data gathered using this checklist can be entered into the "Template for Charting an Itinerary (Strategy)," which is discussed in Chapter 8 and depicted as Figure 8.4. This model is applicable for structuring the project management plan. As a result, it will also contain all answers to the questions that may be asked when held accountable for unintended and unwanted results. After all, people who review your performance want to know what you were thinking. By using this model, you can demonstrate that you did your homework and that you exercised your intellectual integrity.

LEARNING THROUGH OSMOSIS

Although Dr. Peter describes a cause-and-effect relationship between promotion and occupational incompetence, he leaves us guessing regarding the reason why this happens. This omission piqued my curiosity. Why would this phenomenon strike an otherwise competent leader upon their promotion to the position of chief executive officer? After all, occupational competence refers to one's personal effectiveness. So, what does the CEO position do to the aptitude of an individual woman or man?

The significance of promotion is the ability to exercise a greater level of authority to make changes to the processes and business functions of the value chain for which one assumed responsibility. The irony of the Peter Principle is that everyone who reaches their level of incompetence seems to focus their attention more and more on performing activities other than those for which they were hired. This manifests itself in the micromanagement of daily operations to the detriment of what I call *the missing link in the value chain*.

Back in 1937, Napoleon Hill wrote the following in his famous book *Think and Grow Rich*:

> [M]illions of people . . . falsely believe that "knowledge is power." It is nothing of the sort! Knowledge is only potential power. It becomes power only when, and if, it is organized into definite plans of action, and directed to a definite end. This "missing link" in all systems of education known to civilization today, may be found in the failure of educational institutions to teach their students HOW TO ORGANIZE AND USE KNOWLEDGE AFTER THEY ACQUIRE IT.[10]

Diminishing Marginal Utility

The validity of Hill's observation becomes unmistakably obvious in evaluating the curricula of business schools and, more specifically, those with executive development centers. The value chain is broken down into a cafeteria menu of topics for study, which treats every function of the value chain as separate and independent from all other functions. And each function is broken down even further into multiple silos of specialized knowledge. (See Figure 1.15.)

In addition to this analysis of the value chain, there hardly ever is any synthesis—meaning efforts aimed at reconnecting the nine separated business functions in order to form a network or integrated system.

It seems as if the value chain suffers the same fate as Humpty Dumpty in the well-known English nursery rhyme:

> Humpty Dumpty sat on a wall,
> Humpty Dumpty had a great fall.
> All the king's horses and all the king's men
> Couldn't put Humpty together again.

Could this explain why silo managers and executives alike have such difficulties perceiving a business as an organic whole?

Too much emphasis on analysis and specialization exposes students to the effects of Hermann Gossen's first law of Diminishing Marginal Utility, which states, "As a person increases consumption of a product—while keeping consumption of other products constant—there is a decline in the marginal utility that person derives from consuming each additional unit of that product."

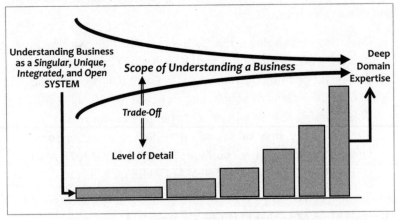

Figure 1.15: Diminishing Marginal Utility of Specialized Knowledge

There is an unavoidable trade-off between the scope of understanding how a business functions, and the level of detailed knowledge one possesses of one or more of the business system's component parts. Executive decision makers will be more effective by widening their scope than deepening their level of detailed analytic knowledge.

Boyd defined the problem of overspecialization in education, in his own succinct manner, as "learning more and more about less and less until you know everything about nothing."

In addition, overreliance on a single deep domain expertise makes one prone to falling victim to the law of the instrument (a.k.a. Maslow's hammer): "It is tempting, if the only tool you have is a hammer, to treat everything as if it were a nail." More precisely, the fact that performance is measured in monetary equivalents and that you happen to have deep domain expertise in financial matters does not mean that every performance problem is a financial problem that warrants investment in or implementation of a financial solution.

CEO Effectiveness

In all likelihood, Maslow's hammer will strike a serious blow to the effectiveness of a new CEO. Let me explain. While grooming oneself for a possible future CEO position, ambitious candidates will study those topics for which they have greatest affinity and aptitude. This is then followed by the pursuit of a career within that specific domain of expertise within the value chain. With every successive promotion to the next higher echelon, hierarchical leaders gain a greater level of influence and power; obtaining more discretionary authority to adjust and shape the character and nature of the processes for which they are responsible. For example, someone with a business degree and a major in finance is most likely to apply for a position dealing with financial matters. This career path reaches its peak at the position of chief financial officer, which is still within the confines of the same business function of the value chain—the firm's infrastructure—where their career path started.

Although promotion within any function of the value chain or any silo of specialized knowledge will increase one's authority and thus one's responsibility, it will always be limited to that specific area of expertise.

Ultimate Authority

However, a promotion to the CEO position is radically different. Any new CEO will experience a giant leap in the level of authority and its corresponding level of responsibility.

The CEO can exercise ultimate authority to shape, adjust, change, renovate, and innovate the design, organization or structure, implementation or operation, maintenance, and management of the entire value chain, and the strategic direction in which it is steered (see Figure 1.16). Therefore, a person in this position is expected to assume ultimate responsibility for the success and failure of the entire value chain, across all hierarchical management levels of the organizational chart. This includes responsibility for solving systemic problems, which is the Achilles' heel of any CEO.

In short, the CEO is responsible for the development—including continual improvement—of a value chain's capability, capacity, and craftsmanship and the volume of work that can be completed successfully per unit of time. However, this cannot be accomplished

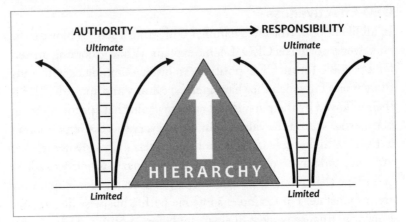

**Figure 1.16: Occupational Competence
(The Peter Principle Explained)**

When climbing the hierarchical ladder, authority and responsibility
go hand in hand. On every next higher level, one's authority
and thus responsibility are still limited. Yet when promoted
to the CEO position, one can exercise ultimate authority
and must thus assume ultimate responsibility.

when trying to understand the business mechanics of a value chain
as an organic whole from the perspective of any of the nine constituent business functions. For example, a company's financial
performance—financial statements and ratios—is not indicative of
the capability, capacity, character, and nature or brand identity of
the value chain. And yet calculations of return on investment or on
assets, or net present value calculations, financial statements, share
price evaluations, and performance forecasts seem to dominate decisions that directly influence the value chain's capability and capacity.
And whack goes Maslow's hammer!

This failure to understand business mechanics impedes a CEO's
effectiveness and decision-making processes, and makes them hes-
itate when asked to provide executive sponsorship for change
initiatives that address systemic problems. A confused mind resists
change and will always say NO.

The CEO Dilemma

Professor Michael Porter and colleagues conducted a study into
the surprises that new CEOs[11] experience on the job; the number
one surprise was how little authority they could actually exercise,

in relationship to their level of responsibility. Suppose a CEO tries to exercise ultimate authority and rule by decree as an autocratic leader. The person will soon lose his or her influence since hierarchical leaders will start to withdraw their support for this CEO. So, when it comes to power, the rule is *Use it AND Lose it.* (See Figure 1.17.)

The CEO dilemma is characteristic of complex organizations. When a business grows (in business volume, number of product lines, geographical areas served, marketing channels, engagement in strategic alliances, and in any other way that increases complexity), new and additional echelons will be inserted within the existing organizational chart.

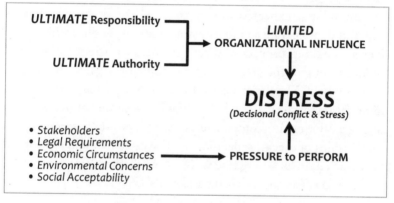

Figure 1.17: The CEO Dilemma

CEOs experience decisional conflict and stress because they feel the pressure to perform while realizing that their organizational influence is limited despite the fact their authority is ultimate.

As a result, the CEO will find himself or herself further removed from the front line where all the action takes place. Changing how individual business functions behave and interact with all other functions within the value chain, in an effort to realize the purpose for which the value chain was created in the first place, is easier said than done.

In addition, most new CEOs have their own agendas with goals and objectives that they want to achieve for the business during their tenure, which often requires steering the value chain in a different strategic direction.

Taking Control of the Business

Contrary to the cockpit of an aircraft, the CEO desk in the corner office is not equipped with a yoke, rudder paddles, trim wheel, throttle handle, or any other physical control mechanisms. Whereas a pilot has the ability to provide planning and control information directly[12] to the engine(s) and control surfaces, a CEO must take the indirect route of written and oral communication—including voice modulation and body language—across the many echelons of the hierarchy.

Piloting a business thus requires that leadership skills be applied in conjunction with organizing knowledge and information into a driving force, and the directing of that force toward the realization of the intended purpose for which the business was created; this organizing and directing is the missing link in the value chain.

The pilot is expected to possess excellent situational awareness and demonstrate sound assessment and foresight in his or her decision-making processes, which requires sufficient insight and understanding of the character and nature of the value chain as an organic whole. More specifically, the pilot is expected to show keen appreciation for the major relationships between the means and ends among a value chain's component parts, and for the cause-and-effect relationships of executive decisions on the capability and capacity of the value chain as an organic whole (see Chapter 10, Figure 10.1, "Cause and Effect versus Means and Ends").

This Is Personal

The rapidly changing global economy is a rich source of new and unforeseen circumstances. These events can disrupt a business's normal operating conditions and generate unintended and unwanted results. Deming said that 94 percent of all results—(un)intended and (un)wanted ones—originate from within the value chain itself. Note that every business system has only one value chain, which means that all unintended and unwanted results are produced by the exact same value chain that also creates the intended and wanted results.

In their study "Capitalizing on Complexity,"[13] IBM revealed that the majority of executives worldwide report being overwhelmed by the complexity of business systems and the disruption of normal operating conditions by events. This is an unfortunate example of the

Peter Principle at work, which is detrimental to CEO effectiveness, and by extension for a CEO's tenure.

CEO Survival Skills

Signs of CEO effectiveness—or the lack thereof—become especially evident in an executive's willingness to provide sponsorship for change, which is of vital importance for the successful resolution of systemic problems in a timely and adequate fashion.

Because CEOs assume ultimate responsibility for the entire value chain, every systemic problem is a challenge to their personal effectiveness as an officer charged with the proper performance of all processes within the value chain. Therefore, systemic business problems are in effect a CEO's personal problems. (See Figure 1.18.)

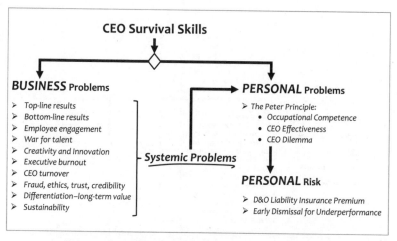

Figure 1.18: Solving Systemic Problems Is Personal

Systemic problems are not just business problems, they are personal problems for the CEO, because failure to address these problems adequately and timely influences his or her performance and thus his or her tenure.

The reason systemic business problems are a CEO's personal problems lie in the fact that only the chief executive has ultimate authority to make changes to the governance of a business's value chain: how it is designed, organized or structured, implemented or operated, maintained, and managed. This is where the rubber meets the road—where responsive executives demonstrate their professionalism and distinguish themselves from their peers with the same education, know-how, and background.

No On-the-Job Learning

Unfortunately, institutions for business education show little to no interest in business governance (see Chapter 9). Somehow, future CEOs are expected to learn through osmosis how to assimilate theories of management for the different disciplines, such as finance, marketing, operations, IT, change, and projects—which I call *management integration* (see Figure 1.19). How else are their students expected to understand the interfaces that transform the nine separate functions of the value chain into a singular, unique, integrated, and open system—safeguarding the value chain's structural integrity?

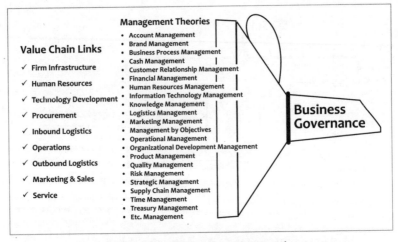

Figure 1.19: Management Integration

For each link comprised in the value chain, a large amount of management theories have been developed. Theories that are valid and true for a single link of the value chain can be expected to conflict with theories that are valid and true for other links of the value chain, and thus conflicting for the value chain as an integrated whole. It is the task of business governance to harmonize or integrate these disparate theories.

However, such a process of absorption—osmosis—requires the respective body of knowledge to be present within the environment in which future CEOs operate, which is highly unlikely given current curricula of business education. Moreover, new CEOs are told there is no on-the-job learning; they are expected, as it is called, to hit the

THE PETER PRINCIPLE AT WORK | 51

ground running. Therefore, it should be no surprise that a majority of executives are overwhelmed by complexity and fail to understand the business as a system, despite all their highly specialized knowledge and highly praised deep domain expertise.

No one should be shocked when I say that failure to understand complex business systems is solved by studying business governance. And yet, the IBM report claims that executives worldwide identified creativity as their preferred solution for:

- Overcoming bewilderment regarding a value chain's complex, interdependent processes and their performance on tightly coupled resources—in other words, dealing with complexity
- Addressing systemic problems as they unfold—that is, adjusting the system to events as they unfold

However, creativity cannot be found in a computer application, an off-the-shelf product that can be bought in a box, a best practice that can be adopted, or a deep domain expertise that can be hired. It is not a thing that can be added to the proverbial "toolbox" to make all your troubles go away. Creativity is not fairy dust that by way of magic gets sprinkled over the organization.

Instead, creativity is just another way of expressing an individual's competence at organizing and directing the value chain's complex, interdependent processes and fulfilling its intended purpose. As such, it refers to CEO effectiveness at business governance, which is a mental skill set based on understanding and appreciating the system's business mechanics. Creativity without understanding complexity is simply trial and error.

Failing to solve systemic problems, resisting efforts to develop the value chain's capability and capacity, and ignoring patterns of collapse result in underperformance for which the CEO is ultimately responsible. Booz Hamilton's annual studies regarding CEO succession indicate that tolerance for a CEO's underperformance is down among board members and shareholders; early dismissal for underperformance is up, and the 10-year moving average tenure for CEOs is declining. In addition, shareholder derivative suits are brought more frequently and their success rate at replacing underperforming executives is not encouraging for the career prospects of any current or future CEO.

Furthermore, studies into the methods of assessing Directors and Officers Liability insurance premiums[14] show that the personality of the insured and the organizational climate the directors and officers create are weighed more heavily than any financial statements. So, yes, systemic problems are personal problems for the CEO!

DEFYING THE PETER PRINCIPLE

Personal success at the top echelon of a business depends largely on one's unique ability to defy the Peter Principle. That means providing executive sponsorship for change whenever the value chain has its integrity disrupted by systemic problems, while demonstrating a sufficient degree of CEO effectiveness in directing the organization.

The only true measure of success at defying the Peter Principle is the experience of peace of mind—the absence of mental stress or anxiety. The person who exercises ultimate authority over every process within the value chain and takes ultimate responsibility for the value chain's performance possesses the right stuff as chief executive.

Trying to solve every manifestation of the same root cause individually and separately of all other manifestations with more and better specialized analytic knowledge is neither effective nor efficient. Therefore, whenever consecutive decisions to implement more and better of the same solutions lead to more and better of the same unintended and unwanted results, you should be courageous enough to conclude that the solution is wrong.

Failing to create a coherent mental image of what one observes here and now, and what one understands rationally about what is going on in real time, is the Peter Principle's root cause. Boyd famously called such a mismatch "a short between the ears."

The root cause cannot be found in the knowledge one possesses, what one thinks, but in how one thinks. One's ability to organize knowledge after acquiring it is called creativity. Mahatma Gandhi said that "the end is inherent in the means," by which he meant that everything we do is infused with the consciousness with which we do it. Therefore, if we make decisions with the wrong mindset or when we are in the wrong frame of mind or when we pursue the wrong ideals, we will end up with unintended and unwanted results.

Now is probably a good time to insert Einstein's most famous quote: "The problems that exist in the world today cannot be solved by the level of thinking that created them."

Given the fact that everything is created twice—first mentally and then in its physical form—systemic problems originating from the value chain's design, organization or structure, implementation or operation, maintenance, and management can only be solved by changing our current level of thinking about governing how to design, organize or structure, implement or operate, maintain, and manage the value chain.

Making a Difference

The notion that shaping and adjusting the physical form of a value chain requires a change in a CEO's mental programming, causing the career path of current and future CEOs to bifurcate into two alternative but incompatible roads. Each path follows its own itinerary in pursuit of its own values and principles and leads businesses toward different destinations (see Figure 1.20).

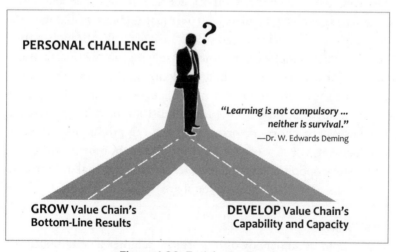

PERSONAL CHALLENGE

"Learning is not compulsory ...
neither is survival."
—Dr. W. Edwards Deming

GROW Value Chain's
Bottom-Line Results

DEVELOP Value Chain's
Capability and Capacity

Figure 1.20: Fork in the Road

The words "growth" and "development" are used interchangeably, yet there is a distinct difference. The personal challenge lies in recognizing this distinction. You can grow bottom-line results without developing or at the expense of the value chain's capability and capacity. On the other hand, you can choose to develop the value chain's capability and capacity, which makes growing bottom-line results practically inevitable.

In addition, the fact that systemic business problems are personal challenges to a CEO's effectiveness raises the question of the purpose of the chief executive officer position and the foundation on which the job performance assessment is based. Is that purpose to grow the value chain's bottom line? Or is it to develop the value chain's capability and capacity to realize its intended purpose?

This fork in the road represents a paradigm shift, with serious and far-reaching consequences for what we believe to be valid and true about executive leadership.

To Be or To Do

Since the eventual path one chooses to follow is a reflection of one's personality and ambition, current and future CEOs should ask themselves what they want their legacy to be. No one could have expressed that choice any better than Colonel John R. Boyd with his famous "To Be or to Do" speech, which I quoted in the Introduction.

To Be Somebody

Desiring to be somebody of importance requires leaders to play along in order to get along. Leaders who pursue this objective maintain the status quo and endeavor to grow bottom-line results through cutting costs, making employees redundant, moving production facilities overseas, investing in (seemingly random) opportunities that promise higher short-term returns on investment—including participation in share buyback programs—and acquisition of other (unrelated) businesses. In short, favoring profits over production, quality, employment, client needs, society, and the environment. Moreover, lavish stock option plans for executives serve as personal incentives to follow this course and increase the share price.

The "Game"

Desiring to be somebody of importance requires a certain attitude that was rather accurately portrayed in the 1999 movie *Instinct*. Cuba Gooding Jr. plays the role of the ambitious psychiatrist Dr. Theo Caulder, who is a careerist within the academic system. He convinced his boss Ben Hillard, played by Donald Sutherland, to give him as his patient the noted anthropologist Dr. Ethan Powell, played by Anthony Hopkins, who is imprisoned for murder. Dr. Powell had left society behind in order to live in the jungle among gorillas.

Although Caulder is tasked with treating Powell who for years lived with primates in the jungle, Powell eventually awakens Caulder to the hypocrisy and lack of fulfillment in his own life. Toward the end of the movie Caulder confesses to Powell what it is that makes him break into a cold sweat in the middle of the night; it's not the work he does, but the *game* he must play—which is all about careerism.

Caulder tells Powell he obsesses about who can advance his career and those who can hurt it; who he should associate with and who he should avoid; and what he can offer to people in power that will put him in their good graces. And, in a moment of honesty, Caulder reveals what frightens him the most: his love of the game. The game is about a person's ambition to be somebody rather than to do something. Long live Machiavelli's cynical disregard for morality and focus on self-interest and personal gain! And he knows this inauthentic form of living is devoid of integrity and destructive to the soul. He knows the price you pay for careerism is nothing short of losing your humanity.

To Do Something

When desiring to do something of importance, and to do that successfully over the long haul and under the most difficult conditions, Boyd explains what is necessary:

> One needs some unifying vision that can be used to attract the uncommitted as well as pump-up friendly resolve and drive and drain-away or subvert adversary resolve and drive. In other words, what is needed is a vision rooted in human nature so noble, so attractive that it not only attracts the uncommitted and magnifies the spirit and strength of its adherents, but also undermines the dedication and determination of any competitors or adversaries.[15]

Such a unifying vision implies a willingness to end conflicts on favorable terms, in order to ensure that peace terms do not provide seeds for (unfavorable) future conflict.

Boyd calls the following ingredients essential for the pursuit of a unifying vision:[16]

1. **Insight.** Ability to peer into and discern the inner nature or workings of things
2. **Orientation.** Interactive process of many-sided implicit cross-referencing projections, empathies, correlations, and rejections that are shaped by the interplay of genetic heritage, cultural tradition, previous experiences, and unfolding circumstances
3. **Harmony.** Power to perceive or create interaction of apparently disconnected events or entities in a connected way
4. **Agility.** Ability to operate inside an opponent's decision-making processes in order to shape and adapt to new or unforeseen circumstances
5. **Initiative.** Internal drive to think and take action without being urged

These ingredients determine the character and nature of the value chain, or, in other words, its capability and capacity. Since capability and capacity determine the value chain's ability to perform predictably, sustainably, and profitably, the more capable the value chain will be at utilizing its capacity, the more money it is going to make.

Please note how developing capability and capacity will help grow bottom-line results. However, growing bottom-line results is by no means a guarantee for developing capability or capacity. After all, money spent on dividend payments and share buyback programs is not spent on system development. Then, the remaining question to pose oneself is: Growing bottom-line results or developing capability and capacity—which way will you go?

WHAT HAPPENS NEXT?

A systemic problem is a mismatch between the current state of a business and its desired state. Failure to solve systemic problems adequately, in a timely manner, and within budget will expose occupational incompetence on behalf of the executive leader, which is another validation of the Peter Principle.

In the next chapter, we'll explore how our orientation (genetic heritage, cultural tradition, previous experiences, and unfolding circumstances) project images of the world around us onto our minds. Note that a change in orientation will change the mental images that we create of the same business system and the same new and unforeseen circumstances.

CHAPTER 2

Top Three Business Gremlins That Sabotage CEO Effectiveness

*The problem is not people being uneducated.
The problem is that people are educated
just enough to believe what they have been
taught, and not educated enough to question
anything from what they have been taught.*

—Professor Richard P. Feynman
1965 recipient of the Nobel Prize in Physics

W hile I was standing in line at the library one day, the picture of a guy in a flight suit and a helmet under his arm caught my eye. It was the front cover of the book *Boyd: The Fighter Pilot Who Changed the Art of War.* I picked it up to have a closer look and read the very impressive accolades on this guy whom I had never heard of before. I don't think I have ever finished reading a book in less time. Apart from my fascination with his personality and his remarkable accomplishments in the face of resistance from the Air Force bureaucracy, I felt I was reading a very good business book. That's why I frequently quote Colonel John R. Boyd USAF throughout this book.

Colonel John R. Boyd subscribed to Carl von Clausewitz's[1] idea that the factors distinguishing real war from war on paper is the concept of friction, which includes the interaction of many factors, such as uncertainty, psychological and moral forces, and effects. "Friction is the force that resists all action and saps energy. It makes the simple difficult and the difficult seemingly impossible," Boyd said.[2] In this sense, he believed, friction is representative of the climate or atmosphere of war.

Similarly, the factors distinguishing real-life business from business in textbooks is the friction and conflict that people experience from how their value chain is governed. In this sense, friction and conflict are representative of corporate culture and the climate or atmosphere in which business is conducted, the methodology by which its processes are organized and executed, the striving toward a clear and concise purpose, and the rationale behind resource allocation.

Imagine the amount of conflict and stress that executive leaders face in their decision-making processes. Already overwhelmed by complexity and events, these executives must cope with yet another layer of uncertainty caused by friction and conflict.

This feeling of uncertainty manifests itself first in failing to discern what's happening in real-time within one's environment and within the value chain and, second, in not knowing how to solve systemic problems by leading the value chain's transition from its current state to an intended new and more advantageous state.

In addition, past business governance practices and trade-off decisions may have eroded the value chain's capacity and capability to adapt to new and unforeseen circumstances as they unfold. An example is relinquishing the value chain's agility—its ability to operate with flexibility and speed—to increase operational efficiency through standardization of work processes and thus the products or services it provides.

Colonel John R. Boyd said, "He who can handle the quickest rate of change survives," in which "quick" does not refer to speed but the amount of time that elapses in transitioning the system from one state to another. Hence, when competitors experience similar challenges, fast transients should be conducted asymmetrically, so as to complete a transition from one state to the next in less time than anyone else. Also, Boyd favored abrupt, fast transients that come as a surprise. Consequently, the antidote to uncertainty is adaptability—not certainty.

CEO effectiveness at solving systemic problems is thus a matter of:

- Discernment of what goes on in real-time within one's environment, including the value chain.
- Knowing how to lead the value chain's transition from its current state to an intended new and more advantageous state.
- Past business governance practices—corporate memory—that shaped the value chain's capability of and capacity for adapting to new and unforeseen circumstances as they unfold with flexibility and speed (i.e., agility). Note that high employee turnover results in a loss of corporate memory.

PERCEPTION OF REALITY IS A MATTER OF CREATING MENTAL IMAGES

Perception is subjective. In other words, awareness of a common environment through physical sensations differs from person to person. Therefore, different people have different experiences of reality. Such differences become especially significant when new and unforeseen circumstances unfold before our eyes, such as when events disrupt a business's normal operating conditions.

In the epic 2004 movie *What the Bleep Do We Know!?*—which served as a dynamic catalyst for consciousness in media—scientists compare human perception with a movie camera. Our eyes are the lens and our visual cortex is the film, or nowadays the memory chip. The visual cortex imprints on the brain only what it has the ability to recognize as real or what it is capable of processing as valid or true according to an individual's predisposition and assessment. What we "see" is the result of a successful matchup of patterns in the reality an individual observes and his or her mental programming, which happens throughout our lives and is affected by our education, schooling, cultural habits, customs and traditions, prejudices, interpersonal relationships, work or industry experiences, exposure to different socioeconomic and geopolitical environments, media exposure, travel, and reading.

Therefore, eyes see much more than the brain is consciously able to project onto the screen of an individual's mind. This means that large amounts of information reaching our brain through the eyes are not integrated with our awareness, and therefore they do not seem to exist or are perceived as untrue, invalid, or even as an impossibility.

An individual's perception of reality is thus a matter of creating mental images. We create mental images by matching the object of our observation, or our experience of a situation or condition, with our mental programming. Therefore, reality is judged according to the beliefs we were mentally programmed to accept as right or wrong, valid or invalid, or true or false. And we apply those beliefs to our interpretation of successful value-chain governance and to interpret events as they unfold before our eyes.

In addition, the validity of our beliefs is reinforced through interaction with our peers, business journals' op-eds and articles by experts, online blogs, discussion groups, and so forth. This constant reinforcement strengthens our beliefs and thus our self-confidence.

What happens to our psyche when our mental programming fails to create a meaningful mental image because our current level of understanding and knowledge is inadequate to explain a specific observation or experience? Suppose you already created a meaningful mental image, and you are presented with a new, competing, and unfamiliar explanation for that same experience or observation?

As illustrated in Figure 2.1, you'll experience a restriction of consciousness either because you don't understand what's going on, or because you start to doubt the validity of your perception of a business system's character and nature. This experience can result in a wide range of emotions, from simple surprise to various combinations of uncertainty, doubt, confusion, self-deception, indecision, fear, panic, discouragement, and despair.

Decision makers who experience a restriction of consciousness are inhibited in their ability to cope with new and unforeseen circumstances, which manifests itself to the outside world in their unskillful behavior. Unskillful behavior can show up as both an error and a violation. We have seen in the news media how a CEO's unskillful behavior in combination with pressure to perform—the CEO dilemma—has the potential of collapsing a business into itself.

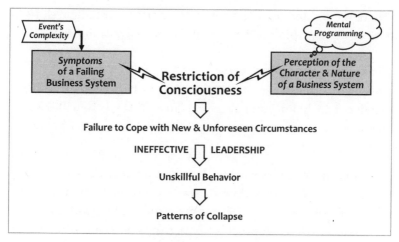

Figure 2.1: Restriction of Consciousness

What we believe about business—our mental programming—is what we accept as reality. Whenever the business system shows symptoms we cannot comprehend—incidents we cannot explain or believe to be possible—we experience a restriction of consciousness. Failure to resolve this restriction of consciousness in an adequate and timely fashion renders a leader ineffective, which leads to unskillful behavior and ultimately in patterns of collapse.

Recognizing Our Dominant Mental Programming

The restriction of our consciousness results from repeatedly asking the exasperated question: "Why does the world behave as it does, even though I know that this is impossible?"

What this line of questioning reveals is an individual's firm belief in their infallible mental programming, which is often reinforced by their social status, advanced education, hierarchical position, or past successes. In other words, the experience of a restriction of consciousness produces moral conflict.

Instead of looking for confirmation of one's mental programming within one's environment, Colonel John R. Boyd suggested looking for mismatches[3] between observed reality and one's mental programming. This can be done by asking, "If the world behaves the way it does, then how should I change my thinking to understand its nature and character?"

By embracing this process of questioning the knowledge we believe to be valid and true, we learn, update our mental programming, and come to terms with significant paradigm shifts in our perception. This is how problems become opportunities.

Temperament and Character

Although people's behavior might appear to be random, Carl Jung, founder of analytical psychology, explained that it is actually consistent with basic differences in the ways individuals prefer to use the following cognitive processes:

- **Perception.** This involves the many different ways of becoming aware of things, people, happenings, or ideas.
- **Judgment.** This involves the many different ways of coming to conclusions about what has been perceived—discernment.

Elaborating on Jung's work, social scientists identified different ways in which different personalities interact with their environment. For example, Katharine Cook Briggs and her daughter Isabel Briggs Myers are known for the Myers-Briggs Type Indicator (MBTI), which recognizes 16 personality types, as distinctive dynamic energy systems. These distinctive dynamic energy systems are derived from one's preferences regarding:

- **Favorite world.** Do you prefer to focus on the outer world or on your own inner world? This is called extraversion (E) or introversion (I).
- **Information.** Do you prefer to focus on the basic information you take in or do you prefer to interpret and add meaning? This is called sensing (S) or intuition (N).
- **Decision.** When making decisions, do you prefer to first look at logic and consistency or first look at the people and special circumstances? This is called thinking (T) or feeling (F).
- **Structure.** In dealing with the outside world, do you prefer to get things decided or do you prefer to stay open to new information and options? This is called judging (J) or perceiving (P).

Since people demonstrate systematically different preferences toward what they perceive and in how they reach conclusions, it should be expected that they show corresponding differences in their interests, reactions, values, motivations, and skills. Apart from the MBTI,

David Keirsey created a Temperament Sorter, which links human behavioral patterns to four temperaments and 16 character types. What these models have in common is the division of personality into temperament and character, explaining how each healthy mature individual will develop a character appropriate to his or her temperament:

- **Temperament** refers to an individual's predisposition or preferences that become recognizable in their talents, passions, and unique ability. This inborn configuration of preferences and inclinations defines how a person will operate and is not likely to change over the course of a lifetime. Temperament is comparable to computer hardware; the way it was designed determines the activities it performs best—form follows function. (See Figure 2.2.)

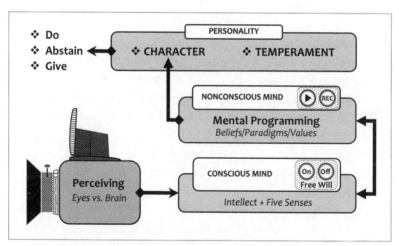

Figure 2.2: The Brain Imprints on the Conscious Mind What It Has the Ability to See

Our nonconscious mind functions as a de facto autopilot. And, most of the time, we behave according to our mental programming. Yet, we can choose to exercise free will and use our conscious mind to learn, unlearn, and relearn, thus uploading new beliefs, paradigms, and values with which to reprogram our nonconscious mind.

- **Character** is a configuration of habits and a disposition toward a certain attitude and interaction with the world. Character is the emergent form that develops through interaction of temperament and environment. Character is the de facto determinant of how a person will function in his or her environment. This relationship between character and temperament is well described with the beautiful French expression *c'est le ton qui fait la musique*—"it is the tone that makes the music." Unlike temperament, character evolves over time, subject to an individual's personal experiences, cultural influences, and education. Therefore, a person hindered in giving expression to his or her temperament—by family members, educators, employers, or political regimes—may develop character defects. As a result, character is comparable to computer software, which can be changed or adapted for new situations. When a person interacts with his or her environment differently from what is expected of that person based on previous experiences, that person is said to behave out of character.

The Nonconscious Mind

Maxwell Maltz said that "a human being always acts and feels and performs in accordance with what he imagines to be true about himself and his environment." In other words, an individual acts according to the programming of their nonconscious mind, which is the repository of our personal beliefs, values, customs, culture, schooling, and habits. Our mental programming contains ideas and concepts with which we are emotionally involved.

Consequently, most "thinking" is a form of deductive reasoning or analysis that keeps the thinker captive inside the box of his or her own nonconscious mind. Therefore, thoughts and images that fail to resonate with a concept or idea with which we have an emotional involvement are rejected as false or an invalid line of reasoning. As a result, it is our nonconscious mind that controls our behavior most of the time. Thus, most of us live our lives on autopilot.

The Conscious Mind

The conscious mind is the thinking mind that acts as the gatekeeper to the nonconscious mind. As such, it has the ability to accept or reject a new idea or concept. The five senses—sight, taste, touch, hearing, and smell—provide us with objective input variables that are given meaning through processing by our six intellectual faculties—reasoning, intuition, perception, will, imagination, and memory. The synthesis of input variables with our intellectual faculties is how we create new ideas and concepts. For example, instead of providing the same products or services better, faster, or cheaper, you now provide similar products and services in a different and unique way, or satisfy similar needs with entirely different products or services the likes of which no one ever saw before.

Free Will

It is by exercising our free will that new concepts or ideas are rejected as false, accepted as true, or accorded a temporary suspension of disbelief—such as when we read a novel or watch a movie. In its role as gatekeeper to the nonconscious mind, the conscious mind has the ability to record new ideas and concepts and integrate them into our awareness. Recording new ideas is usually expressed as thinking outside the box of our nonconscious mind. It is said that instructions for thinking outside the box are written on the outside, thus requiring an outsider to read them to you. (See Figure 2.2.)

There are countless historical examples that have changed our beliefs of what is true and false. Think of notions such as the Earth is flat, metal ships cannot float, or "640K ought to be enough for anyone." (said by Bill Gates in 1981).

PRINCIPLES THAT EXPLAIN CAUSE-AND-EFFECT RELATIONSHIPS

When faced with systemic problems, the person who was given the right to exercise ultimate authority to restore integrity to the value chain must understand causality or causation. Causality concerns itself with relationships of cause and effect, which states that absolutely everything happens for a reason, that for every outcome or effect in one's life, there is a specific cause. Since all actions have consequences and produce specific results, this law provides answers to the question "Why" things happen the way they do. Note that the reason why an effect occurs should not be equated with the consequences or meaning of that effect for an individual or an organization.

Answers to the "Why" question provide explanations in the form of principles that can be found in moral values, formal logic (philosophy), laws of physics, laws of men, procedures, regulations, theories, and beliefs. Hence, knowledge of principles that explain cause and effect also serve as predictors of the outcome of one's actions and behavior. Experience alone, learning "what" to do and "when" to do it is not enough. Dr. W. Edwards Deming said, "Experience without theory teaches nothing."

The impact of principles on natural and manmade systems is well captured by Marianne Williamson[4] when she wrote:

> There are objective, discernable laws of physical and non-physical phenomena. These laws merely describe the way things are. You don't exactly have faith in the law of gravity, so much as you just know that it is. These laws aren't invented; they're discovered. They are not dependent on our faith. Faith in them merely shows we understand what they are. Violation of these laws doesn't bespeak a lack of goodness, just a lack of intelligence. We respect the laws of nature in order to survive.[5]

Failure to make an effort to discover the principles that enhance or reduce the capability of the value chain for which you are responsible, ignoring those principles, or attempting to overrule them with force or by instilling fear among employees demonstrates "just a lack of intelligence." This includes the nowadays all-too-common reluctance or omission to initiate a root-cause analysis when faced with a systemic problem.

Knowing Why

Mechanical systems are often more easily understood than organic systems such as the human body or organizations and other social structures. Therefore, let me provide a real-life example from a car mechanic with ample hands-on experience but a lack of understanding of the principles that make a four-stroke reciprocal gas engine fire on all cylinders. (See Figure 2.3.)

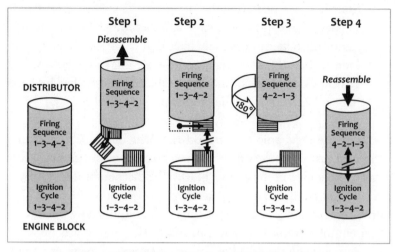

Figure 2.3: The Importance of Knowing Why

In order to solve a problem, you need to understand its function in relationship to the whole. Minor mistakes made on the level of a single component part can have significant ramifications for the system as an integrated whole.

Step 1. The mechanic pulled the distributor assembly from the engine block. The spindle connecting the distributor to the camshaft is divided into two sections that are connected like a tenon and mortise. Each section is slotted and holds a peg half the width of the slot. Pegs are positioned opposite of each other in order to prevent incorrect assembly. However, when the mechanic removed the distributor from the engine block, the peg on the distributor side fell from its slot in the spindle.

Step 2. Upon replacing the peg inside the slot, he inadvertently put it on the opposite side of its intended position, causing a conflict with the other peg in the other spindle section connected to the camshaft.

Step 3. He resolved the conflict by rotating the spindle on the distributor side 180 degrees to make it fit, and he secured the distributor to the engine block. He failed to recognize that he was creating a systemic problem by misaligning the ignition cycle and thus the firing sequence.

Step 4. When he started the engine, it was misfiring, causing it to buck, shake, poof, and smoke. This shows how a seemingly minor mistake can have an effect that is noticeable in all cylinders, the exhaust system, and the air intake system. As the vehicle shook from side to side, the mechanic scratched his head in bewilderment and called for help.

Had the mechanic understood the principle of a four-stroke reciprocal gas engine, he would not have treated the distributor as just a cap to fill a hole in the engine block. The distributor is an integral part of a gas engine. It directs an electrical current to the spark plug of the right cylinder at the right time, as determined by the design of an engine's crankshaft and camshaft. The engine was bucking because spark plugs sparked out of sequence and at the wrong time. This shows that there is more to making an engine run than having all the necessary parts connected to each other at all the designated places.

Just like mechanical systems, social systems, businesses, and a business's value chain operate according to certain principles or laws. Violation against such principles causes friction and conflict and eventually failure or collapse.

Let's take a look at the airline industry, which failed to appreciate the principle behind Southwest Airlines' policy of not issuing boarding passes with assigned seats and not serving meals. The principle was not so much to save money—as imitators assumed erroneously—but to speed up turnaround time at the gate. Turnaround time matters because air traffic control reserves precise time slots for the departure of each scheduled flight. Having to wait for caterers to arrive and passengers to find their assigned seats costs time and risks delaying push-back from the gate. Missing the assigned departure time slot means being placed at the back of the line—waiting, burning fuel, causing passengers to miss connecting flights, and possibly requiring additional crew rotations. The operative principle for airlines is that they make money when they are in the air flying—not when on the ground waiting, especially at airports with a large number of aircraft movements.

Entering the Twilight State

When struggling to make sense of new and unforeseen circumstances, executive decision makers can become unglued. The effects of disruptive events on normal operating conditions often lead executives to justify the decisions they made that led up to this moment in time. They rationalize their actions with theories, case studies, and best practices, which convince them that what they did was a textbook example of good leadership.

Nonetheless, their disbelief regarding the current state of the business is disconcerting. They did all the right things for all the right reasons and they most certainly did not slip-up. And yet, they are faced with an unforeseen, unintended, and unwanted situation. It's like they just entered a twilight state, where everything they thought to be true is turned upside down and inside out. Subsequently, their conscious mind attempts to open one corner of their mind to considering the possibility that they might have made mistakes or violated some elementary core business principles.

Business Gremlins

All of a sudden, they start noticing those pesky *business gremlins*—outside forces that are messing with their minds and thereby sabotaging their occupational competence. Business gremlins serve as a temporary veil for the fact that their intellectual integrity was breached. There is a bug in their mental programming.

British novelist Roald Dahl, who served as a fighter pilot in the Royal Air Force during World War II, recounts in his book *Going Solo* his encounters with "Gremlins," the little creatures that while in flight, stood on his Spitfire's wings, cowlings, and propeller, drilling holes with a hefty pneumatic hammer.

Here is the *Tale of the Gremlins*, a story told in the form of verse, which was published in RAF bulletins during the war, and often sung to a familiar tune:

This is the tale of the Gremlins
    As told by the PRU
    At Benson and Wick and St Eval—
    And believe me, you slobs, it's true.

When you're seven miles up in the heavens,
    (That's a hell of a lonely spot)
    And it's fifty degrees below zero,
    Which isn't exactly hot.

When you're frozen blue like your Spitfire,
    And you're scared a Mosquito pink.
    When you're thousands of miles from nowhere,

And there's nothing below but the drink.

It's then that you'll see the Gremlins,
    Green and gamboge and gold,
    Male and female and neuter,
    Gremlins both young and old.

It's no good trying to dodge them,
    The lessons you learnt on the Link
    Won't help you evade a Gremlin,
    Though you boost and you dive and you jink.

White ones will wiggle your wing tips,
    Male ones will muddle your maps,
    Green ones will guzzle your glycol,
    Females will flutter your flaps.

Pink ones will perch on your perspex,
    And dance pirouettes on your prop,
    There's a spherical middle-aged Gremlin,
    Who'll spin on your stick like a top.

They'll freeze up your camera shutters,
    They'll bite through your aileron wires,
    They'll bend and they'll break and they'll batter,
    They'll insert toasting forks into your tyres.

And that is the tale of the Gremlins,
    As told by the PRU,
    (P)retty (R)uddy (U)nlikely to many,
    But a fact, none the less, to the few. [6]

The reality of rapid, violent, unexpected, and dramatic changes in one's circumstances was just too hard to comprehend. Once a pilot entered this twilight state, it was easier to accept that those imaginary blooming gremlins were compromising the airworthiness of their formidable aircraft than the truth of being shot at by a faceless enemy.

Making Excuses

Business executives faced with systemic problems have similar experiences when the euphoria of personal success and a subsequent succession of promotions is overtaken by the experience of occupational incompetence, brought on by complexity of the value chain as an organic whole, and events that disrupt business as usual.

Business gremlins are just an excuse for the failure of one's mental programming to understand and adapt to new and unforeseen circumstances that cause systemic problems and compromise business performance.

Decision makers who look for confirmation that they made no mistakes in the hope of finding redemption for their leadership usually take refuge in their mental programming and, as result, experience a restriction of consciousness. In that twilight state of mind, the concept of a meddling interference by a vicious outside force for which no one can be held responsible becomes an attractive explanation for a sudden onset of occupational incompetence.

Soon, other executives start noticing how the same business gremlins are sabotaging their effectiveness as well. This twilight state experience draws attention to effects rather than the actual causes—which remain a mystery to everyone.

Faced with hard economic times, many executive leaders commit to *doing more with less* by stiffening their resolve to *doing more and better of the same* by *working smarter not harder*. Does that sound like rational and sane advice to you? See where it has gotten us today!

THE FIRST BUSINESS GREMLIN: COMMITTING TO THE CORE BUSINESS PURPOSE

Core business is about the purpose of a business: its raison d'être, or the reason it was created. Every enterprise starts with an idea and the business system is the vehicle for the pursuit of that idea. In other words, the business system is a means to an end. Consequently, its success is determined by the extent to which the business system succeeds at realizing its purpose. Therefore, it's of paramount importance that a business system has what Deming called "Constancy of Purpose." This means avoiding the unintentional replacement of the system's core purpose with ad hoc opportunities, fashionable fads, or solutions for temporary challenges. While tempting, these options can:

- Sabotage your current strategy.
- Undermine the alignment of the value chain with its purpose and strategy.
- Attempt to realize the new purpose with the old and now ill-suited value chain.

Recognizing Our Dominant Mental Programming

There seems to be consensus that the purpose of a business is to make money. In other words, success is equated with money. Therefore, everything is given a price tag including people, humanity, health, safety, organizational culture, work climate, values, morality, ethics, pride of workmanship, and the environment.

Consequently, based on theories of operational efficiency, decisions are reduced to an analytic process of determining which solution is economic and which is uneconomic. The one that costs less wins. Similarly, note how consultants attempt to calculate the return on investment of employee training, and how business schools are ranked based on the salary or income of its alumni. How would you feel if that same method were used for assessing the success of medical practitioners, legal professionals, or civic engineers?

Principles that Explain Cause-and-Effect Relationships

No one denies the necessity for a commercial enterprise to pursue revenue and a healthy profit margin. The criticism against "making money" is that it should not be professed as the purpose of a business system.

Rather, earning a profit margin is not the purpose of a business but a "prerequisite" for operating a sustainable business (see Figure 2.4). Please do not disregard this distinction between purpose and prerequisite as a matter of semantics, for it is nothing of the sort. Profits are the applause for a job well done, and receiving a standing ovation is the cry for an encore. It is a show of being in demand; it is the proof of a success!

Wallace D. Wattles, author of *The Science of Getting Rich,* wrote: "You cannot give every man more in cash market value than you take from him, but you can give him more in USE VALUE [emphasis added] than the CASH VALUE [emphasis added]of the thing you take from him."[7]

Use value is the sum of the applied resources and the utility that users derive from that product or service. Utility is the added value that differentiates one brand from another. Utility can be expressed and experienced either in a lower price or in unique benefits.

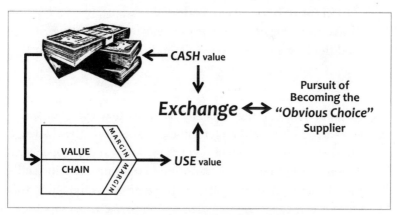

Figure 2.4: The Core Business Principle

The core principle of business is the exchange of use value for cash value. The amount of use value executives choose to create determines whether their business becomes the obvious choice supplier to their target audience or not.

Utility or Profit Margin

The price people are willing to pay for a product or service is equal to the perceived use value they anticipate receiving from their purchase or investment. Because not everyone has the same perception of what constitutes use value, not everyone is a prospective buyer of your brand or your kind of product or service—hence the recognition of market segmentation and the identification of different target audiences.

Rather than creating use value similar to one's competitors, different expressions of use value can be created by changing the business's transformation process. As Figure 2.5 illustrates, you can perform one of the following:

- **Similar activities in different ways.** For example, taking advantage of opportunities in the transformation process and becoming the lowest-cost producer (think Costco and Southwest Airlines). By transferring these cost advantages to buyers, you create additional use value for them without eroding your profit margins. Even though this strategy commands an average profitability as a percentage of the sales price per transaction, this strategy aims to increase income, thus increasing net profits.
- **Different activities from rivals.** For example, by creating unique tangible or intangible user benefits. By creating additional utility that exceeds its additional cost, you increase your profit margin (think name brand products by Apple, Starbucks, or haute couture fashion designers).

The profit margin is thus equal to the utility that a product or service delivers to its intended target audience. Therefore, the challenge of any business, with the exception of monopolies and oligopolies, is to add more utility to its value proposition targeting a specific audience than its immediate competitors. In other words, pursuing this strategy to become that target audience's "obvious choice" supplier—and thus standing out as the *only* choice in the hearts and minds of your market segment.

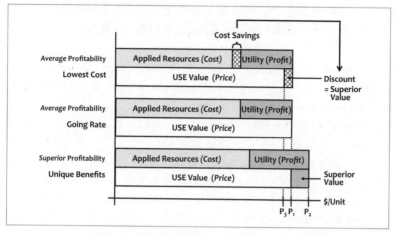

Figure 2.5: Creating Superior Use Value

The price you pay for a good or service (P_1, P_2, P_3) is a function of the cost of production plus a profit margin. The profit margin buyers are willing to pay is in direct proportion to the utility they anticipate to obtain from that purchase. Price is thus equal to use value. Superior use value can be delivered in the form of cost savings due to being the lowest-cost producer or by creating unique benefits, which allows for charging a higher profit margin.

Entering the Twilight State

A booming economy increases the margins for error, which allows everyone to experience success. Whenever economic conditions cause margins for error to dwindle, errors and violations against vital core business principles are exposed.

Without being *the* obvious choice supplier for a specific target audience, you'll have to market and advertise to a much wider audience, which increases cost. In the absence of superior use value, you have no competitive advantage, which can only be compensated by giving discounts to buyers at the expense of your profit margins.

This is when the business gremlin will blunt the reality of your environment and tell you to follow your mental programming. So, in order to make more money, you'll increase operational efficiency. Once the slack is taken up, you'll have to standardize your value propositions, which tends to cut off the differentiating qualities that distinguish you from your competitors. Eventually, when the only redeeming differentiator is price, a price war of attrition is inevitable. And, those with the deepest pockets win.

THE SECOND BUSINESS GREMLIN: FORM FOLLOWS FUNCTION

What is the idiosyncratic answer of a management consultant when asked which of two strategies, investment options, or solution alternatives to choose? Answer: *"It depends!"*

Instead of comparing alternatives based on their respective specifications, design, origin, or principle, they need to be judged on the basis of their suitability or fit, which depends on the specific function the chosen alternative answer has to perform under the given circumstances. The right choice will need to take the form that is best aligned with the function it is expected to perform when integrated within a system. Form follows function!

The importance of form was already recognized more than 2,500 years ago in a script called *The Art of War*, which is attributed to the ancient Chinese strategist Sun Tzu, who wrote:

Of old the skilled first made themselves invincible to await
the enemy's vincibility.
Invincibility lies in oneself.
Vincibility lies in the enemy.
Thus the skilled can make themselves invincible.
They cannot cause the enemy's vincibility.
Thus it is said, "Victory can be known. It cannot be made."[8]

Recognizing Our Dominant Mental Programming

Executives are expected to grow the business, and their success is measured in expressions such as earnings before interest, taxes, depreciation, and amortization (EBITDA); earnings per share (EPS); return on investment (ROI); return on assets (ROA); net present value (NPV); or just net profits—the bottom line.

Growth implies an increase in size and form and the pursuit of becoming the number one in whatever goal is identified: market share, market penetration rate, industry leader, and so forth.

Principles That Explain Cause-and-Effect Relationships

In order to perform an economic service for society that is scalable, sustainable, and profitable, all activities involved in fulfilling that service will have to be systematized (i.e., organized into processes, business functions, and jobs), and then directed toward the realization of that service. In other words, you want those processes and functions to be repeatable so that you don't have to reinvent the wheel every time you make a sale.

A system is successful when it succeeds at achieving its purpose or raison d'être. Therefore, every system must have a succinct, well-defined, and openly stated purpose in the absence of which it would make little economic sense to spend any time, money, or effort on creating and maintaining that system.

However, there is more to success than just realizing a specific purpose. Processes, business functions, and the products and services they deliver should comply with certain rules and regulations, moral standards, and ethics. They will be required to demonstrate a sense of common decency, humanity, social responsibility, and environmental conscientiousness. Therefore, the performance of processes and business functions need to be guided by certain prerequisites, and the design of products and services need to comply with specific critical success factors.

Character and Nature of Systems

In a sense, prerequisites and critical success factors determine the character and nature of each individual business system. They are an expression of an individual business's brand identity.

Consequently, the appropriate and distinguishing critical success factors and prerequisites for the system's design, organization or structure, implementation or operation, maintenance, and management (a.k.a. its business governance) must be derived from the system's purpose—hence form follows function.

By the way, this is very similar to a variety of sports that have the same objective of passing a ball into a goal. These games differentiate themselves from each other through their rules and regulations that stipulate the size, shape, and material of the court, ball, and goal and how the ball must be handled. In addition, there is a dress code and there are specific restrictions to a player's conduct on and off the court. Therefore, there is much more to success than winning or losing.

When thinking of success, I want you to remember the elegant prose written by Grantland Rice, an early-twentieth-century

American sportswriter for the Nashville daily newspaper the *Tennessean*: "For when the One Great Scorer comes to write against your name, He marks—not that you won or lost—but how you played the Game."

In conclusion, the purpose of a business system, in conjunction with its derivative prerequisites guiding the organization of people, ideas, and hardware into a value chain, and the critical success factors defining the value proposition it delivers, differentiates one business from another.

The Input → Process → Output Model

Imagine the input-process-output (IPO) model, a widely used approach in systems analysis and software engineering, for two different business systems that are catering to a similar target audience with a similar value proposition.

Competing businesses with similar value propositions that draw on similar input variables are very likely to have similar value chains. As a consequence, such value propositions have few distinguishing qualities other than price and make you susceptible to attrition price wars. And, when you can only entice people to buy from you by lowering prices time and again, your profit margins will suffer. Only those competitors with the deepest pockets—financial stamina—will survive. (See Figure 2.6.)

When discussing use value, we saw that superior use value originates from the following:

1. **Being the lowest-cost producer.** This can be either due to superior cost-effective procurement of input variables or superior operational efficiency within the process of transforming input variables into output variables, or a unique method for delivering use value to the buyer or end user.

   Note that in many instances, a competitive advantage based on cost-effective procurement has proven to be relatively easy to copy, with outsourcing of labor-intensive processes to lower-wage countries as the most well-known option. And within lower-wage countries, we now see a trend of outsourcing work to their rural areas where wages are even

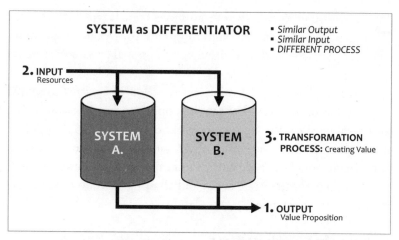

Figure 2.6: How to Succeed in a Competitive Market

The means by which buyers and users experience doing business with you depends on your proprietary transformation process. Similar products or services, created from similar resources, result in distinctly different user experiences that determine your customer's satisfaction, brand loyalty, and obvious choice supplier status.

lower. How sustainable will that competitive advantage prove to be in the long run?

2. **Creating unique benefits.** To create a distinguishingly different value proposition, there must be a distinguishingly different process for transforming input variables into output variables. The benefit of a high-quality transformation process is a consistently high predictability rate of delivering high-quality products and services, which require less re-work and incur fewer warranty claims. Being more effective at satisfying customer needs goes hand in hand with higher operational efficiency. In short, improving the quality of the transformation process can offset the additional cost of providing more utility. This form of creating superior use value is the aim of Deming's life's work.

An additional benefit of developing proprietary processes and business functions that create superior use value is the difficulty they pose to competitors who want to copy your success. After all, if we assume that a competitor manages to copy each individual process of your value chain with 95 percent accuracy, then after copying only five successive processes, the overall success rate is reduced to a mere 77 percent, which is not enough to imitate your value proposition. The success rate goes down with every additional process that needs to be copied.

Creating superior use value is a function of creating a unique transformation process that requires ongoing development of the entire value chain through a process known as continual improvement. Developing the value chain in this manner involves a coordinated increase in capability and capacity of all business functions throughout the value chain and aligning them to the purpose for which it was intended.

Entering the Twilight State

An established business system is powerful because it possesses significant amounts of internal momentum that can act either as a constructive or destructive force. Therefore, one wants to work *with* the system's internal force rather than *against* it.

The concept of form follows function implies that the form of a business system aligns with the function it is expected to perform. Consequently, misalignment between form and function will cause unnecessary friction and conflict within the business system, which turns its internal momentum into a self-destructive force.

Misalignment originates from one of the following:

- Changing the function(s) the current business system is designed to perform without adjusting or changing its form accordingly in an adequate and timely manner
- Undermining the business system's capability and capacity of realizing its function(s) by deferring maintenance in order to save money and by implementing efficiency measures that undermine the system's effectiveness

Adopting a strategy for the pursuit of (hyper) growth and/or becoming the number one in the market alters a business system's de facto purpose. Since growing the system requires capital, executives tend to resort to cutting cost to finance future growth internally.

Growing faster than one can generate the necessary cash to pay for the expansion is a well-documented hazard. Nonetheless, every shortfall in cash is met with another attempt at improving operational efficiency. No wonder most people erroneously proclaim that the purpose of a business is to make money; that's how their minds have been programmed. Imagine a business plan competition where every participant says, "The purpose of my business is to make money." Where is the use value in that for prospective investors and clients?

Maintaining System Integrity

However, repeated and sustained cost-cutting measures will eventually erode the business system's capacity and capability of creating superior use value, which is the exact ingredient that attracts customers and makes them willing to pay the desired superior profit margin.

Needless to say, a business system that is expected to realize multiple purposes—making money and creating superior use value—which are sometimes mutually exclusive, experiences serious internal friction and conflict.

Without crystal clarity about a business system's function, executives risk making the wrong decisions regarding its form. They need this clarity to design, organize or structure, implement or operate, maintain, and manage the value chain, also known as business governance. Mismatches between a system's form and function show up as systemic problems, which render any business system vulnerable to failure in a competitive marketplace.

When held to account and asked to explain the current state of the business and to propose a short-term course of action for restoring the business system's integrity, the business gremlin appears right out of the blue. Clearly, someone or something is messing with the system. It cannot be you because you followed your mental programming: you did everything in your power to grow the business and to increase bottom-line results.

Once hypervigilance (more commonly known as anxiety or panic) subsides and vigilance returns, errors and violations against vital core business principles become evident. It does not require rocket science to figure out that a value chain in which capability and capacity are not at par with the function it is expected to perform, is prone to failure. Increasing operational efficiency of an ineffective system is a lost cause.

THE THIRD BUSINESS GREMLIN:
THE MEANS AND ENDS

Dominant economic markets demand that everything and anything is given a price tag, including noneconomic values such as humanity, culture, environmental health and beauty, and clean air and water and soil. In order to attach a price tag to the perceived benefits of these noneconomic values, economists conduct cost-benefit analyses. With the distinction between economic and noneconomic values reduced to a single entity—money—the destruction, pollution, or annihilation of noneconomic values can now be justified with a trade-off against economic benefits such as net profits, gross domestic product (GDP), infrastructure, employment, regional development, and tax revenue. This all-too-common practice demonstrates that money is now perceived as the highest of all values, and the purpose of any for-profit enterprise is to make money. The most successful business is the one that makes the most money.

Because decision makers are expected to behave economically, they are expected to base their decisions on simple calculations to determine whether a proposal is economic or uneconomic. Therefore, any proposal in which the projected income, investment, or cost fails to meet certain predetermined financial standards should be rejected. Subsequently, executives who approve such uneconomic proposals expose themselves to shareholder derivative action suits aimed at their replacement.

Because the purpose of any commercial enterprise is defined as making money, or raising bottom-line results, every hierarchical leader is expected to maximize the amount of money that their part of the value chain contributes to the overarching aim of making money. Success is then measured from one quarter of a year to the next.

Because each resource, and every link in the value chain is a means to achieving the purpose for which the value chain was created, decision makers will evaluate and judge the choice of every alternative based on its ability to perform effectively and efficiently. The alternative with the highest anticipated NPV or ROI wins.

Short-Term Gains

Effectiveness tends to be expressed in terms of specifications, such as a job description, properties of a commodity or tool, or a request for proposal (RFP). Specifications become less precise when their prerequisites and critical success factors cannot be expressed quantitatively. When the pros and cons of each competing resource is expressed in preferences, and when each preference is given a weight to determine its importance to the acquisition or investment for the business, assessments become rather subjective.

Efficiency tends to boil down to the lowest possible price—the least amount of up-front or out-of-pocket cost, or the lowest NPV. Price tags do not reveal a resource's accuracy, reliability, security, dependability, longevity, sustainability, trustworthiness, and loyalty. Price does not provide any value judgment regarding the capability and capacity of any of the competing resources as a suitable means to an end.

When certain distinguishing specifications of a competing resource cannot be translated into immediately obvious short-term contributions to a business's financial performance, efficiency concerns tend to trump those regarding operational effectiveness.

Principles That Explain Cause-and-Effect Relationships

The raison d'être of any commercial business venture is to satisfy customer needs; hence, the money one desires to make must be obtained from those customers. However, what an individual customer needs depends on personal preferences that are determined by many factors, such as their nationality, culture, geography, climate, weather, fashion, disposable income, social standing, social responsibility, environmental friendliness, sustainability, age, sex, personal values, and beliefs. Therefore, any attempt at being everything to anybody is doomed to fail.

Consequently, you'd better identify a clearly defined target audience of people who believe what you believe and who believe that the things you do can help them. Imagine doing business with people who resonate with your value proposition because they experience the value you provide on a visceral level. This experience is what Bo Burlingham identified as *mojo* in his fascinating book *Small Giants: Companies That Choose to Be Great Instead of Big*. Mojo refers to the effect you have on buyers and users rather than a specific behavior, which, incidentally, cannot be captured in any prescription or best practice. Instead of using words related to price, quality, service, and features, these people use words to describe your value proposition such as "love," "adore," and "trust." For them you are their obvious choice supplier.

Obvious Choice Supplier

Being their obvious choice is all about *What's in It for Me* (WIIFM)— meaning the utility that users of the products or services anticipate to receive. These benefits exceed the physical product or service delivery and are mostly intangible in nature (e.g., beauty, confidence, security, safety, femininity, masculinity, avant-garde, prestige, and coolness). Although economists tend to regard such benefits as noneconomic values, the users, on the other hand, are more inclined to perceive these benefits as priceless. Therefore, such unique benefits are part and parcel of a brand identity, or how buyers and users experience the relationship with their provider or supplier of choice.

This experience of being the obvious choice provider/supplier can only be derived from integrating the design, organization or structure, implementation or operation, maintenance, and management of the means of production. Means must have the capability and capacity to realize the end, or purpose, for which the value chain was created. Different ends require different means. And your choice of a means to a generic end such as making money is less critical than choosing a means to satisfy specific customer needs. In addition, hardly any potential customer resonates with a business leader's desire or goal to make money; what buyers care about is the effectiveness with which a business delivers on its (marketing) promises to them. Period.

Holding individual hierarchical leaders accountable for their contribution to a value chain's bottom-line results, without sufficient influence over the business's overall revenue generation capability and capacity, forces them to focus their attention on the acquisition of specialized knowledge, skills, and tools to maximize operational efficiency of all processes for which they are directly responsible. Because of this, development of individual means has become an end in its own right. (See Figure 2.7.)

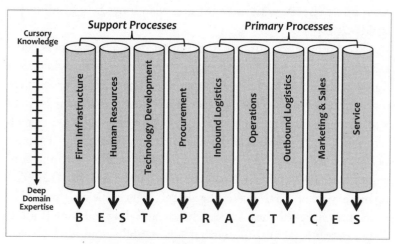

**Figure 2.7: The Perfection of Means Within
Each Link of the Value Chain**

When every link in the value chain is perceived and treated as a silo of
specialized knowledge, and develops its own best practices to optimize
its own standards, deliverables, procedures, and tools, separately and in
isolation of all other value chain links, the business will be yanked in multiple
directions. Perfecting the means while confusing the silo's purpose for that
of the business as a whole creates unnecessary friction and conflict.

Practitioners within each individual link of the value chain
develop their own silos of specialized knowledge, each with its own
silo-management techniques, best practices, and promotion of creativity and innovation to increase its financial contribution to the
business's bottom-line results. For each link in the value chain,
there are countless professional service organizations to support
and encourage the development of their own form of specialized
knowledge, including certification of practitioners, accreditation of
training, consulting and coaching professionals, conferences, webi-
nars, podcasts, and newsletters.

Gold Plating Silos of Specialized Knowledge

Silo managers confuse the pursuit of silo optimization with the purpose of the business system. This unfortunate trend is not unique
to the world of business. Boyd, known for designing the successful F-16 fighter jet, recognized a similar pattern within the world
of fighter aircraft design. He called this pursuit of silo optimization
the "Bigger, Higher, Faster, Farther Syndrome." And he called efforts

to equip an aircraft with more features than it needs to fulfill its job "gold plating."

Boyd proved scientifically that gold plating a fighter jet is detrimental to the rationale behind the procurement and deployment of a fighter jet, which is to obtain air superiority. The price to pay for turning a fighter jet into a dazzling piece of technology is an increase in its size, diameter, drag coefficient, fuel consumption, weight, wing loading, and so forth. Note how these factors are all correlated. To make her faster, she will need a bigger engine that weighs more and consumes more fuel, which in turn requires a larger fuel tank that takes up more space and thus makes the aircraft bigger. The weight of additional fuel makes her heavier, which increases drag and wing loading. This is detrimental to an aircraft's maneuverability and agility, which are critical success factors for air superiority. So, how much air superiority are you willing to trade for extra speed? Apart from speed, designers can opt for a more advanced radar system with a larger radar dome, which increases the diameter of the fuselage, which causes more drag, which decreases fuel efficiency and thus its range. How much range is enough for attaining air superiority?

Remember, in system design there are must-haves, should-haves, and nice-to-haves. Therefore, the follow-on question becomes: How much speed and radar range are enough for attaining air superiority?

The same principle applies to businesses: optimizing one or more of its business functions independently and in isolation of each other and disregarding the purpose of the business as a whole is detrimental to overall performance. Too many silo managers are quick to adopt and implement the latest-and-greatest specialized tool, technology, or methodology without thinking through its impact on the rest of the business. The problem with this logic is what Einstein called *"perfection of means and confusion of ends."*

Optimizing operational efficiency within a single department, independently of all other intricately interdependent departments, will cut cost. However, such uncoordinated efforts tend to spill over to other departments in the form of unintended consequences. As a result, these departments might have to adjust their work flow in order to accommodate for these unforeseen circumstances—and the costs of those adjustments might exceed the costs saved by the first department.

A common approach to cutting cost is standardization, which implies reducing differentiation. When this occurs, your value proposition starts to look more like that of your competition. When price is the only remaining differentiating factor, you risk unleashing a war on price.

Value Chain Integration

Executives can only succeed at becoming the obvious choice supplier to their intended target audience when all business functions within the value chain cooperate and interact with each other as they continually develop the capability and capacity of the value chain as an organic whole, as shown in Figure 2.8.

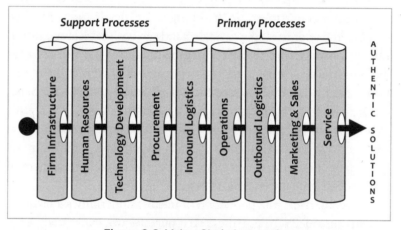

Figure 2.8: Value Chain Integration

Value chain integration is an expression of the missing link in the value chain (see Chapter 1). All links are organized into an integrated system, which is then directed toward the realization of the purpose for which it was created.

This means that although each business function pursues its own objectives, those objectives must support and contribute to the realization of the purpose of the value chain as an integrated whole. In other words, there is a hierarchy of objectives within the value chain. Having hierarchical leaders of silos of specialized knowledge compete among themselves for the allocation of resources and budget is an unintended source of friction and conflict within itself that should be avoided at all cost.

Entering the Twilight State

Back in 2008, when the banking debacle started to dominate the news, I attended a meeting that was called "Doing Business in Bad Economic Times." Right off the bat, keynote speaker Paul Brown, CEO of Expedia, said: "Doing business in bad economic times is no different from doing business in good economic times!" I could not agree more.

The only difference between doing business in good and bad economic times is the margin for error: in bad economic times a business system's tolerance for mistakes is less than in good times. To illustrate this point with an analogy, imagine driving your car under good and bad weather conditions and under good and bad road conditions. The car does not require its driver to perform any additional or "secret" activities in order to arrive at the intended destination. But bad weather and poor roads put extra demands on both vehicle and driver. Drivers must exercise their best judgment in assessing a situation as it enfolds and in choosing the right course of action given the condition of the road, the weather, traffic, the vehicle, and the task at hand.

Remember, a business system is a means to an end. It is a vehicle for the production and delivery of use value to its intended target audience. Even though specialization is essential for progress in the development of means, we cannot let the continual development of means determine the ends we pursue.

Specialization (the perfection of means) undermines a business system's intended purpose (the ends it pursues) when it is used for:

> **Gold plating,** which refers to increasing a business system with state-of-the-art features that are nonessential for continual improvement of a system's capability. Gold plating is an unnecessary drain on resources and a drag on overall system performance.

> **Predatory cultivation,** which means perfecting operational efficiency beyond the point of picking-up slack within the system and when any amount of incremental efficiency can only be gained at the expense of the system's overall effectiveness. This reckless chopping away at operational cost to the point where it infringes upon the business system's capacity and capability for realizing its intended mission is what I call the "Black Knight

Syndrome" (after a scene from the British movie *Monty Python and the Holy Grail*). Moreover, its rationale flies in the face of Gossen's first law of diminishing marginal utility.[9] Revenue is determined by buyers, and by eroding the use value that attracted people to your products and services, you are eroding brand loyalty. And it's no secret that retaining an existing loyal audience is cheaper than attracting new buyers who come and go.

There Are No Secrets or Silver Bullets

With every link in the value chain pursuing its own goals in isolation from all other silos, hierarchical leaders pull the value chain apart. For example, operations can save money by standardizing products and services, whereas marketing and sales can generate more income by diversification. Or, firm infrastructure may decide to save money by reducing inventory of spare parts, whereas service may want to improve customer satisfaction by keeping any spare parts in stock for prompt delivery.

Substituting the purpose of a value chain with the pursuit of separate goals for each of its links is like playing golf on a course where every green has multiple holes, expecting a player to hole-out with one ball, in all cups, with one single stroke. In addition, hierarchical leaders will demonstrate a greater reluctance or resistance to cooperating with change initiatives that enhance the capability of the value chain as an organic whole but which cannot be chalked up as an individual achievement on their profit and loss statement, which forms the basis for their annual performance review.

Whenever there is a downturn in the economy, when buyers are reevaluating the cash value of their disposable income, they are more critical in their evaluation of the use value offered by competing suppliers of products and services. They couldn't care less about their supplier's level of operational efficiency or their gold-plated means of production. Because of this, the suppliers' margins for error are narrower, which make the mismatches between means and ends more obvious and a more compelling choice for immediate action than ever before.

No matter what the business gremlins whispered in your ear—about how you adhered to best practices, how a penny saved is a penny earned, how you took the advice of an industry thought leader, how you followed the example of those who should know what they are doing—you are experiencing systemic problems. Since something went wrong, and because you did everything right, someone else should take the blame. Maybe you can get by with, "It's the economy, stupid!"

There must be a secret for doing business in bad economic times, and so we keep searching for that one-size-fits-all silver bullet solution that can be implemented in a few easy steps and without having to change our level of thinking about the relationship between means and ends and not requiring any effort from executives. We keep hoping for a different outcome until we can no longer escape accepting the inevitable truth of the principle of means and ends. You cannot expect your intended target audience to support you when cash value exceeds use value. That is when you stopped being their obvious choice supplier.

WHAT HAPPENS NEXT?

The twilight state exposes a mismatch between how a business system behaves in reality and how our mental programming tells us that it should be behaving. Instead of casting blame on someone other than oneself or on something outside one's sphere of influence, we might want to examine our own mental programming, especially when operating within a social system where many principles and values are in flux constantly.

In the next chapter, we'll explore four other business gremlins that handicap executive performance.

CHAPTER 3

Four More Business Gremlins That Handicap Executive Performance

The illiterate of the 21st century will not be those who cannot read and write, but those who cannot LEARN, UNLEARN, and RELEARN.

—Alvin Toffler
American writer and futurist; from *Future Shock*

Jared Diamond explained in his book *Collapse: How Societies Choose to Fail or Succeed* that decision makers have no incentive to change their behavior for as long as they can insulate themselves from the consequences of their actions or inactions, and thus of the principles, methods, theories, or beliefs they accept and reject by exercising their free will.

As cunning as business gremlins may be in denying the small still voice within a fair hearing, sooner or later, unexpected events will cause you to listen. Then, you'll realize that solving systemic problems requires more training on how to think than what to think, demanding we think deliberately rather than leaving our nonconscious mind in charge, similar to flying on autopilot.

THE FOURTH BUSINESS GREMLIN: WHOLENESS VERSUS SEPARATENESS

We live our lives within one system or another, whether that is a family, economic, political, cultural, technological, or any other form of organization including a business. Please note that a system is a network of nodes and connections—component parts and their interfaces. And systems derive their unique ability from the connections and interdependent relationships between their component parts rather than the gold plating of any or all of their individual constituent part(s). Therefore, "wholeness, interconnectedness, and change are not theoretical; they make possibilities."[1]

Separateness is the idea that a single component part with its own distinct identity, while belonging to a system, can exist independently and in separation from that system.

Wholeness is the recognition that the identifiable character and nature of a system originates from the integration and interconnectedness of that system's component parts, the processes they perform, and the focus and direction of their application toward a common purpose.

On the flip side, wholeness loses its signature character and nature when the interconnectedness among component parts is disrupted by the unfolding of new and unforeseen events. An organic whole that has lost its integrity will experience friction and conflict.

Wholeness and interdependence are more commonly known as complexity. Studies show that nothing befuddles and bewilders executives more than complexity.

In short, wholeness is the recognition that the identifiable character and nature of an organic whole originates from the integration and interconnectedness of the processes performed by a system's component parts and the focus and direction of their application to a common purpose.

Recognizing Our Dominant Mental Programming

Business systems are becoming increasingly more complex. Effective control over the behavior and performance of such complex systems requires that leaders comprehend a system's *business mechanics* (see Part II of this book) and internal dynamics. To that end, our schooling has imprinted our minds with the notion that a business system is comparable to a mechanical machine. Thus, according to Newtonian physics, we are informed that:

- The business system is comprised of physical component parts only, and that all performance and outcomes are the result of material interactions (commonly known as *materialism*). Such material parts include all forms of organizational structures ranging from hierarchical, functional, or geographical departments and its human resources—a euphemism for human beings or personnel—to the specific hardware they use, the nature of their workspaces, and their physical locations.
- The role or function that each component part performs inside a business system can be understood by studying how each separate individual part interacts with any of the other parts, i.e., by identifying the business system's functional structure. Therefore, a complex system is nothing but the sum of its parts (which is commonly known as *reductionism*). Think of the value chain and how each of its links can be reduced ever further down to the level of a single task (see Chapter 1, Figure 1.4, "Translating Processes into an Organizational Chart").
- The behavior and performance of a complete business system can be understood by gaining insight into the chain of cause-and-effect relationships among its component parts (commonly known as *determinism*). Since every part is interchangeable, any malfunctioning part will just be replaced with a new one, including a human resource. Therefore, as long as every part just does the job for which it is intended, leaving the thinking and decision making to those in charge, everything will function like clockwork.

Human Fallibility

Because of our fallibility, people are perceived as the weakest link in the value chain. The fact that we make mistakes is not compatible with management's desire for engineered system reliability, requiring performance to be quantified as precisely as possible, often expressed in probabilistic terms. Therefore, it has become common practice to automate processes and to replace people with machines if and when possible.

In addition, since labor tends to be the single largest cost of production, it has become common practice to replace expensive local labor with cheaper labor overseas or with a machine. Therefore, decisions to replace people are based on a cost–benefit calculation. Note that the calculated cost of replacement depends on the scope of the inquiry—which affected independent processes, separate departments, the value chain as an integrated whole, or a community are included in those calculations. Replacing people with machines or with other people overseas brings its own challenges and cost in the form of adoption time, composing service level agreements, the need for specialized personnel, adapting to time differences, and misunderstandings due to language barriers and cultural barriers, to name but a few. These challenges and costs—such as the loss of corporate memory—are often not anticipated and thus not included in the deciding cost–benefit calculation.

Principles That Explain Cause-and Effect Relationships

Separate parts that are organized into a coherent entity and directed toward the realization of the purpose of the system to which they belong, is called a network. Networks consist of nodes (the separate parts that perform their activities, processes, and functions on tightly coupled resources) and network links (the interfaces or connections between the nodes). (See Figure 3.1.)

Network links allow work flow to pass from one node to the next, where it is either redistributed to one or more other nodes, collected from one or more other nodes, or where it enters or exits the network.

Therefore, every node contributes to the capability and capacity of the network as an integrated whole to realize its intended purpose. Consequently, any attempt at ranking the importance of one part over another is meaningless because removing any node from the network diminishes its ability to realize the purpose for which it was created. Ranking suggests that a system could survive without a node of lesser importance. However, a node that does not contribute to realizing the system's purpose should not have been integrated within the network to begin with.

Unfortunately, some operational efficiency measures are based on eliminating one or more nodes for the sole purpose of "saving" money and thus increasing profits, as goes the line of reasoning. Decision makers who approve the adoption of such measures suffer from the aforementioned Black Knight Syndrome because their desire to make money undercuts their business system's capability and capacity.

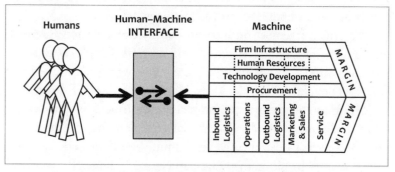

Figure 3.1: The Network or Business System

A business system is a network of nodes—human and machine—and its interpersonal connections and the Human–Machine Interface (HMI). Note: the HMI can also be a node.

Although nodes cannot be ranked according to their level of importance within the network, they can be divided according to similarities in their nature and then aggregated into three main categories: humans, machine, and the human–machine interface (HMI).

Human

Business executives who identify money as the highest of all values often train their crosshairs on employees. After all, they are usually the largest business expense. Therefore, according to their mental programming, people are the eminent target for cost-cutting measures such as replacing people with machines. Lisanne Bainbridge, author of the study "Ironies of Automation," points out:[2]

> The designer's view of the human operator may be that the operator is unreliable and inefficient. So should be eliminated from the system. There are two ironies of this attitude. One is that designer errors can be a major source of operating problems.

> The second irony is that the designer who tries to elim-
> inate the operator still leaves the operator to do the tasks
> which the designer cannot think how to automate.

We need to acknowledge that the real challenge before us is neither the cost of a labor force nor human fallibility. The real challenge
is a decision maker's proficiency at solving systemic problems in a
timely fashion, which is empirically inadequate!

America's foremost military strategist, Colonel John R. Boyd,
was famous for saying: "Machines win no wars. People do and they
use their minds." Boyd would equate a business system to a force,
which he defined as "People, Ideas, Hardware: in THAT order."

Humans are thus not the problem; even though employees are
often made out to be. As a matter of fact, humans are impressive
problem solvers whose effectiveness diminishes when working under
time pressure. In his study on human error, Dr. James Reason concluded, "Although we cannot change the human condition [human
fallibility] we can change the conditions under which humans work."

Reason's studies have proven that it is not uncommon that the
conditions under which humans work forbid or prevent employees
from using their minds and judgment to do what the current state
of the business demands. A lack of manpower and training, inadequate or improper tools, poorly maintained equipment, safety hazards,
shortage of spare parts, insufficient time, being told to leave the thinking up to management, or fear of being let go are just some examples.

Business governance is responsible for creating the conditions—
good and bad—under which humans work, which makes the
effectiveness and efficiency of all employees an executive's
responsibility.

Machine[3]

"Machine" represents the organization of tasks into activities, activities into processes, processes into business functions, and business
functions into a single coherent value chain. Critical success factors
serve as organizational principles for the look and feel of the products
and services, while prerequisites serve as organizational principles for
the machine's production and delivery processes. Critical success factors and prerequisites are derived from the purpose of the business

system, which is to guarantee the integrity of the network as an organic whole.

The interconnectedness of tasks, activities, processes, and business functions becomes pertinent when deciding on a change management initiative. Such an initiative is either warranted by the need for a solution for a systemic problem, by a change in strategic direction, or by the desire to renovate or innovate the existing business system.

It is during this decision-making process that the scope of an intended change management initiative and its temporary disruptive effect on business as usual tends to be grossly underestimated. Some decision makers erroneously believe that the scope of a change management initiative and its temporary disruptive effect on business as usual can be limited to a single organizational component.

Take the C.H.A.F.P.I.L.O.T.™ test (shown in Figure 3.2) as a rule of thumb for estimating the scope and impact of a change initiative on a business system and the time until completion. (C.H.A.F.P.I.L.O.T. is an acronym for Commercial, Housing, Administrative Organization, Finance, Personnel, Information, Legal, Organization, and Technology and Tools.)

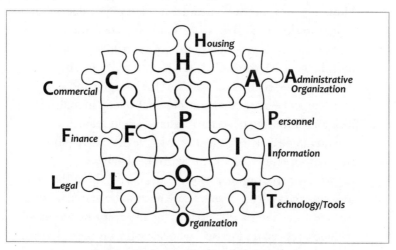

Figure 3.2: The C.H.A.F.P.I.L.O.T. Model

Every business system adheres to the C.H.A.F.P.I.L.O.T. design principles. A change in one of those principles cannot fail to affect one or more other design principles.

As said before, decision makers have a tendency to downplay the impact of a proposed change initiative on the business system as a whole. Many such initiatives involve the introduction, upgrade, or replacement of computer hardware and software, and the collection, maintenance, and manipulation of data. Consequently, people jump to the conclusion that it is just an information technology (IT) project.

For example, assume your business is highly data driven. Currently, your data is stored on five separate databases. Access is limited to five people at a time only, and those people must have received special training. You want to replace the separate databases with a single one that is web-based and thus accessible to all authorized users. Is this just an IT project or not? The following list is only an example of possible aspects to consider per organizational component and is thus by no means intended to be complete:

- **Commercial.** The nature of one's business dictates a system's capability and capacity. Alternatively, improved access to a single integrated database opens up possibilities for use in other applications or by other lines of business. Licensing access can be an additional source of revenue.
- **Housing.** Any piece of hardware needs a physical location. Access to the physical location that houses hardware for the storage of proprietary data of a sensitive nature must be secured, controlled, and monitored. Certain data sources—such as transactions for banking and asset management—require remote system back up in multiple locations. Housing of certain systems might require an emergency electricity generator. Mobile devices require Internet access for connecting with the database.
- **Administrative organization.** Users need to be authorized to access the system. Terms of use need to be drawn up that include procedures and measures for enforcement and must include a procedure for users who leave the business. Layout of system output needs to be designed to reflect the corporate image and brand. Contracts need to be drawn up and monitored for equipment or the purchase, leasing, licensing, and maintenance (Service Level Agreements—SLA) of

software, as well as housing (location, specification, and access), security, and other services required.

- **Finance.** Change management initiatives need to be financed. Procurement of equipment, services, and rights need to be paid for in full up front or over time. The project requires manpower to execute the change management initiative. Additional expertise might have to be hired on a temporary basis, which requires funding. Once the project has been implemented, it needs to be operated, maintained, and managed, which needs to be paid for. There is hardly any conceivable change management initiative that does not require involvement of the organizational component of finance. And yet, not all change management initiatives are finance projects. (See Figure 3.3.)

- **Personnel.** To authorize people for the use of the system, the project will need a list of names of employees who need to receive access and what level of security clearance they need to receive. It might be necessary that those people receive a background check. Users will need to be trained on the proper use of the system and sign a users' agreement.

- **Information.** Data needs to be migrated from the old databases to the new one. Before doing that, the data might have to be scrubbed for mistakes and duplicate entries. Also, a decision needs to be made regarding the sort of data to collect and store, in which order it is to be displayed, its compatibility with other data systems, the exchange of data with outside vendors, the onscreen display of data, and the format of reports.

- **Legal.** Change management initiatives involve many commercial transactions and long-term financial obligations or commitments that require examination by legal experts. In addition, there are legal restrictions on the rights to collect and use data, either by law or by contract. Legal includes tax implications, and available government subsidies and incentives.

- **Organization.** Change management initiatives can change which activities, processes, and business functions are to be performed within the value chain. When access to data is extended beyond a small group of employees who provide data services to the entire business, for which they received special training, their services might be no longer required and their department might have to be reorganized or even eliminated. In other cases—think of the advent of on-line business and social media—new business functions and even departments might have to be created.

• **Technology and tools.** Mission critical and expensive equipment are normally procured by means of a Request for Proposal (RFP). This document will stipulate all requirements and specifications—including its implementation, maintenance, operations, and management—with which the new technology or tool needs to comply for it to be considered a viable candidate in the procurement process. Apart from the tool itself, its interface(s) with other tools and technologies need to be seriously considered for compatibility.

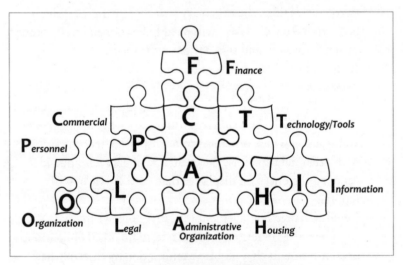

Figure 3.3: The Role of Finance

Ultimately, every C.H.A.F.P.I.L.O.T. design principle affects finance. Yet not every problem is a financial problem in need of a financial solution. Solutions can be chosen from any of the design principles as warranted.

Human–Machine Interface

A HMI is a shared boundary across which employees and the value chain interact with each other to affect each other's behavior and performance. The HMI encompasses all the elements a person will touch, see, hear, or use to perform control functions and receive feedback on those actions. (See Figure 3.4.)

Human beings possess the spark that brings the value chain to life! The uniqueness of every single human being can be described by means of his or her distinct preferences (personality type; see Chapter 2 under "Temperament and Character") for the way in which each of them wants to (1) interact with the world in which they live (**E**xtraversion or **I**ntroversion), (2) gather information (**S**ensing or i**N**tuition), (3) make decisions (**T**hinking or **F**eeling), and (4) relate to their outside environment (**J**udging or **P**erceiving).

Note that these preferences represent a continuum, which implies that every personality type inhabits both aspects but not always in equal amounts. Every human being tends to demonstrate a bias towards one of the aspects.

Apart from an individual's qualifications and general aptitude for a specific job, personality type serves as an indicator for the kind of job and environment in which an individual can perform to the best of her or his abilities.

The way in which a value chain is organized and directed is based on a wide array of assumptions. These assumptions contain the prerequisites for the value chain's effective and efficient performance and the critical success factors for its intended output.

In conclusion, for the achievement of an effective, sustainable, humane, predictable, and profitable network, accommodating the specifications or requirements for people to excel within a network—the conditions under which humans work—is as important as facilitating the assumptions regarding the organizing and directing of the value chain.

Perhaps the best-known HMI is the GUI, or graphical user interface between people and an electronic device. The common criterion for the design of a GUI is user-friendliness. Similarly, hand tools, desk chairs, dashboards, and cockpit layouts are assessed on their ergonomic properties.

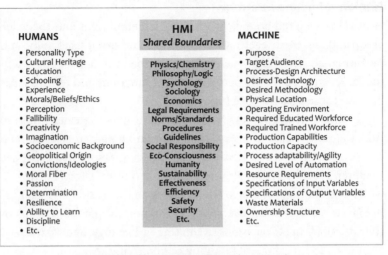

Figure 3.4: The Human–Machine Interface

The shared boundaries—interfaces—between humans and machines are governed by concepts, mental constructs, or intangible and nonquantifiable factors.

On the other hand, the effectiveness and efficiency of a business network's HMI are rated on many factors, such as the openness of internal and external communications, the level of trust, organizational culture, cooperation, interaction, productivity, work climate, best place to work, pride of workmanship, employee loyalty, being a target audience's obvious choice, creativity, innovation, inspiration, authenticity, and brand identity.

Note that most of these factors are intangible, nonquantifiable benefits—they are *not* things or component parts that can be hired, bought and sold, or leased. They are the result of proper business governance. The fact that they have no price tag does not mean that they are valueless and that they can be used as cheap bargaining chips in negotiations for internal reorganization or merger and acquisition transactions.

Keep in mind the following key principle: *What really matters happens at the edges—that is, where one surface or material meets or changes into another—is a key principle of architecture. The action is not in the centers or areas of sameness.*

Entering the Twilight State

Because a rising tide lifts all boats or, as I've heard many times in presentations, in a hurricane even turkeys will fly, no one questions an executive's business governance acumen when bottom-line results meet or exceed expectations. Any attempted criticism is countered with the clincher, "Who can argue with success?" Note that this implies equating success with profits, not the system's capability and capacity for becoming the obvious choice supplier to one's target audience.

As we saw before, the difference in governing a business system under good and bad economic conditions is the margin for error. Consequently, executive decision makers are escorted into the twilight state by their dwindling profit margins.

Instead of investigating the root cause of one's dwindling profit margins, executive decision makers rely on their mental programming. Instead of addressing the cause, they jump on addressing the effect—dwindling profit margins. When there is this kind of confusion about cause and effect, the root cause is thus often mistakenly perceived as a financial problem. Because increasing income (sales volume and profit margins) is more difficult to achieve in an economic downturn, lowering cost is the only remaining logical conclusion.

In general, there are two preferred approaches to cutting costs:

- **Cutting cost across the board.** This indiscriminate method reduces the budget of every department with the same percentage. The Dutch call this approach "the cheese-slicer method;" like a cheese slicer, you cut the budget with a small percentage across all line items on the profit and loss statement. This method is presented as being more equitable because the pain is shared by everyone.
- **Targeted.** This differentiating method reduces the budget through downsizing, postponing, or eliminating certain projects, activities, processes, functions, or departments. The criteria for selecting the targets to cut are usually financial.

Quality Improvement

Cutting cost based solely on financial parameters denies the interconnectedness of separate component parts and the wholeness of the network to which they belong. Cutting certain change management initiatives, operational activities, processes, business functions, or departments carries the risk of tearing the network. Unfortunately, due to the nature of complex systems, the possible consequences of tearing the network are unknown and often unknowable. Although possible consequences cannot always be predicted, successful management must take account of them nevertheless.

The minute you demonstrate the slightest intent of making cuts to a complex network, business gremlins start showing up because with every cut something else gets killed in the process.

All of a sudden, you will experience resistance to change that manifests in a decline in trust, an increase in disengaged employees, top talent resigning, a decline in organizational culture and brand identity, a drop in customer loyalty, and ethics violations. Despite trying to do what you believe is right, things go from bad to worse. Remember that prescribing cost-cutting measures before diagnosing any root cause(s) is malpractice.

Business gremlins will keep trying to reinforce the validly of your mental programming until you recognize the wholeness of the system to which all separate component parts belong or until you appreciate the interconnected structure of your network.

Once you start conducting root-cause analyses, you might discover that you can actually save cost by reallocating resources and by continual improvement of the network's quality (its effectiveness and efficiency). Quality is not a separate part that is added to the network at an additional cost, but it is a methodology for organizing separate component parts into an organic whole.

THE FIFTH BUSINESS GREMLIN: INTERACTION VERSUS ISOLATION

Two common approaches to making the network of a business system visible are an organizational chart and a process chart.

The organizational chart is focused on visualizing the level of authority delegated to leaders of individual hierarchical positions within the organization, and therefore on the activities and the outcomes for which those leaders are responsible. The organizational chart shows that an organization has an unbroken line of command from top to bottom and that there is unity of command. No one has more than one hierarchical leader. And the span of control of each hierarchical leader—how many people report to a single hierarchical leader—is defined.

The focus of a process chart is on visualizing the work flow from end to end within a business process, a business function, the value chain as a whole, and between the value chains within the same value system. Process charts resemble an electrical home wiring diagram, showing the flow of electrical current through all of its component parts. *End to end* means following the electrical current as it flows through the hot wire from each breaker on the circuit breaker panel to every connected electrical component—such as switches, lights, appliances, and electronics—*and* back through the neutral wire to the circuit breaker.

The same principle applies to data as it flows through a business process such as the compiling of a monthly profit and loss statement. It starts with the old P&L statement and ends with the creation of a new P&L statement—end to end within a closed circuit. I once mapped out such an end-to-end process for a client and discovered information was flowing through 12 departments, belonging to three divisions, at multiple geographical locations. I don't think anyone involved in this end-to-end process was previously aware of the number of participating departments; everyone was just concerned with doing their own jobs.

How people from inside and outside the organization experience their relationship with a business system as an organic whole is not the exclusive realm of hierarchical leaders' interpersonal behavior—their leadership skills—as seems to be a fashionable posture of many of today's business articles, books, seminars, and coaching sessions.

A business system's behavior—its character and nature—is largely determined by the design, organization or structure, implementation or operation, maintenance, and management of all business processes performed by all component parts, including their mutually interdependent relationships, or interfaces. I call this shaping and adjusting a business system's character and nature business governance, which is an exclusive executive responsibility (see Chapter 9).

Nonetheless, it is not uncommon for a hierarchical leader to become defensive when issues regarding the work flow within his or her department are raised by a peer. Failing to see the workflow for which one is responsible just as a part of an end-to-end process creates an invisible wall between departments and threatens to sever direct lines of communication.

Hence, the nature and character of interpersonal relationships among hierarchical leaders can be described on a continuum that has isolation and interaction as its extremes. Whereas interaction refers to an open business system that allows interactions and exchanges between its internal elements and the environment, isolation refers to a closed business system, which denies such interactions and exchanges.

Recognizing Our Dominant Mental Programming

Regardless of their size or scope, almost all businesses feel the effect of today's global 24/7 economy upon their individual operations. Therefore, hierarchical leaders give ample consideration to the impact of external forces on internal operations in formulating strategy and executive decision-making processes. Examples of such external forces can be found in the bargaining power of rival businesses, the bargaining power of vendors and suppliers, buyer preferences, purchasing power, socioeconomic and geopolitical conditions, social responsibility, environmental awareness, financial and economic markets, government regulations, trade policies, and many others.

Business systems are perceived as inanimate, mechanical machines that consist of many distinct component parts—including human beings. Since each part interacts with other parts of the machine, these parts must adhere to strict specifications to guarantee that they will perform their unique functions to the best of their abilities. This makes each part interchangeable and allows for any part that is broken or does not function properly to be replaced by a spare part. Nonhuman spare parts are obtained through the procurement department, and humans are obtained through the human resources department.

The major challenge to operating an inanimate for-profit system is maximizing its efficiency. This demands that the collective component parts operate inside very narrow margins for error and require the least amount of additional energy input and influence from outside the business system. In other words, the machine will reach maximum efficiency when every hierarchical leader optimizes the efficiency of every component part(s) or department within the system for which they are personally responsible.

Best Practices

Business authors, students, researchers in academia, industry groups, and professional associations have come to the aid of hierarchical leaders by analyzing the processes of individual silos of specialized knowledge to achieve possible efficiency gains. Researchers interview hierarchical leaders of a particular silo of specialized knowledge within a sample group of businesses that successfully increased their efficiency over a certain period of time (see Figure 3.5). Their aim is to discover an attitude, habit, decision, or methodology that can be attributed to that hierarchical leader's success—how she or he contributed to the business' goal to make more money. The answer of each participant on each question is analyzed for statistical correlation. Any correlation found is then formulated into another "best practice" for increasing efficiency within a specific silo of specialized knowledge. Note that correlation is not the same as causation.

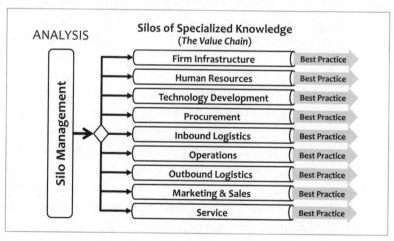

Figure 3.5: Creating Best Practices

The business system is broken up into its component parts, and every part is analyzed separately and in isolation of all other parts in search of potential cost-cutting best practices aimed at boosting bottom-line results. Consequently, silo management must now compete for influence and budget with every other silo.

Principles That Explain Cause-and-Effect Relationships

Any business is a living system, or organism, which is comprised of multiple process structures. The definition of a process structure is a network of intricately interdependent and dynamically balanced processes. These structures are capable of adjusting or changing their behavior when new and unforeseen circumstances unfold, and yet their processes remain in the same relationship to one another. This allows a living system to reconstitute, self-renew, and reinvent its structure without altering the system's (brand) identity.

The energy for maintaining dynamic relationships among all processes within a human-made system is provided by human beings. Human energy comes in many forms, such as biological, chemical, physical, emotional, moral, mental, creative, and spiritual energy. Each form can be converted into another and vice versa. For example, moral energy—the conviction of one's beliefs—can be translated into the mental energy that is one's will power and determination, which can be converted into creative energy, and this in turn can be converted into physical energy, thus maintaining the system's dynamic balance. Note that this conversion of one form of energy into another can work in both directions. Because people have this amazing ability to convert energy, they are the glue that hold processes together, especially when the system is stressed beyond its capability or capacity. However, there is a limit to the amount of time people are able and willing to hold things together. And, when they let go, when they let the chips fall where they may, the system collapses.

Even though business systems are autonomous from their environment, their identity, just like that of any other living entity, is defined by their relationships with that environment. Business systems interact with their environment through an intricate web of relationships with buyers, vendors, suppliers, government entities, labor markets, economic trends, cultural expectations, fashion, state of technology, discretionary income, and positioning within the value system, among others. This web guarantees that changes inside and outside the system, even when a part is lost, can be adjusted, compensated, or substituted without affecting the business system's (brand) identity. The sole purpose of this web is to continually reproduce the living system's structure—organism—as a form of self-renewal. There is one caveat though. As stated earlier, energy for maintaining dynamic relationships among all processes within a human-made system is provided by human beings. Once the number of people who are disengaged from their work—which is today's most frequently heard complaint from executives—reaches a critical mass, the system will start to become unglued.

The Need for Open Systems

The major challenge to keeping a living system alive is allowing the system to evolve from its old state to a new state, which happens to be the essence of solving systemic problems as well! Business systems can evolve from one state to another only if hierarchical leaders interact with their environment openly or when their business is an open system.

According to the Russian-born Belgian scientist Ilya Prigogine,[4] the quintessential characteristic that distinguishes an open system from a closed system is what he called a "far from equilibrium" environment. He defined equilibrium as the maximum state of entropy—a state in which all useful energy has dissipated. Let me try to translate this scientific language into an understandable format for business applications.

For a living system to cope with complexity and the disruptive effects of events, human energy must be converted from one form into another. However, in some human energy conversions, some amounts of energy, such as engagement, creativity, imagination, enthusiasm, pride of workmanship, and love, become temporarily tied up elsewhere, typically in different forms of friction and conflict—for example, general frustration, dissatisfaction, power tripping, political gamesmanship, discrimination, sexual harassment, whistleblowing, retaliation, employee disengagement, immoral and unethical conduct, sabotage, and fraud. Employees who experience any of these symptoms of friction and conflict for an extended period of time will disengage themselves from their job and employer. The scientific name for this efficiency loss of human energy is entropy. It means that a certain amount of human energy will, temporarily, be unavailable for making a positive contribution to the realization of the business system's purpose. (See Figure 3.6.) Note that this conversion of human energy works both ways—nonproductive energy can be converted back into productive energy.[5]

Figure 3.6: Generating Entropy

Competition among silos of specialized knowledge for influence and budget reinforces the fifth business gremlin, interaction versus isolation. Isolation results in entropy—energy that is temporarily not available to be productive.

Business systems that operate within a far-from-equilibrium environment are commonly known as open systems. Far-from-equilibrium environments are characterized by a high flow of energy and the influx of new information, knowledge, people, ideas, tools, technology, and materials. This constant input of new energy is used to increase the business system's capability and capacity for solving systemic problems—evolution as a living organism—and it stabilizes the shape of the system's process structures. For this reason, open systems must constantly dissipate entropy, the human energy that is temporarily not available, so it won't build up inside the system and "kill" the system by establishing a state of equilibrium.

A Challenge to Open Systems

The challenge, however, is that too much inflow of new energy and thoughts (such as best practices, the perfection of means, and flavor-of-the-month business theories or leadership practices) threatens to overwhelm the system and radically alter the relationships among its processes. Therefore, open business systems must constantly balance their need to remain safe from intense fluctuations within their environment and their need to remain open to an ever-fluctuating input of energy from that fluid environment.

Giving people new challenges through education, job rotation, promotion, and continual business system development are good examples of methods by which entropy is dissipated from a business system's current state while injecting new energy into the creation of its desired state. This combination of constant energy input and dissipation of entropy enhances the effectiveness of open systems.

On the flip side, businesses that experience an extraordinary amount of entropy for extended periods of time (e.g., due to a poor culture and working climate) risk losing key employees with hands-on experience and corporate memory. Such a drain on production capability and capacity—the war for talent—often proves devastating to business systems.

The Risk of Closed Systems

On the other hand, systems become closed when they are isolated from their environment and subsequently demonstrate equilibrium or near-equilibrium situations. Without input of an independent amount of power or energy to compensate for the near state of maximum entropy, the living system is doomed to die.

Typically, such situations arise within a business system when its leaders try to solve systemic problems with the same knowledge that created those systemic problems, fully expecting to succeed this time around by doubling their efforts. In fueling this maximum effort by converting human energy from one form into another—preferably creativity as indicated in a recent IBM study[6]—a significant amount of energy is tied up elsewhere. For example, creative human energy will be tied up in irritation, frustration, indifference, anger, or even contempt when people with the most knowledge about day-to-day processes are deliberately ignored and excluded from the problem-solving process. Consequently, the fact that these employees disengage themselves from their jobs, which they now call "just a paycheck," is a clear indication of the presence of entropy. Other common examples of entropy are people who speak up, complain, or blow the whistle on management errors and violations, and are therefore derided as "troublemakers." Subsequently, these people are demoted, are fired, or decide to leave of their own volition. Either way, their talents are no longer available to save the business from itself. And those who remain behind take notice of such decisions and their incidence.

Management teams of closed business systems are usually rather homogeneous with regard to their members' sex, ethnicity, socioeconomic background, academic and professional credentials, political and religious persuasion, personality types, and many other personal traits, preferences, and characteristics. As a result, they are seduced to see what their mental programming wants them to see, thereby confirming what they already believe to be valid and true.

Colonel John R. Boyd warned against this kind of behavior, which he called "incestuous amplification."[7] The danger in this behavior is that hierarchical leaders will dismiss offhand any new concept that is foreign to them without even contemplating its validity. They always seem to justify their rejections with the same argument: "We just don't believe that the major premise(s) on which the new concept is based is true!" They simply cannot even begin to contemplate the suggestion that any major premise that does not acknowledge money as the highest value, such as becoming the obvious choice for one's target audience, improving process and product quality, promoting pride of workmanship and joy of work, livable wages, equal pay for equal work, and so forth, could ever constitute a sound and defendable business practice.

Entering the Twilight State

Process maps and organizational charts form a kind of matrix, which means that the hierarchical responsibility for a single end-to-end process is distributed over multiple organizational units, each with their own hierarchical leader.

Therefore, executives who pursue business growth by setting tight operational efficiency goals for all departments and who hold hierarchical leaders personally accountable for reaching those goals, risk playing a game of Whac-A-Mole. After all, this approach to running a business motivates hierarchical leaders to only implement measures that are the least intrusive to those parts of an end-to-end process for which they are accountable, and that generate the biggest efficiency gain in the shortest possible time frame. The fact that those measures might disrupt the work flow of other departments working on different parts of the same end-to-end process is par for the course. Within such an "every man for himself, and God for us all" corporate climate, "Not my problem" becomes the excuse for causing trouble for other people in other departments. The ensuing friction and conflict among different departments is praised as internal competition, which is generally regarded as healthy. What do you think?

Resistance to Change

Erich Jantsch, an organizational theorist who applied Prigogine's theory to evolution, notes that "biological organizations put innovation and creativity at the 'top' of the hierarchy (in the brain), just the opposite from their position in most human-made organizations (such as corporations or nations), where structure becomes increasingly rigid toward the top."[8]

Rigidity in the executive suite is the result of members' resistance to having the validity of their personal and collective mental programming questioned by revolutionary thought patterns, new concepts, and fresh perceptions of their business system and its environment.

Consequently, their executive decisions, policies, procedures, rules, and regulations keep the entire business system hostage to mediocrity when it comes to reconstituting the business system's capability and capacity for adapting to new and unforeseen circumstances.

It should be abundantly clear that "the end of one problem may be the beginning of another. To manage a system effectively, you might focus on the interactions of the parts rather than their behavior taken separately."[9]

THE SIXTH BUSINESS GREMLIN: EVERYTHING IS CREATED TWICE

Stephen Covey said, "All things are created twice: first mentally, then physically. The key to creativity is to begin with the end in mind, with a vision and a blueprint of the desired result."

People with a vision for future manifestations demonstrate an unwavering belief in what is possible. For example, Wilbur Wright wrote the following in his letter of May 13, 1900, to Octave Chanute (a French American railway engineer and aviation pioneer):

> For some years I have been afflicted with the belief that flight is possible to man. I have been trying to arrange my affairs in such a way that I can devote my entire time for a few months to experiment in this field.

Because of these experiments, the Wright brothers discovered the principles of flight, which are still valid today. Later, Orville writes about their experiments: "Isn't it astonishing that all these secrets have been preserved for so many years just so we could discover them."

It is hard to deny that these principles were always there and that it took a visionary to see what is possible to do to turn beliefs into truths. Unfortunately, in the words of Arthur Schopenhauer: "All truth passes through three stages. First, it is ridiculed. Second, it is violently opposed. Third, it is accepted as being self-evident."

Recognizing Our Dominant Mental Programming

Most business leaders are relying on the theory of *Management by Objectives* (MBO), which was first popularized by management guru Peter Drucker in his 1954 book, *The Practice of Management*. Top-level managers must determine the mission and the strategic goals for the entire value chain. The goals they define are based on an analysis of what the business system can and should accomplish within a specific time frame. Some objectives are collective (for a whole department or the whole company); others can be individualized.

A goal is defined as an outcome toward which effort is directed. Therefore, a key tenet of management by objectives is having a management information system for measuring and comparing an employee's actual performance against the goal. Consequently, goals must be **S**pecific, **M**easurable, **A**ttainable, **R**ealistic, and **T**ime-related; in short, they must be SMART.

Executives who define the purpose of their business as making money will choose financial goals that are expressed in some form of ratio, such as productivity, profitability, return on investment, return on assets, earnings per share, solvability, liquidity ratio, or net present value. Therefore, popular solutions tend to favor short-term gains in operational efficiency, which can be calculated in advance. The choice between competing alternative solutions is thus a matter of arithmetic; the solution forecast to produce the highest short-term profitability gain wins.

Solutions thus tend to be products and services that can be bought and added to the existing business system on relatively short notice, such as innovation with advanced tools and technology, or coaching for holding individual hierarchical leaders accountable for their efforts toward the realization of their goals.

Principles That Explain Cause-and-Effect Relationships

Business is a mental phenomenon. In other words, the vehicle for conducting business—a business system—is structured and governed according to the thoughts, beliefs, values, schooling, theories, dogmas, ideologies, perceptions, emotions, and interpretations of the environment of its executive decision makers.

Although it is often believed that one can just jump from the decision to initiate change to the actual implementation of change, our brain will stubbornly refuse to cooperate until it has a clear visualization of what you're planning to do and why that's important to you.

Here is an example from an aviation accident investigation. Pilots get disoriented when they lose sight of the horizon. This means that without the aid of a flight instrument—the artificial horizon—pilots cannot tell the attitude of the aircraft or whether they are flying straight and level or climbing, diving, or banking.

An accident investigation report relates the story of a pilot who became disoriented and survived the subsequent accident. He told investigators how he yanked the yoke back with all his might to pull up the nose of his aircraft because the artificial horizon indicated he had entered a steep dive. He blamed crashing the aircraft on the yoke being stuck, although examination of the wreck could not corroborate his claim. It was concluded that the pilot's mind was conflicted between the information from the artificial horizon and that of his disoriented senses. Believing that his senses were more reliable than his artificial horizon, his brain could not visualize a dive and thus refused to cooperate in commanding the big muscles of his arms to effectively pull back the yoke.

This aviation example shows the importance of having a clear and fully crystallized vision of what conditions will amount to success. Using that image, the brain can then start figuring out alternative strategies for departing from the current state and arriving at the envisioned state. Having just a theory is not enough because a theory always needs to be translated into practice—tactics—which is the hardest part of change and where most advisors tend to leave you to your own devices.

In conclusion, there is a cause-and-effect relationship between the decision maker's mind (the level of cause) and solving a systemic problem (the level of effect). The creation of the intended effect—the relationship between means and ends—is dependent on having a coherent and well-articulated vision for the future state of the business.

Entering the Twilight State

As usual, the rubber meets the road when dealing with systemic problems becomes inevitable. That happens when the management information system shows that current performance is lagging behind the goals as set per the theory of management by objectives.

All of a sudden, the pressure to perform is palpable and the need for an instant solution is sky-high. This is when the Black Knight Syndrome strikes again; more and better of the same cost-cutting measures are implemented, and employees are somehow expected to increase the system's capacity and capabilities without making any structural and integral changes to the business system. Using the exhortation "doing more with less," people are basically expected to outperform the current system's capability and capacity. Hence the call for so-called A players and A teams. If that is not bad enough, everyone is held accountable for achieving the goals as set under management by objectives. When a "zero-tolerance" policy is in effect, people even risk losing their jobs when failing to meet such unrealistic and arbitrary goals.

Because regular employees have no authority to initiate improvements to the system's capacity and capabilities, which are necessary to achieve the management demanded results, people become rather creative and resourceful. It is a well-known fact that there are lies, damn lies, and statistics. So, employees will have to fudge the numbers if they want to satisfy management and keep their job. That's what happens when leaders care more about the numbers than the processes that produce those numbers.

Business gremlins start to appear out of thin air when someone, eventually, discovers that the actual results are worse than the official quarterly and annual results reported to owners and shareholders. Now look who is left holding the bag? Those who have been responsible for the system's success and failure all along.

The Small Still Voice Within

Despite business gremlins whispering in your ear that you managed the business as you were trained to do (apart from the cheating), you might hear a little voice casting doubt. Perhaps you should have analyzed the system to learn why it failed to live up to its expectations, rather than seeking to blame the people working within that system.

This little voice is telling you that different results are generated by different behaviors. However, you will need to provide an emotional context for people to change their behavior; failure to communicate *why* creates nothing but doubt, friction, and conflict.

The appropriate emotional context can be found in the basic principles of business. The most basic one is not to demand of people what you are not willing to do yourself. Would you accept responsibility for improving the business system's capability and capacity without any authority for making any structural and integral changes to that system? Of course not!

Because our thoughts, beliefs, values, principles, schooling, theories, ideology, and cultural heritage tend to be implicit, one can only start examining their validity after making them explicit. Thought patterns that are derived from a counterproductive emotional context need to be changed. Consequently, executives who are able and willing to change the thought patterns with which they conduct business governance will be able to change the conditions under which people work, thereby influencing how people behave in their job, and thus how they generate different results. Soon enough, those explicit thought patterns become implicit again—the new normal. (See Figure 3.7.)

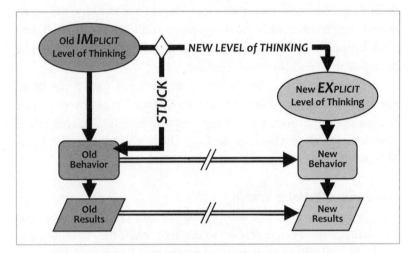

Figure 3.7: Manifesting New Outcomes

Results cannot be changed after the fact. Results are the effect of a decision maker's behavior. People need a solid reason before they consider changing their behavior. Behavior is informed by our mental programming or implicit thinking. Decision makers have a choice to either change their level of thinking, thereby creating new results, or they stick to their guns and get stuck thus perpetuating old behavior resulting in the same old results.

As a matter of fact, the driving force behind innovation is an executive who changed his or her thought patterns regarding business governance. After all, innovation involves only the implementation of a new or significantly improved product, service, or process that creates unique value for its target audience. The prerequisites for creating new processes that will produce and deliver new products and services are an executive with both a fully crystalized vision and keen insight into the principles of business governance (see Chapter 9).

THE SEVENTH BUSINESS GREMLIN: AUTHENTIC SOLUTIONS

We know from Dr. W. Edwards Deming that 94 percent of all problems are systemic in nature. Authentic solutions are the only remedies that prevent systemic problems from lingering and recurring. They are the best guarantee for restoring a business system's integrity. However, management by objectives practices seem hostile to any attempts at solving systemic problems. Though Peter Drucker warned managers that a systemic view was required, it goes largely unheeded by the practitioners of MBO (see the fifth business gremlin, interaction versus isolation).

Recognizing Our Dominant Mental Programming

The purpose of a business system is to make money in order to grow the business. The preferred management method for measuring progress is MBO.

Objectives are set and measured quarterly, and the outcome of one's individual annual performance review depends on hitting the mark quarter after quarter. This means the challenges that hierarchical leaders encounter on a daily basis are generally defined in terms of operational efficiency or short-term solutions for short-term financial gains.

Because systemic problems do not seem to register on hierarchical leaders' radar screens, they have no need for any integral approaches aimed at implementing structural changes to the business system. Instead, they deal with a variety of persistent, recurring, unintended, and unwanted symptoms (caused by systemic problems) on a day-to-day basis. Among their daily decisions are the continual firing of (allegedly) unqualified personnel and the hiring of new recruits. The suggestion of training employees is rejected by arguing that people come and go, so why bother spending money on those who are bound to leave sometime soon only to go work for one's competitor?

The only solutions that are of real interest to hierarchical leaders are what they themselves describe as "painkillers"—anything that suppresses bad symptoms that could interfere with quarterly performance measurements instantaneously. Solutions aimed at improving a business system's overall long-term health are perceived as too costly and too time-consuming. Derided as "vitamins," they are not even taken into consideration.

After all, hierarchical leaders are held to account for their quarterly contribution to bottom-line results. Therefore, they preoccupy themselves with activities over which they can exercise immediate control. These are most notably costs (resource allocations such as labor, materials, fuel, or power) that are directly related to the product, process, or cost center for which they are responsible.

Principles That Explain Cause-and-Effect Relationships

We know by now that a business system has integrity when its organizational behavior is aligned with the governance thinking of its executives. That means that system performance is at par with its leadership's intentions and expected performance outcome.

Systemic problems occur as the result of misalignment between organizational behavior and governance thinking—when there is a discrepancy between the business system's current state and that of its desired state. They are experienced as symptoms or unintended and unwanted effects. As explained in the previous chapter, the significance of this discrepancy can be measured, and the outcome is called the problem. Thus, the desired state performance equals the current state performance minus the problem.

At this stage, all we know is that something has changed in either the business system's organizational behavior or in the governance thinking of its executives. Therefore, we need to identify the root cause(s) of the problem. After all, there are countless events that are all capable of causing the same problem or the same measured shortfall in performance. So, which one is it?

Discovery of Root Causes

A root cause is an event that, triggered by internal or external stimuli, creates either an active failure or a latent condition within the business system. Please note that although other organizations might experience similar symptoms, those are very likely the result of different root causes, unless they have identical process structures, which is rare. After all, organizations that want to boost their unique brand identity differentiate themselves from the pack with their unique process structures for transforming input variables into products or services.

Conducting a root-cause analysis is a discovery process. To calculate the problem's significance, you need to establish:

- Insight into the current state of the relevant process structures
- Consensus among executives regarding the desired state of the entire value chain
- Agreement from the problem owner regarding the applicable norms and standards for measuring performance of the processes for which they are responsible

This discovery process should reveal sufficient data and information for creating an authentic solution that will be:

- Creating buy-in from the problem owner, and . . .
- Addressing the root cause, and . . .
- Reinforcing the business system's purpose, and . . .
- Aligning with the chosen strategy for realizing that purpose, and
- Supporting the business system's brand identity

Authentic solutions are by far the best guarantee for solving systemic problems and thereby restoring a business system's integrity and alignment with its purpose and strategic direction. (See Figure 3.8.)

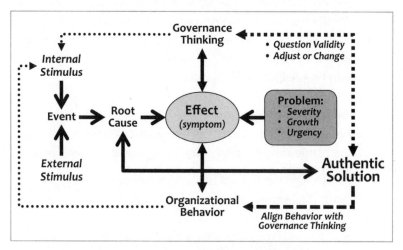

Figure 3.8: Creating Authentic Solutions

Solutions for systemic problems become authentic if and when they reduce or remove the root cause(s) and align with current governance thinking, including strategy. Authentic solutions are aimed at changing organizational behavior and/or governance thinking—that is, the current state of the business and/or the desired state.

Entering the Twilight State

The core tenet of any business system is the exchange of a specific value proposition for money. Performance is defined by the system's effectiveness and efficiency and challenged by complexity and events that disrupt the system's integrity. Any conflict with or violation of a core business principle—as explained in seven business gremlins introduced here and in Chapter 2—will affect organizational behavior and thus performance. Any adjustments or changes to the business system that are made in an effort to restore its integrity should thus adhere to those principles in order to succeed.

Earlier, I referenced an IBM report in which executive leaders worldwide stated that complexity perplexes them more than any other aspect of business. Imagine a similar statement from a surgeon about the human body or an airline pilot about an aircraft! Without understanding complexity, all they *can* do is trial and error, and one can only hope for the best. Just sit back, relax, and enjoy the flight!

Executive leaders who are perplexed by complexity are more likely to provide executive sponsorship for solving symptoms that they can experience themselves rather than analyzing unknown root causes. While demanding to see results quickly, pressing issues are solved with creative quick-and-dirty solutions that probably violate other core principles, thus propelling a problem throughout the entire value chain for the foreseeable future.

From Bad to Worse

Poor decision-making processes can wreak havoc on the business system as an organic and integrated whole, in particular when decisions:

- Are made on the basis of how much money it makes
- Impair the business system's capability and capacity
- Gold plate idolized means (a.k.a. sacred cows)
- Treat process structures separately from their environment
- Isolate process structures from each other
- Fail to question current beliefs, values, and assumptions
- Ignore root causes

In addition, patching up symptoms within one hierarchical unit only creates new and different symptoms in another hierarchical unit. Because of this robbing-Peter-to-pay-Paul syndrome, everyone is busy putting out fires instead of doing their jobs. There simply is no tool, technology, methodology, or best practice that can compensate for any of the unintended and unwanted consequences brought on by such poor decision-making processes. Such decision makers need a miracle—that is, a new level of thinking about business.

In the absence of an adequate leader (someone who would cut the losses and search for the root dysfunction), everyone is pointing fingers at everyone else and blaming each other for making their jobs impossible. As a result, relationships among people with the combined knowledge and expertise to solve systemic problems are polarized; they are not talking to each other. Now the business gremlins rush to everyone's aid, providing hierarchical leaders with arguments that demonstrate why they are not at fault by quoting common business practices.

General George Patton, US Army, once said: "If everyone is thinking alike, then somebody isn't thinking." This frequently applies to business executives.

Until someone starts to think critically for oneself and questions common assumptions, values, beliefs, business theories, practices, and other dogmas and ideologies, we are held hostage to mediocrity.

WHAT HAPPENS NEXT?

Although all business gremlins are distinctly different from one another, they are closely related. The mere fact that a decision maker is listening to one of them is a pretty good indication that she or he is probably also listening to what others are whispering in their ear. They seemingly make good sense because they are different manifestations of the same root dysfunction: choosing money as the highest of all values, to the detriment of quality and the striving to become the obvious choice supplier to members of one's target audience.

In the next chapter, we'll explore how authentic solutions for systemic problems can be found when we submit ourselves to a *mind shift*. Conducting a mind shift involves changing firmly held beliefs, principles, values, theories, ideologies, and habits that stand in the way of solving persistent and recurring problems. To that end, we'll explore the mythological phenomenon of a hero's journey[10] because the traveler's ultimate quest is transformation of his or her perception of life, reality, or what the traveler believes to be valid and true, or possible.

CHAPTER 4

Mind Shift: The Antidote to the Peter Principle

Sometimes it's the very people whom no one imagines anything of, who do the very things that no one can imagine.

—Christopher Morcom
close friend of Alan Turing, OBE FRS,
and World War II codebreaker at Bletchley Park, England, UK

The Peter Principle strikes decision makers who, in the face of systemic problems, feel conflicted. They experience a restriction of consciousness (recall Figure 2.1) when their old and familiar principles fail to explain or predict current organizational behavior, while being unaware, or having rejected the validity of principles that would explain and predict their current situation. No wonder they experience confusion, which was described by American writer Henry Miller as a word we have invented for an order which is not yet understood.

Therefore, the answer to not understanding is to *develop* understanding. Hence, the antidote to the Peter Principles is to create insight into the cause-and-effect principles that facilitate a business system to function successfully. This sounds like a commonsense approach, yet the popular method is to perform more analysis on a single silo of specialized knowledge, in search of deeper deep domain expertise. However, no amount of additional knowledge of a single component part can explain or predict the behavior of the system to which it belongs.

Furthermore, every problem carries within it the seeds of its solution. And harvesting these seeds requires understanding the principles that explain and predict *why* a problem occurs, and *why* a solution will succeed or fail. Systemic problems only seem to be without solution for as long as we resist changing our mental programming—to learn, unlearn, and relearn new principles, whether they are physical, chemical, biological, social, or spiritual in nature.

A NEED FOR DISCERNMENT

Characteristic of systemic problems is an enterprise-wide disruption of work flow. Something inherent to the business system's design, structure or organization, operation or implementation, maintenance and management is out of alignment with the business's purpose and strategy. And reaching a diagnosis for the root cause(s) is complex because many successive intermediary steps may have taken place, by multiple executives, over an extended period of time, between the incidence of a cause and the experience of its effect(s).

Diagnosing root causes becomes even more complex when no one denies the existence of a recurring problem, and no one confesses to having made any mistakes. Our minds just cannot comprehend having problems when everyone is just doing their job. Executives who firmly believe in holding someone accountable are likely to assume that frontline operators are not telling the truth about their role in the problem. What else could it be?

However, the firing of those scapegoats—in a demonstrable pose of zero tolerance—is, in most instances, only an act because, in all likelihood, the system will continue to produce the same unintended and unwanted results! Not only that, setting a precedent of firing people for no good reason undermines morale.

In case you were wondering, yes, a business *can* experience systemic problems while every employee is just doing her or his job, because responsibility for solving systemic problems is not part of their job—they have no authority to change the system.

When our mental programming falls short on usable knowledge, it's time for research, which requires a very different usage of the mind—the brain in action. "Research is what I'm doing when I don't know what I'm doing," said Wernher von Braun, the German American aerospace engineer.

Research requires discernment. Discernment is a cognitive ability to perceive precisely and/or to comprehend well what is obscure, especially subjects that are often overlooked by others. This acuteness of observations about properties or qualities (which can be psychological, moral, or ethical in nature) is used to distinguish or appraise a person, statement, situation, or environment.

Principles for Principals

Phenomena that disrupt system integrity can be explained once the underlying cause-and-effect relationships are known. Such explanations (principles) help decision makers (principals) solve systemic problems.

Principles help us to explain behavior of all kinds of systems—natural, biological, social, and manmade. Although we would like to believe those principles are universally valid, they are not set in stone. After all, there was a time when we believed the Earth was flat, that the sun revolved around the Earth, that steel ships would sink, and that "there is no reason for any individual to have a computer in their home."[1] Anyone who professed otherwise was either a heretic or insane; they were said to be out of touch with reality.

Whereas the principles that explain the behavior of natural systems are called laws of physics or biology, those governing the performance of manmade systems are social constructs. Examples of principles used in the governance of a business system are a stated purpose, a mission statement, strategy, legal frameworks, morality, humanity, cultural traditions, norms, values, beliefs, customs, genetic heritage, previous experience, written contracts, oral agreements, ideas, theories, dogmas, ideologies, best practices, common sense, and decency.

Because principles are based on cause-and-effect relationships, not only do they explain certain behaviors, they also predict certain outcomes (see Figure 4.1).

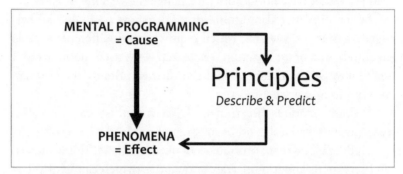

Figure 4.1: Recognizing Cause-and-Effect Relationships
Instead of asking in bewilderment why did this happen, identify the principle(s) that explain and predict the underlying cause-and-effect relationships—nothing happens by accident.

"Fingerspitzengefühl"

Once our mental programming includes a certain principle, it can be recalled to explain an observed phenomenon, or predict a certain outcome. However, the extent of our education, experience, curiosity, and the scope of our general interest—our willingness to learn, unlearn, and relearn—puts a limit on the scope of our mental programming, thereby limiting our power of discernment.

Furthermore, many principles have proven to be subject to change. For example, principles involving child labor have disappeared and the 40-hour workweek, a two-day weekend, minimum wage, paid vacation and sick leave, equal pay for equal work, and other benefits became new norms. In addition, a heightened sense of social responsibility and environmental consciousness have changed our attitude toward the pollution of soil, air, and water with industrial waste products. We are no longer ignoring the social cost of doing business.

Moreover, certain principles are sensitive to economic conditions. Some will generate positive outcomes during good economic times when margins for error are wide. Others are indispensable during poor economic times only, prompting some decision makers to suggest during good economic times that these are useless and should therefore be eliminated. But who bemoans having paid for fire insurance because their house did not burn down?

Also, not all business principles are universally applicable across all industries and every cultural, socioeconomic, and geopolitical condition. Consequently, the principles for the governance of a man-made system should be selected based on their appropriateness for the prevailing economic conditions of the regions and countries in which one intends to operate. This requires discerning leaders—people who heed Mark Twain's warning to not let your schooling interfere with your education. Discerning leaders have wisdom and an innate ability to cope with the vagaries of life.

Discernment includes a mental ability that Colonel John R. Boyd identified with the German word *Fingerspitzengefühl*, which literally translates as "fingertips feeling." It describes a great situational awareness, and the ability to respond intuitively, appropriately, and tactfully to new and unforeseen circumstances as they unfold.

Fingerspitzengefühl becomes evident in one's ability to generate mental images one after another in a rapid pace until one finds a match between an observed phenomenon and a principle programmed in one's mind. Alternatively, strategic opportunities can be found in one's implicit recognition of a mismatch between unfolding new and unforeseen circumstances and a competitor's reaction—his or her ability to interpret or make sense of what is happening in real time. This mismatch reveals the operative principle programmed in the competitor's mind—his or her deficient level of thinking. Hence, *Fingerspitzengefühl* underscores the vital importance of one's mental programming in accurate discernment, and its need for constant updating through learning, unlearning, and relearning.

The Importance of Personal Beliefs to Business Outcomes

Principles work whether you believe in them or not. However, decision makers apply them only when they believe them to be valid and true, or beneficial to their cause. Marianne Williamson, teacher of *A Course in Miracles*, says, "We are heir to the laws that rule the world with which we identify." We can identify with a world in which money is the highest of all values, or one in which quality is the highest of all values—a world that prioritizes either profits or quality and humanity.

Therefore, it is up to the chief executive officer to discern the beliefs with which she or he wants the business system to identify. With which world do you think your intended target audience identifies itself?

Whenever a systemic problem defies any solution, you should accept that a principle with which you identify and that is firmly programmed in your mind is at the heart of the difficulty. Consequently, that principle must be broken, rewritten, or replaced by a new one. Be reminded of Einstein's suggestion to avoid insanity by staying the course.

Decision makers who either believe they can pay lip service to or ignore or violate those vital principles—or who believe that principles are sacrosanct—will do so at their own peril. The risk involved is equal to the probability of an unfavorable outcome, multiplied by the severity of unintended and unwanted consequences: Risk = Probability × Consequences.

How to Challenge a Dilemma with Formal Logic

Whenever confronted with two arguments that affirm or deny something, which is either true or false, while reaching mutually exclusive irreconcilable conclusions, you are faced with a dilemma (see Figure 4.2). In order to examine this mystery, both arguments are best presented in the form of a syllogism,[2] which consists of the following components:

Major premise. Defined as the predicate of the conclusion, most major premises—also referred to as hypotheses—are presented in the form of a cause-and-effect relationship. If A happens, then B will be its consequence. These statements are based on a principle—true or false—that explains why a proposed decision will render the intended result. That principle is reflective of an individual's mental programming and beliefs as stated in the hypothesis or theory.

Minor premise. Defined as the subject or object of the conclusion, a minor premise is what it is; reality as perceived by the individual constructing the argument. Even though we believe we are not deceived by our eyes, what registers on the brain depends on the individual's mental programming. We can only "see" the patterns—phenomena—with which our brain is already familiar. All else is, by default, filtered out.

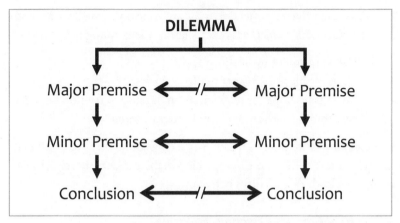

Figure 4.2: The Dilemma

Dilemmas create a state of uncertainty or perplexity especially when one is forced to choose between two valid arguments whose conclusions cannot be reconciled.

Conclusion. Defined as a conjunction of the subject or object of the first premise with the predicate of the second, a conclusion is a reasoned judgment. However, this judgment is only valid when it complies with the rules of logic, that is, when the argument is logically consistent. And the validity of an argument expresses no opinion regarding the truthfulness of that argument's major premise.

Let's examine the following two lemmas, argument 1 and argument 2:

Argument 1	Major premise	If you automate, you'll be *less* dependent on people.*
	Minor premise	You have automated.
	Conclusion	Therefore, you'll be less dependent on people.

Argument 2	Major premise	If you automate, you'll be *more* dependent on people.**
	Minor premise	You have automated.
	Conclusion	Therefore, you'll be more dependent on people.

* Dominant belief and argument for automating more business processes.
** Lisanne Bainbridge, "Ironies of automation," *Automatica* 19(6), 1983, 775–779.

Assuming that arguments 1 and 2 are logically correct, we are confronted with a dilemma that is excruciatingly frustrating because:

- Each argument by itself is valid.
- Their conclusions are mutually exclusive.
- There is no hope for reconciliation because of friction between two conflicting sets of mental programming.

Dilemmas are potential causes of a decision maker's restriction of consciousness, which, as discussed in Chapter 2 (see Figure 2.1), can result in a leader's unskillful behavior.

When Best Practices Become Fallacies

The successful use of a scientific method (displayed in Figure 4.3) in the world of science was not lost on the world of social studies. Subsequently, people studying management and leadership started to compile their own best practices.

However, the validity of general theories intended to explain social phenomena should not be equated with the validity of scientific laws explaining natural or physical phenomena such as Buys Ballot's law, Bernoulli's principle, the laws of thermodynamics, or Ohm's law. After all, human behavior is less predictable than that of matter and energy—people can exercise free will.

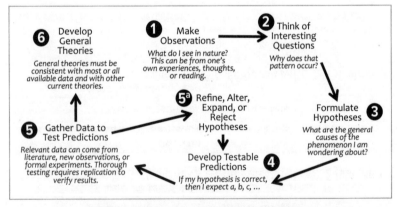

Figure 4.3: The Scientific Method Protocol

The scientific method is used to solve problems and explain phenomena. This procedure has characterized natural science since the seventeenth century. "Scientific Method 3" by Whatiguana-Own work. Licensed under CC BY-SA 4.0 via Wikimedia Commons. http://commons.wikimedia.org/wiki/File: Scientific_Method_3.jpg#/media/File:Scientific_Method_3.jpg

However, there is an essential difference between science and social studies, and therefore between natural systems and human/ social systems with regard to the validity of their hypotheses. A scientific hypothesis or principle is only valid when repeated attempts at disproving its validity have failed, or when repeated experiments fail to identify a possible observation or an argument that proves the scientific hypothesis is false (see Figure 4.3).

Arguments that are not logically consistent—fallacies—should also be discarded as false. Examples of fallacies—most notably the fallacy of *affirming the consequent*—can be found in many management and leadership best practices.

Typically, this kind of research is conducted among a limited number of executives who are all asked the same set of questions. Based on their answers, researchers infer a general theory *about* management, which they translate into a theory *for* management. In other words, many if not most general theories about business are based on merely statistical correlations among the results of repeated observations from a relatively small sample group. The correlations should not be mistaken for causality. In addition, the mere fact that no two businesses in the sample group are equal—operating under identical conditions, experiencing the same situations, within comparable environments—violates a major tenet[3] of scientific research.

To demonstrate the mistake these researchers make, we need to write their method for formulating management best practices as a generic syllogism, which appears to be a prime example of the fallacy of affirming the consequent:

> **Major premise.** If our theory is true for ALL, then this theory must be true for SOME.
>
> **Minor premise.** We have proven that it is true for SOME.
>
> **Conclusion.** Therefore, it is true for ALL.

Writing a business best practice *after* interviewing executives in their sample group is no substitute for formulating a proper hypothesis *before* conducting interviews. Then they could have used that hypothesis as their major premise against which to test their observations.

Fallacies apart, many discussions about management and leadership focus on minor premises—effects or symptoms—which are the result of individual observations, perceptions, justifications, interpretations, beliefs, and opinions. People who participate in these discussions often display an obsession for ranking specific things or ideas to establish which is the most or least important or valuable. They completely lose sight of what really matters—the major premise or predictive principle—and the correct structuring of the syllogism.

In the preceding example of a dilemma, people are bound to experience great difficulty agreeing on definitive properties and characteristics that constitute automation, in particular, those that constitute "good" automation, let alone finding consensus regarding the appropriateness of any measuring methods and standards.

Note that the source of frustration originates from our mental programming—what outcome or effect we perceive as the consequence of our intended course of action. Anticipating a different outcome—the consequent of a major premise—from the same intended course of action cannot fail to result in a different conclusion.

Realizing that our perceptions are but beliefs that we can choose to change, the real question becomes which major premise—cause-and-effect relationship—do you perceive to be valid and true? This discussion is all too often neglected, thus remaining unexamined.

These are the lessons learned from our discussion of a syllogism:

- Arguments formulated as a fallacy are invalid or untrue.
- Major premises based on flawed cause-and-effect relationships can still result in valid arguments.
- Most debates and discussions are about minor premises (individual perceptions of reality), while disregarding the importance of major premises (cause-and-effect relationships). However, the soundness of well formulated major premises is the most critical aspect in choosing a course of action—a relationship between means and ends—that produces the intended and wanted outcomes.

THE CRUX OF SOLVING STUBBORN ENTERPRISE-WIDE PROBLEMS

The obstacle to solving systemic problems is not the supposedly secretive or scarce nature of solutions, as is often professed by their advocates. Rather, it is the executive decision maker's disbelief, doubt, aversion, reluctance, resistance, or utter refusal to even contemplate updating and expanding their mental programming with a new principle because it conflicts with those already firmly programmed into their mind and already implemented throughout the business system.

This lack of curiosity or apathy is not new or unique to anyone. For example, in 1615, the Roman Inquisition investigated the Italian astronomer Galileo Galilei, who championed Copernican heliocentrism (the Earth rotating daily and revolving around the sun), and concluded that heliocentrism was foolish, absurd, and heretical since it contradicted Holy scripture. Eventually, in 1992, Pope John Paul II acknowledged that the Church was wrong. More recently, after World War II, American managers rejected Dr. W. Edwards Deming's System of Profound Knowledge because he bluntly told them that poor quality products resulted mostly from their failures, not from worker ineptness. Deming, the vanguard of American production experts, was told to get lost—and he did, in Japan. Yet when Japan penetrated Western markets with high-quality products at competitive prices, corporate America accused Japan of dumping. And some 70 years later, I met with an executive adviser who rejected Deming's principles because he did not believe they are true—end of story.

Only the closed mind is certain. Therefore, "to argue with a man who has renounced the use and authority of reason, and whose philosophy consists in holding humanity in contempt, is like administering medicine to the dead, or endeavoring to convert an atheist by scripture." [4]

Two quotes attributeed to Einstein come to mind: "Insanity is doing the same thing over and over and expecting different results" and "The problems that exist in the world today cannot be solved by the level of thinking that created them." Although these quotes are used ad nauseam, too few people recognize the problem-solution contained therein; the antidote to this insanity is to change one's level of thinking.

Most decision makers fail to recognize an authentic solution when it presents itself because they resist even examining its principles on their merits. "It is the mark of an educated mind to be able to entertain a thought without accepting it."[5] They dismiss it offhand saying that they just don't believe that it will work. Consequently, solutions for systemic problems that proclaim quality as the highest of all values take an awfully long time to gain recognition in a world that prioritizes economic principles over humanitarian ones. And we are all too familiar with the business variant on the golden rule; those who own the gold make the rules. Hence, nothing changes significantly until the ultimate decision maker provides his or her sponsorship for change.

Have you noticed the structure of this book? Part II is about rethinking your approach to solving stubborn enterprise-wide problems, while Part I provides reasons why you would want to do that—even if you don't care about humanistic principles and just want to advance your own career. It works either way.

Different Levels of Thinking

When alternative courses of action conflict with each other, their major premises are probably not part of the same continuum. That means that studying the old principles or theories harder, longer, or more in depth will never result in arriving at the new principles. They simply exist on different continuums—they are two lemmas, which we identified earlier as a dilemma.

The current dominant mental programming that is set for the pursuit of making money as the purpose of a business conflicts with principles of developing operational process and product quality—to increase the system's capability and capacity. Quality is perceived as an unaffordable expense that will reduce short-term earnings.

On the other hand, improving operational effectiveness by exercising one's free will to pursue continual quality improvement—in an effort to become the intended target audience's obvious choice supplier—cannot fail to increase operational efficiency and thus increase net profits; albeit in the long run.

The mind shift challenges every executive decision maker to let go of old, familiar, but outdated, principles and to embrace new and unfamiliar ones (see Figure 4.4). It does not offer a cafeteria menu from which to pick and choose the courses that one likes or the option to mix and match ingredients for the purpose of avoiding what one dislikes. It's a take-it-or-leave-it proposition to shift one's mind from a previously limiting level of thinking to an enhanced level of thinking, resulting in greater clarity of mind, insight, understanding, and appreciation for the complexity of a modern business system.

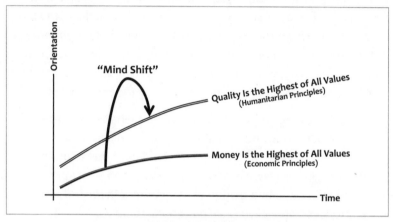

Figure 4.4: Different Levels of Thinking

Examining one's current level of thinking more frequently and revisiting its underlying principles in much greater depth will not and cannot develop into a radically different level of thinking. Changing one's level of thinking requires a mind shift—a willingness to observe a phenomenon, such as business, from a different perspective.

A mind shift makes all the difference in one's decision-making processes, one's interactions with people and the environment, and ultimately in one's outlook on the future well-being of the business system and its stakeholders. Profitability should not be attained at the expense of quality, humanity, and sustainability. And short-term gains should not be pursued by sacrificing the development of long-term value. Remember, "a man who knows the price of everything and the value of nothing" was Oscar Wilde's description of a cynic.

A Sure Sign of Mature Leadership

The experience of systemic problems nudges us to get out of our comfort zones and widen our inventory of moral ideas, to question our assumptions and to fill the gaps in our knowledge.

I believe that what many designate as an economic crisis is in fact a moral crisis. Colonel John R. Boyd described morality as "cultural codes of conduct or standards of behavior that constrain, as well as sustain and focus, our emotional and intellectual responses." Hence, we need to think critically and creatively, and be willing to break with established rules and norms. Yet for many, diverging from generally accepted levels of thinking is difficult. Consequently, as Sir Karl Popper[6] cautioned, people look with disdain on people who differ with us: "There is an almost universal tendency, perhaps an inborn tendency, to suspect the good faith of a man who holds opinions that differ from our own opinions. It obviously endangers the freedom and the objectivity of our discussion if we attack a person instead of attacking an opinion or, more precisely, a theory." Popper also said:

> If we are uncritical we shall always find what we want: we shall look for, and find, confirmations, and we shall look away from, and not see, whatever might be dangerous to our pet theories. In this way, it is only too easy to obtain what appears to be overwhelming evidence in favor of a theory which, if approached critically, would have been refuted.

And,

> Whenever a theory appears to you as the only possible one, take this as a sign that you have neither understood the theory nor the problem which it was intended to solve.

Thus, the idea that creativity is the answer to executives' bewilderment because of complexity and unforeseen events seems to be paradoxical. If it weren't for the consistency in their thought processes—as whispered in their ears by business gremlins—they would already be creating authentic solutions for the many systemic problems that are plaguing them today. "Consistency is the last refuge of the unimaginative."[7]

The Root Cause is a journey to expand one's imagination—the act or power of creating a mental picture of something not present to the senses or never wholly perceived in reality. Understanding complexity and events is a function of one's mental programming. Exposure to new and unfamiliar principles expands the range of mental pictures one can produce.

In short, the mind shift is the antidote to the Peter Principle (occupational incompetence), and the experience of the CEO dilemma, which makes executive sponsorship for change so excruciatingly hard to obtain. Conducting a mind shift is a sure sign of mature leadership.

THE HEROIC CHIEF EXECUTIVE

Search for a solution to overcome the debilitating state of decisional conflict and stress was researched by Joseph Campbell and shared with us in his epic book *The Hero with a Thousand Faces*. It is about mankind's coming to maturity—a transformation of consciousness within the psyche of individual adventurers, better known as a hero's journey.

This kind of journey is a cycle of separation or departure from the world of common day, fulfillment—trials and victories of initiation within a supernatural world—and return followed by reintegration with society.

Call to Adventure

Every hero's journey starts with a call to adventure—an invitation to leave behind the safety and familiarity of home so that one can embrace a strange, unpredictable, and dangerous world, where the rules are different and the cost of failure is high (see Figure 4.5).

Destiny summons the hero to transfer his or her spiritual center of gravity from within the pale of society to a zone unknown:

> This fateful region of both treasure and danger may be variously represented: as a distant land, a forest, a kingdom underground, beneath the waves, or above the sky, a secret island, lofty mountaintop, or profound dream state; but it is always a place of strangely fluid and polymorphous beings, unimaginable torments, superhuman deeds, and impossible delight.[8]

The call represents either an internal drive that compels individuals to embark on the journey of their own volition, a situation in which they are forced to go or lured away from their community, or perhaps where they blunder into an unintended and unfamiliar situation.

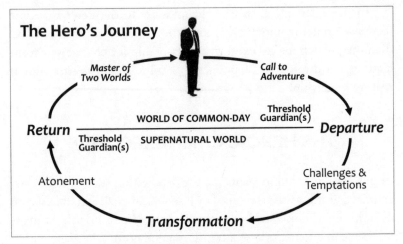

Figure 4.5: Influences on the Hero
The hero's journey is the story of mankind's coming to maturity—a transformation of consciousness within the adventurer's psyche.

On the threshold between the visible world of common day and the region of supernatural wonder, the hero-to-be must decide to accept or reject the call to adventure. Acceptance signifies the beginning of the hero's journey, whereas rejection means damnation to living a life of mediocrity.

Campbell writes about those rejecting the call:

> His flowering world becomes a wasteland of dry stones and his life feels meaningless—even though, like King Minos, he may through titanic effort succeed in building an empire of renown. Whatever house he builds, it will be a house of death: a labyrinth of cyclopean walls to hide from his Minotaur. All he can do is create new problems for himself and await the gradual approach of his disintegration.[9]

Fulfillment

Those accepting the call to embark on the hero's journey are often summoned to "Go find your father." The actual meaning of this father quest is to discover your Self, with capital *S*.

Having to discover one's Self is a matter of one's awakening to the activities, conditions, and situations that provide the most exalted experience of being alive. These experiences do not necessarily refer to the things that one does best, or that come naturally, but they refer to the purpose one is intended to fulfill during one's life on Earth—results an individual is destined to create with the unique qualities one was given.

These qualities of one's personality are present from birth and are known as one's id.

According to the Bhagavad Gita:

Even as a person casts off worn-out cloths and puts on others that are new, so the embodied Self casts off worn-out bodies and enters into others that are new. Weapons cut It not; fire burns It not; water wets It not; the wind does not wither It. This Self cannot be cut nor burnt nor wetted nor withered. Eternal, all-pervading, unchanging, immovable, the Self is the same forever.[10]

Therefore, finding one's Self does not mean that anything is missing or lost. Rather, it expresses the need to recognize one's life potentialities and a deliberate decision to realize those potentials, given the circumstances in which one finds oneself then and there. It's a matter of removing the impediments we created for ourselves by listening to our ego and superego. Hence the notion that a hero receives the journey for which she or he is ready, not the one that she or he is waiting for or planned to receive.

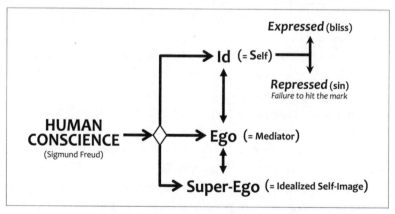

Figure 4.6: The Human Conscience
Human conscience—the object of transformation during the hero's journey.

The id, which was first named and described by Freud as one of the three elements of the human personality along with the ego and superego, is an individual's hardwired personality structure—temperament—that acts on life instincts, without judgments of value, organization of instinctual trends, or incitement of a collective will. Id just strives to bring about satisfaction of instinctual needs, which can be both altruistic and selfish in nature.

Therefore, the id can be described as an individual's personality structure that purposefully equips an individual with the gift, significant skills, or unique abilities, for the fulfillment of a specific role or function that one is destined to perform in their lifetime.

People who work in a profession or trade in which they can express their id are said to be following their bliss; they are doing what they were intended to do from birth for the benefit of something bigger or other than oneself. By following their bliss, they find themselves on the hub of the Wheel of Fortune, where they are not subjected to the humbling roller-coaster ride of life. They are not at the hands of fate—the experience of being *Himmelhoch jauchzend, zum Tode betrübt*: flying high one minute, and low the next.[11]

Those who repress their id, in obeisance of their ego, are said to commit sin; they miss the mark of their destiny or purpose in life. Consequently, they find themselves on the outside, on the rim of the Wheel of Fortune, going up and down, experiencing highs and lows, going from one extreme to the next. Rejecting the call to adventure, refusing to realize one's human potential is the true meaning of sin, which has real-life consequences. Therefore, we are punished *by* our sins not *for* our sins.

The superego is that part of the human mind that acts as a self-critical human conscience that punishes an individual's misbehavior by instilling feelings of guilt, anxiety, and inferiority. It controls one's sense of right and wrong by criticizing and prohibiting the id's instinctual drives, urges, fantasies, feelings, dreams, ideals, and actions. As such, it helps an individual fit into society, by getting a human being to act in socially acceptable ways.

The original conditioning of the superego stems from parental imprinting and later from people who take on the role of parents, such as educators, teachers, coaches, mentors, and other people chosen as an ideal, idol, or role model.

The ego is the organized part of the personality structure, which mediates between the superego's morals and norms for a socially appropriate and realistic manner of behavior, and the id's drive to fulfill its instinctual passions.

Although conscious awareness resides in the ego, not all of the operations of the ego are taken consciously. The ego represents what may be called reason and common sense, thus acting as a filter for determining what one believes to be true or false, helping us to make sense out of the world around us.

Sigmund Freud used the word "ego" to mean a set of psychic functions such as judgment, tolerance, reality testing, control, planning, defense, synthesis of information, intellectual functioning, and memory. This includes interpersonal skills—a central aspect of leadership studies and executive coaching.

From time to time, the ego will experience anxiety in trying to balance the influences that the external world—the superego—and the id exert onto it. In order to counteract this experience of anxiety, the ego is equipped with ego-defense mechanisms such as denial, casting blame, rationalization, intellectualization, dissociation, fantasy, suppression, regression, or repression. These mechanisms are used to conceal the unconscious demands of the id as it remains rigid and unyielding. The ego-defense mechanism is known to fail when the development of an individual's character is prevented from aligning itself with his or her temperament. It is no wonder such individuals demonstrate dysfunctional behavior.

In conclusion, the ego keeps the mind occupied, thus preventing a mind shift from taking place, and closed to new ideas, creativity, and innovation, with which systemic problems could be solved. The outcome is that executive leaders remain unable to shape and adapt the business system, for which they assume ultimate responsibility, as new and unforeseen circumstances unfold. They are doomed to repeat the same mistakes *until* they exercise their free will enabling them to conduct a mind shift.

Conducting a mind shift requires quieting the chatter of the ego-mind. It is through the practice of meditation and prayer that one attains a mentally clear, emotionally calm, and stable state of mind. The need for this emptying of the mind is expressed best with the anecdote of a cup of tea:

In the early 20th century, Zen master Nan-in received a university professor who came to ask about Zen. But instead he only talked on and on about his own ideas. Nan-in served tea. He poured his visitor's cup full, and then, while the man continued to speak, Nan-in kept on pouring the tea. The professor watched the overflow until he could no longer restrain himself. "You fool! It is overfull. No more will go in!" Nan-in replied, "Like this cup, you are also too full of your own opinions and speculations. How can I show you Zen unless you first empty your mind?"[12]

The letting go of the attachment to the ego is the hardest and most difficult task to accomplish. "The agony of breaking through personal limitations is the agony of spiritual growth."[13]

Return
Having completed the assignment, the hero faces the daunting task of returning to the kingdom of humanity, where he will bestow the boon that he garnered from the deities from the realm of supernatural wonder onto the community, society, and nation from where the hero came. Single-hearted, courageous, and full of faith that the truth, as he finds it, shall make us free, he is responsible for knitting together two worlds: the world of common day and the spiritual world—economic principles and humanitarian principles.

But, as Campbell writes, "The boon brought from the transcendent deep becomes quickly rationalized into nonentity, and the need becomes great for another hero to refresh the world."[14]

Normal waking consciousness instilled in us a fear of assimilation between self (ego) and otherness. As a result, the world of common-day experiences a divorce of opportunism from virtue, which fuels the degeneration of human existence. We witness this sentiment in the platitude, "Every man for himself and God for us all."[15]

And yet, as Campbell explains, "The realm of the gods is a forgotten dimension of the world we know."[16] Consequently, the heroic deed is intended for the hero to experience that the reality of the spiritual world is not contradicted by that of the material world. With the acquisition of this knowledge and insight comes the realization that he has become a Master of Two Worlds. The true mark of a master of two worlds is revealed in the reply to your calling him or her a hero: "I just did what was the right thing to do."

MASTER OF TWO WORLDS

In order to explain—in nonscientific terms—the nature of the cosmos, mythology created the following anthropomorphic figures:

- **The Universal Mother.** "The goddess is red with the fire of life; the earth, the solar system, the galaxies of far-extending space, all swell within her womb. For she is the world creatrix, ever mother, ever virgin. She encompasses the encompassing, nourishes the nourishing, and is the life of everything that lives. She is also the death of everything that dies. The whole round of existence is accomplished within her sway, from birth, through adolescence, maturity, and senescence, to the grave. She is the womb and the tomb: the sow that eats her farrow. Thus, she unites the 'good' and the 'bad,' exhibiting the two modes of the remembered mother, not as personal only, but as universal. The devotee is expected to contemplate the two with equal equanimity. Through this exercise his spirit is purged of its infantile, inappropriate sentimentalities and resentments, and his mind opened to the inscrutable presence which exists, not primarily as 'good' and 'bad' with respect to his childlike human convenience, his weal and woe, but as the law and image of the nature of being."[17]

Hence, the nature of the visible world is just *it is what it is*. We need to accept that.

- **The Universal Father.** He is the creator of all that lives, fueling the universe's cyclical process of renewal—creation, maturation, and dissolution. That means, the energy behind elemental pairs of opposites, such as fire and water, is one and the same force, supplying life to life.

Whereas the Universal Mother is the universe itself—which is what it is—the Universal Father is the Universe's Life Force. Opposite the discrediting acclamation that "all life is sorrowful," there is the world-begetting affirmative of the father: "Life must be!"

Because the son is to become the father—through the process of initiation; an introduction of the candidate into the techniques, duties, and prerogatives of his life's vocation—there arises an element of rivalry between the two, for the mastery of the universe. Campbell writes:

> The mystagogue (father or father-substitute) is to entrust the symbols of office only to a son who has been effectually purged of all inappropriate infantile cathexes—for whom the just, impersonal exercise of the powers will not be rendered impossible by unconscious (or perhaps even conscious and rationalized) motives of self-aggrandizement, personal preference, or resentment. Ideally, the invested one has been divested of his mere humanity and is representative of an impersonal cosmic force.[18]

The Force of Life

The force of life—the power to give life to life—brings into existence what we think in our mind's eye to be possible. Our minds are thus very powerful because every thought creates form that we will experience on some level—one way or another—in our everyday life. This mental power cannot be decreased, but it can be mismanaged and misused. By exercising our free will, we can direct our consciousness either in the direction of heaven, which we experience as inner peace, the zone, effortless achievement, and the experience of our oneness with others, or hell—conflict, struggle, pain, and the experience of our separateness from others.

Therefore, we can choose to identify ourselves either with the light side or with the dark side of the force of life. We can choose to contribute or to detract from the universal will of helping all of humanity to attain its highest level of creative possibility—to actualize its full potential. In *A Course in Miracles*, it says there is a limit beyond which the Son of God cannot miscreate. This means that using our minds in a loveless (i.e., miscreative) way will not last long before the whole thing falls apart.

Light Side of the Force of Life

Masters identifying with the light side of the force of life perceive business systems as a vehicle, a means to an end. They rely on a qualitatively different type of mental functioning, which the Greek philosopher Aristotle called *practical wisdom*.

Practical wisdom is described as:[19]

- The **moral will** to do what is right for humanity's attainment of its highest level of creative possibility—to actualize its full potential (which equals stewardship; see Chapter 5).
- The **moral skill** to discover the meaning of what is right for humanity's attainment of its highest level of creative possibility—to actualize its full potential (which equals craftsmanship; see Chapter 5). Note that what is legally right does not automatically make it morally right, and vice versa— unfortunately. Furthermore, what is right in one instance may be wrong in another.

Hence, the light side facilitates development of the quality of life (an index of development) and the standard of living (an index of growth) for all human beings. Russell Ackoff, an American organizational theorist and a pioneer in the field of operations research, systems thinking, and management science, says:

Growth refers to an increase in size or number, whereas development refers to an increase in one's ability and desire to satisfy legitimate needs and desires of oneself and others. A legitimate need or desire is one the satisfaction of which does not reduce the chances of others satisfying their legitimate needs or desires. Although growth and development can effect each other, they can also occur independently of each other: An entity can grow without developing (for example, a rubbish heap), and a person can continue to develop long after he or she has stopped growing. One can grow without wisdom but one cannot develop without it. Growth and increases in standard of living do not necessarily entail increases in the value of what is obtained; but development and increases in quality of life do.[20]

Let's be honest, we know in our gut what is morally right because it gives us peace of mind—it makes us free from decisional conflict and stress.

According to Buddhism, executives who want to experience peace of mind with their tough decisions need to develop the following two qualities:

- **Compassion (*karuna*).** Love, charity, kindness, tolerance, and such noble qualities on the emotional side, or qualities of the heart
- **Wisdom (*panna*).** The intellectual side or the qualities of the mind

It is said that the Buddha gave his teachings "for the good of the many, for the happiness of the many, out of compassion for the world."

Compassion and wisdom are inseparable and should thus be developed in equal measure. Should one develop only the emotional side, while neglecting the intellectual, one may become a good-hearted fool. And should one develop only the intellectual side, while neglecting the emotional, one may turn into a hard-hearted intellect without feeling for others.

At its extreme form, deep domain expertise is an ideology: a form of nonthinking that asserts that one already knows the answer to everything. Being deluded by the certainty of personal infallibility, decision makers shield ideologies from being penetrated by new facts and deny critical discussion, which makes it impossible for them to learn from mistakes. Ideology is absolutism. The German language uses the word *Fachidiot*[21] to describe such a one-track specialist and expert in his or her field who takes a blinkered approach to multifaceted problems.

Discerning what is morally right requires an enhanced state of understanding of the fundamental principles upon which wisdom itself is founded. The operative word in the attainment of wisdom is understanding. According to Buddhism, there are two sorts of understanding:

- **Knowing Accordingly (*anubodha*).** Knowledge as an accumulated memory that can easily be regurgitated when needed; an intellectual grasping of a subject according to certain given data.

- **Penetration (*pativedha*).** Seeing a subject, object, or concept in its true nature, free from our filters, interpretation, naming or labeling. Deep understanding is an inspirational—"in-spirit"— and context independent form of synthesis of a diverse range of knowledge. How we understand someone or something beyond a shadow of a doubt cannot be explained.

Unfortunately, the fundamental principles upon which wisdom is founded is not normally associated with schooling (see Figure 4.7). Wisdom is preceded by:

- **Data.** Products of observation by people or measuring devices, instruments—such as thermometers, speedometers, odometers, or voltmeters—representing objects, subjects, concepts, events, and their properties. Thus, gathered and measured data is, by itself, without significance or meaning. It is what it is: a collection of facts.
- **Information.** Data processed into a usable format. Information is contained in descriptions, most notably in answers to questions beginning with words such as "who," "what, "where," "when," and "how many." Hence, information fosters understanding of relationships such as means and ends and cause and effect among subjects, objects, concepts, and data. This is what makes information usable in deciding *what* to do—not *how* to do it.
- **Knowledge**. Answers provided to how-to questions, which are contained in instructions. Knowledge facilitates the maintenance and control of objects, systems, and events. Knowledge fosters understanding of patterns of behavior among subjects, objects, concepts, and information that predict the consequences of certain actions and behavior.

We can define wisdom as the ability to perceive and evaluate the long-term consequences of one's actions and behavior, which requires ethical judgment. Such judgments can only take place when legitimate options are available, increased, and preserved. Legitimate options are those that neither reduce access for others nor for oneself.

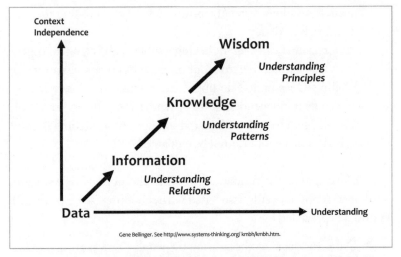

Figure 4.7: Hierarchy of Increasing Value in the Content of Learning

Not only does data, information, knowledge, and understanding presuppose each other, they are acquired and developed interdependently. This model shows their hierarchy of increasing value in the content of learning—that what is learned from others or through experience—yet none is more fundamental than the others. The adage "An ounce of information is worth a pound of data; an ounce of knowledge is worth a pound of information; an ounce of wisdom is worth a pound of knowledge" reflects this hierarchy.

Wisdom—including ethical judgment—is a distinctively human concern, and this is what E. F. Schumacher, an internationally influential German-born British economic thinker, said on the topic:

> The neglect, indeed the rejection, of wisdom has gone so far that most intellectuals have not even the faintest idea what the term could mean. As a result, they always tend to try and cure a disease by intensifying its causes. The disease having been caused by allowing cleverness to displace wisdom, no amount of clever research is likely to produce a cure. But what is wisdom? Where can it be found? Here we come to the crux of the matter; it can be read about in numerous publications but it can be found only inside oneself. To be able to find it, one has first to liberate oneself from such masters as greed and envy. The stillness following liberation—even if only momentarily—produces the insights of wisdom which are obtainable in no other way.[22]

In order to find wisdom within oneself, Buddhism dedicated three of its Noble Eightfold Paths to ethical conduct:

- **Right speech.** Speak the truth; abstain from wrong and harmful speech.
- **Right action.** Conduct oneself morally, honorably, and peacefully.
- **Right livelihood.** Make a living through a profession that brings no harm to others.

Ultimately, wisdom leads to understanding, which consists of a capacity for rational thought or inference or discrimination containing explanations that are the answers to *why* questions. Understanding—of relationships, patterns, and principles—is a core aspect of wisdom that facilitates and accelerates the acquisition of knowledge. This implies we do not learn *how* to do something by doing it correctly because, evidently, we already know how to do it. The most we can get out of doing something right is confirmation of what we already know. However, we can acquire knowledge from doing something incorrectly, but only if we can determine the cause of the error and then correct it. Mistakes can be corrected by trial and error, but this is often very inefficient. A mistake that can be explained by identifying what produced it is understood.

Russell Ackoff admonishes every decision maker, saying:

> Management . . . requires knowledge as well as information, but information and knowledge are not enough. Understanding is also required. Management suffers more from lack of knowledge than it does from lack of information and more from lack of understanding than it does from lack of knowledge. Most managers suffer from information overload, not from either an overload of knowledge or understanding.[23]

The Dark Side of the Force of Life

Masters identifying with the dark side of the force of life perceive the system as an end in its own right; the system has become its own purpose. Such systems demand strict enforcement of the rules, regulations, legislation, and sanctions that shape and adapt the system's behavior with the sole objective of preserving the system for itself and by itself. Obeisance to the needs of the system rules the day. Needs of humanity and society are subordinated to its own needs, and that of its owners—shareholders. Poor social responsibility is justified with amoral, and even immoral, beliefs and ideologies. Hence, questions regarding effectiveness, morality, understanding, or wisdom are suppressed with slick ego-defense mechanisms.

Chances are that whenever you hear a phrase like "The 'system' made a mistake" or "The 'system' cannot afford it; it's too expensive" or "The 'system' cannot handle this kind of enterprise-wide change," a leader is justifying a decision to not doing the right thing, because the person chooses to identify himself or herself with the dark side of the life force.

Being cut off from any influence of the spiritual world, business systems will create and are creating a wasteland, which Campbell defines as follows:

> The waste land, let us say then, is any world in which (to state the problem pedagogically) force and not love, indoctrination, not education, authority, not experience, prevail in the ordering of lives, and where the myths and rites enforced and received are consequently unrelated to the actual inward realizations, needs, and potentialities of those upon whom they are impressed.[24]

In a wasteland, people are fulfilling purposes that are not properly theirs, but ones that have been put upon them as inescapable laws. They experience conflict and stress when work-related decisions require them to apply a set of values and beliefs different from what they apply to their personal decisions. Because of this, they are living inauthentic lives and complain, "I've never done a thing I wanted to in all my life. I've done as I was told." No wonder there is a strong yearning for work–life balance—to align their values and beliefs with their behavior both at home and at work.

Leaders who govern their business systems with the energy of the dark side are incapable of solving systemic problems, all the while running the risk that, sooner or later, the system will implode or collapse into itself.

In writing *The Root Cause*, I recognized that people undeniably have a design problem—a lack of interest, attention, and curiosity for business system design, which is an integral aspect of business governance, which I discuss at length in Chapter 9.

The Need for Business Design

Peter Senge, a professor at MIT's Sloan School of Management, told his CEO students that the leader on a ship crossing the ocean is not the captain, navigator, or helmsman. "The leader is the designer of the ship because operations on a ship are consequences of design."[25]

Similarly, business executives are the designers of a value chain, and all those executives within an industry are designers of the value system (see Figure 4.8). Whether you call it design, redesign, continual improvement, reorganization, change, renovation, or innovation, it is part and parcel of business governance—a unique executive responsibility.

Since form follows function (see the second business gremlin, form follows function), design should follow or, better still, should anticipate the needs of members in its target audience. This is what Steve Jobs (cofounder of Apple) said on this topic:

> Some people say, "Give the customers what they want." But that's not my approach. Our job is to figure out what they're going to want before they do. I think Henry Ford once said, "If I'd asked customers what they wanted, they would have told me, 'A faster horse!'" People don't know what they want until you show it to them. That's why I never rely on market research. Our task is to read things that are not yet on the page.

Apart from capturing an audience's imagination and reading market trends, some of the biggest challenges business leaders face are how to increase employee engagement, encourage employee loyalty, and recruit and retain talented employees. Many employees have become disengaged, disillusioned, and indifferent, and they see their jobs as "just a paycheck."

In addition, the general public has become disenchanted with the corporate world and executives who seem to cater to the interest of shareholders only. There is a noticeable cognitive dissonance between the image brands present of themselves through advertising, sponsorship of events, and cultural expressions, and how they are actually

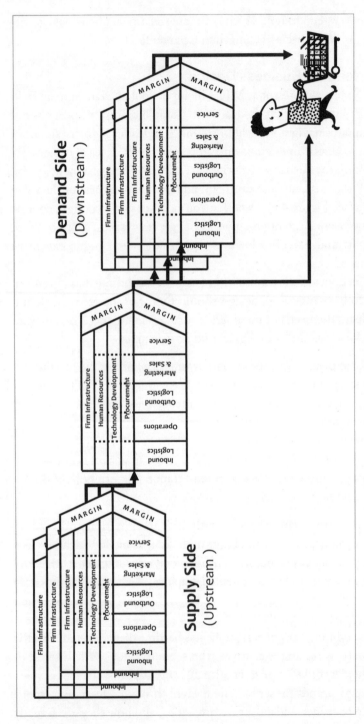

Figure 4.8: The Value System

A business's value chain is embedded in a larger stream of activities. Prof. Michael Porter called this stream of activities the *value system*.

perceived by their surrounding constituency. This dichotomy is eroding trust.

Given the many business systems suffering from stubborn systemic problems that create too many unintended and unwanted results, it's high time for a new design of the business system, which should not be confused with its business model.

In conclusion, Campbell describes as a characteristic of a master of two words the "freedom to pass back and forth across the world division, from the perspective of the apparitions of time to that of the causal deep and back—not contaminating the principles of the one with those of the other, yet permitting the mind to know the one by virtue of the other."[26] In other words, business governance requires being comfortable when experiencing the discomfort of holding in one's mind two or more contradictory beliefs, ideas, or values at the same time, or when new information conflicts with existing beliefs, ideas, or values.[27]

At times, when you feel confused and irritated, you can take solace in these words by Campbell: "Furthermore, we have not even to risk the adventure alone; for the heroes of all time have gone before us; the labyrinth is thoroughly known; we have only to follow the thread of the hero-path." So, knowing that any current or future chief executive officer who undergoes a transformation of consciousness is indeed a hero, will you accept the call to adventure?

WHAT HAPPENS NEXT?

This chapter revealed the inevitability that every chief executive officer who is about to fall victim to the Peter Principle must come to terms with and answer Colonel John R. Boyd's well-known question regarding human maturation which is: to do something important or to be someone important.

For those who accept the call to learn, unlearn, and relearn, the next part of this book is dedicated to painting a bigger-picture perspective of a business system within its natural environment and the interdependent relationships between its major component parts.

Deciding to embark on this journey is of vital importance to anyone's process of self-actualization because, as Mark Twain said, "Travel is fatal to prejudice, bigotry, and narrow-mindedness."

PART II

Business
Mechanics

*The single story creates stereotypes, and
the problem with stereotypes is not that they
are untrue but that they are incomplete.
They make one story become the only story.*

–Chimamanda Ngozi Adichie
Nigerian novelist; from
"The Danger of a Single Story," TED Global 2009

CHAPTER 5

Stewardship and Craftsmanship

*You never change things by fighting the existing
reality. To change something, build a new model
that makes the existing model obsolete.*

—Buckminster Fuller
American architect, systems theorist, inventor, and futurist

It is not necessary to change. Survival is not mandatory.

—Attributed to Dr. W. Edwards Deming
America's eminent scholar, on the methods
for management of quality

The assignment of a returning heroic chief executive—master of two worlds—is knitting together the spiritual world with the world of common day. That means creating synthesis among a business system's attributes such as people (their capacity to think critically and creatively), the quality of operational processes (their capability and capacity), resource management (its efficiency and effectiveness), customer satisfaction (being their obvious choice supplier), profitability, sustainability of business practices, social responsibility, environmental consciousness, and brand identity, to name but a few. In other words, making trade-off decisions rather than favoring features of one world to the exclusion of any of the other.

Note that trade-off decisions that disrespect humanity, society, and the environment are bound to create friction and conflict on some level and at some point in time—most likely when the system is already experiencing unusual levels of stress.

Making trade-offs requires discernment, which relies on insight and understanding of the business system's purpose and its capability and capacity to become its target audience's obvious choice supplier. For example, during an economic downturn, one could decide to reduce the labor force, defer system maintenance, and halt research and development activities to reduce cost, thus maintaining or even boosting short-term profitability. Alternatively, one could decide to compensate for a drop in the labor force's time spent on routine work flow by catching up on back maintenance, initiating new product development, and conducting employee training. The difference between these two decisions becomes particularly evident in a business system's readiness when economic conditions improve again.

Another difference between these two decisions is evident in the decision-making process—using quantitative or qualitative arguments. Quantitative arguments are firmly rooted in dominant thought patterns of the world of common day—the level of thinking that brought us to where we are today. Decisions are then rationalized with easy to corroborate performance ratios that rely on setting arbitrary numerical goals, in what is known as Management by Objectives (see the sixth business gremlin, everything is created twice).

Qualitative arguments, on the other hand, are based on theory, principles, values, opinions, personal experience, gut feeling, intuition, instinct, or mojo. The following quote, often attributed to Albert Einstein, is rather apropos: "The intuitive mind is a sacred gift and the rational mind is a faithful servant. We have created a society that honors the servant and has forgotten the gift."

I believe that intuition and instinct are closely related to the spiritual world in the sense that they contain wisdom, an unwavering knowing, which does not involve reason or any cognitive process. And their benchmark for success is one's experience of inner peace. Now, be honest with yourself; how many times have you rejected your intuition or instinct and come to regret it? What I am advocating here is that a master of two worlds uses both quantitative and qualitative arguments as demanded by current conditions and unfolding new and unforeseen events. Practical wisdom, remember?

BRIDGING THE DIVIDE BETWEEN NEEDS AND WANTS

Every sales course advises its students to engage a prospective client at the point where his or her mind is at that time. Prospective clients should not be expected to do any mental gymnastics—such as performing a mind shift—so they can catch up with the seller's level of thinking. For this reason, I observe a divide between the nature of education, management advice, and leadership coaching that executives say they "want" and what they actually "need." Professor Philip Kotler[1] defined a human *need* as a state of felt deprivation in a person, and a *want* as a culturally defined product or service that will satisfy that need.

We know what executives' wants are from market research in the form of studies, questionnaires, and reports—such as the one conducted by IBM on dealing with complexity—and focus groups. Typically, wants are technological tools—electronic devices and software applications—or a leadership and management methodology. What is missing from most of those research efforts is addressing any specific executive needs that those wants are supposed to fulfill. Then, what *is* an executive decision maker's need when confronted with a stubborn systemic problem? What are the critical success factors and prerequisites that make a solution—a want—into an authentic solution? How can anyone identify a want when the need is still unknown?

As discussed in Chapter 1, business problems become personal problems for the chief executive. Consequently, executive decision makers' needs are for stewardship and craftsmanship, a topic discussed briefly in Chapter 4 under the heading "Light Side of the Force of Life."

In order for a CEO to practice stewardship and craftsmanship, the leader will need to develop a keen appreciation for the flow of energy and information between a business system's key component parts, which is ultimately responsible for its behavior, performance, and outcome. This flow of energy and information is what I call *business mechanics*. Once decision makers develop this value consciousness for business mechanics, they are less likely to harm or undermine good business mechanics with their decisions. What I mean to say is that many solutions could satisfy a decision maker by blunting specific symptoms, but only a few will enhance a system's business mechanics as well—to realign the system's capability and capacity with the purpose for which the system was created.

Consequently, executives' needs for solving stubborn systemic problems is the moral will (*stewardship*) to practice business mechanics correctly, and the moral skill (*craftsmanship*) to explore which practices make for good business mechanics.

The notion about what is right—what makes for good business mechanics—is similar if not equal to what Robert M. Pirsig describes as quality, in his epic book *Zen and the Art of Motorcycle Maintenance: An Inquiry into Values*. According to Pirsig, "Quality is the continuing stimulus which our environment puts upon us to create the world in which we live."

This is no definition of quality because, as Pirsig explains, "to take that which has caused us to create the world, and include it within the world we have created, is clearly impossible. That is why quality cannot be defined. If we do define it, we are defining something less than quality itself."

Pirsig continues with an explanation for why he believes that what is right for one should not necessarily be right for all. "In a sense . . . it's the student's choice of quality that defines him. People differ about Quality, not because Quality is different, but because people are different in terms of experience. . . . [I]f two people had identical a priori analogues they would see Quality identically every time."

Needless to say, not every decision maker has the same interpretation of what is right because not everyone has the same experiences.

Rather than applying prescribed solutions, or wants, without any serious investigation of their appropriateness given the current state of the business and its desired state, learning the principles of business mechanics is what bridges the divide between needs and wants. In the words of Benjamin Franklin, "Being ignorant is not so much a shame, as being unwilling to learn." [2]

STEWARDSHIP

Stewardship is an appointed position of authority that is bestowed upon the person who accepts responsibility for the management of assets that are given in his or her trust by its beneficiary. Stewardship is also a discipline regarding the responsible planning and management of resources. Stewardship—the moral will to do what is right—relies on a theory or system of moral principles and values to assess whether a course of action is good or bad. A steward is held accountable for the soundness of their discernment in their decision-making processes.

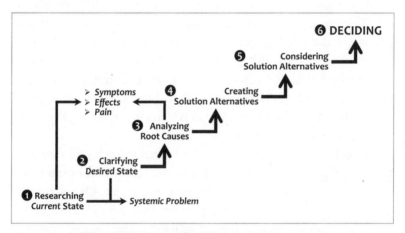

Figure 5.1: Sound Decision-Making Process

Decision makers are held accountable for their decisions, which they can only justify successfully when they have done their homework—when they can explain convincingly how they arrived at their decision.

We obtain a better understanding of the meaning of the verb *to decide* by considering its Latin origin, *decaedere*, which means "to cut off" (derived from *de* [off] and *caedere* [to cut]). What is cut off are alternative options or courses of action. In other words, it means coming to a resolution or choice in the mind as a result of discernment, consideration, or settling an argument. Reaching a successful decision takes many steps (see Figure 5.1).

The role of a chief executive is that of a steward who is responsible for the sustainable development of a business system's capability and capacity in order to realize the system's intended purpose for which that system was specifically created. CEOs are thus expected to leave the company in better shape—which includes more than simply its financial health—for their successor than when it was handed over to them by their predecessor.

The immediate monetary beneficiaries of a business system are the owners or shareholders, who share in the profits when the company does well but lose, to a maximum of their invested amount, when the company does poorly. Hence, the naming of their investment as risk capital. Ultimately, the potential reward should be commensurate with the potential risk, which is an integral part of an investment decision.

Shareholders are part of an extended group called stakeholders, which is any individual or group of people who can affect or is affected by the achievement of the organization's objectives. In addition to shareholders, this group includes indirect beneficiaries, or people whose livelihoods and well-being are tied to that of the business system, such as employees, vendors, buyers, users, professional service providers, the community in which it operates, local government, and trade associations.

Stakeholders and enterprises are bound to each other by contractual relationships. Each party gives up something in return for something else, which makes it a two-way street. Of course, the numerous stakeholders in an enterprise have various self-interests that may not always be properly aligned with each other. In fact, they may be conflicting. Solving such conflicts is the exclusive domain of the system's steward, which demands of him or her the moral will to do what is right and thus to avoid and resolve friction and conflict, making sure that a chosen solution does not provide seeds for future conflict.

Moral Compass

We already established that a steward knows a solution is "right" when she or he experiences peace of mind. Will, as in moral will to do what is right, refers to a steward's intention—informed by the voice of the id—to value humanity more than shareholders' desire for money. This matters because by eliminating humanity—the spiritual world or the path of the heart—from the equation, decision makers can defer the defense of their decisions to cold-hearted mathematical calculations.

The certainty that universally verifiable mathematics provides is intended to unburden a decision maker's conscience, which is often expressed to stakeholders in the all too familiar advice: "Don't take this personally, this is business." This line of reasoning wants us to believe that emotion should be separated from business (that is, when it suits a decision maker). After all, employees are expected to be fully engaged and motivated, and to have heart for the business. Yet such emotional investment *is* personal.

However, morality is not a luxury (the affordability of which is debatable); it is critical to the successful resolution of any conflict, large or small, in private, public, and among nations. As Einstein said, "Not everything that can be counted counts and not everything that counts can be counted." A lack of moral fiber, demonstrated by either an individual or a corporation, influences public opinion and thereby people's behavior toward the culprit. Don't underestimate the influence of globalization and social media on your reputation.

Although the consequences of such a change in behavior, as measured in monetary terms, is unknown and unknowable, successful stewards must nevertheless take these into account during their decision-making processes. After all, employees who trust that management will do the right thing and will fight for the success of their employer instead of "looking out for number one," which is the main reason the war for talent exists.

To paraphrase Colonel John R. Boyd: tools and technology do not increase bottom-line results; employees do when they use their minds.[3] Employees have finely attuned antennae for picking up cause-and-effect relationships between their experience of friction and conflict and executive decisions. They use their own moral compass to discern what is right and wrong, and they will act accordingly. In addition, they are willing to do the near impossible to make a wrong decision work, up to a certain point and for a limited amount of time only. So, don't tick them off unnecessarily—that is, without a defensible reason.

CRAFTSMANSHIP

Trying to determine the essential attributes of craftsmanship is, perhaps, an attempt at defining what may prove to be indefinable.

Craftsmanship is not the only indefinable concept in the English language. This is how Supreme Court Justice Potter Stewart described, rather than defined, hard-core pornography in his opinion in the 1964 case *Jacobellis v. Ohio*: "I shall not today attempt further to define the kinds of material I understand to be embraced within that shorthand description, and perhaps I could never succeed in intelligibly doing so. But I know it when I see it."

While we all recognize craftsmanship—the moral skill to identify the right thing to do—and while we can describe what it looks like and how it makes us feel, we cannot formulate a conclusive definition of those succinct qualities that turn performing a trade or profession into craftsmanship. Craftsmen possess an inner knowing about what constitutes doing something the right way. They do not question whether they should be doing it any other way. Moreover, cutting corners goes against their natural disposition; it violates their integrity and thereby the id of who they are. Because there is pride and honor in their work, you cannot even force them to do what is wrong—it is just not done, period.

In developing my own craftsmanship in root-cause analyses and change leadership, I learned to identify the complex interdependent relationships among the major tangible and intangible aspects of a business system, and how to make them visible with simple and easy-to-comprehend models as you see throughout this book. Note that the relationships between separate individual parts are what turn individual value links into a value chain. Therefore, a value chain is only as strong as the weakest relationship—interface—between two value links.

Communication

Responsibility for the successful maintenance of these relationships is often incorrectly ascribed to the discipline of communications—an academic discipline that deals with processes of human communication. This silo of specialized knowledge is just a channel or medium for passing messages between a sender and a receiver—it is the faucet, not the water. Its main concern is to accurately convey the sender's intent and to avoid or reduce noise from garbling the content.

However, relationships (connections) that tie separate value links (nodes) into a value chain (network) are shared boundaries across which information is exchanged. These shared boundaries are commonly known as interfaces. Although proper communication processes may improve clarity of transmissions, the essence of an exchange of information is in its content, which demands familiarity with the principles of business mechanics.

Unfortunately, few silo managers possess that kind of knowledge. In fact, interfaces have become a no-man's-land between two or more links of the value chain for which very few leaders feel any sense of responsibility. Why? Because we have committed ourselves to the process of managing the actions of individual links of the value chain rather than their interactions. As a result, issues that remain unattended are falling in the cracks between two silos of specialized knowledge. These issues make themselves known enterprise-wide in the form of acute or latent problems, and they will persist, recur, or become acute until they are addressed with an authentic solution.

In a worst-case scenario, latent problems can become acute, and acute problems can grow in severity, or even reach a fatal date—urgency—after which their detrimental power skyrockets or can no longer be corrected and causes a business to implode. This was discussed in Chapter 1, under the subheading "Measuring a Problem." By now you should understand why alleged performance improvement measures such as benchmarking, accountability, and cultivating "A" players/teams are ineffective; no individual value link can outperform the capability and capacity of the value chain as a whole.

Establishing and maintaining properly working interfaces within a complex network of business processes requires a give-and-take decision-making process that is cognizant of what needs to be done three to five steps into the future and across multiple value links, which is a key characteristic of craftsmanship. Imagine the feeling of extreme frustration when finding oneself in pursuit of an intended outcome (effect) that requires a specific course of action (cause) that is no longer available because of a past decision by you or your executive? This is the message made visible with a decision tree.

Pursuing the creation and implementation of prescribed generic deliverables and milestones as a precondition for changing a specific system's behavior and performance are doomed to fail because no two business systems are identical in their level of complexity and their reaction to unfolding events. However, once you understand business mechanics, you don't need to memorize tricks, procedures, or best practices because you are capable of figuring out what the system requires here and now by yourself.

Knowing Why

Performing one's trade or profession the right way does not imply a faithful reliance on following a strict protocol that prescribes when, where, and how specific tasks must be performed and which tools should be used. Craftsmanship is about knowing the goal of a methodology, what it aims to accomplish, why something is done, when, how it works, where to apply what practice, and by whom. The *why* is informed by circumstances, such as the task at hand, the materials or substrate with which to work, critical success factors that determine the success of the end result that a principal intends to achieve, and prerequisites that determine the success of the production and delivery process, including cultural, environmental, social, and ethical aspects.

Typically, artisans require fewer specialized tools because they know how to perform a greater variety of tasks with the same tool. Just visit Colonial Williamsburg in Virginia, where modern-day craftsmen are still making exquisite colonial furniture with period hand tools—no computer-controlled routers or laser-guided power tools in sight. They are testimony to the fact that craft is in the man (or in the woman), not the tool. Craftsmanship is, first and foremost, a way of thinking with some tools attached. And, executives who invest more in tools and technology than in craftsmanship are themselves the cause of complexity, which they decry as the source of their bewilderment.

In *Understanding Variation: The Key to Managing Chaos*, Donald J. Wheeler discusses the uses and limitations of tools:

> While it is easy to focus on the tools, and while it is easy to teach the tools, the tools are secondary to the way of thinking. Learn the tools and you have nothing. You will not know what to do. You will not know how to use the tools effectively. Learn and practice the way of thinking that undergirds the tools and you will begin an unending journey of continual improvement. Without major capital expenditures you will discover how to increase both quality and productivity, and thereby improve your competitive position.[4]

Craftsmanship in business is an individual executive's unique ability to translate performance theories (relationships between cause and effect) into their intended physical results (relationships between means and ends). The success of such translations depends on understanding the principles that govern business mechanics and the possession of sufficient insight to predict the outcome of one's actions—tools are just a means to an end, not an end in their own right. Success depends on the design of the business's facility, organizational climate, and corporate culture, which are unique executive responsibilities.

Quality

In other words, craftsmanship is an individual's expression of quality. Therefore, craftsmanship is expressed differently by different individuals, because each has different experiences with properties that constitute quality for them.

Quality is the path one chooses to walk through life, and the experience of peace of mind is its sign of success; that is how you know you are on the right track. Pirsig says about peace of mind: "That which produces it is good work and that which destroys it is bad work."

Therefore, executive decision makers must possess the ability to see what *looks good* and an ability to understand the underlying methods to arrive at that good, which is not a one-size-fits-all criterion. Expecting that good will naturally follow when applying the underlying methods is an illusion. Pirsig writes, "The way to see what looks good and understand the reasons it looks good, and to be at one with this goodness as the work proceeds, is to cultivate an inner quietness, a peace of mind so that goodness can shine through."

This goodness occurs when subject and object become one and their activities effortless. Athletes describe this experience of concentration on the present moment as "being in the zone." In classical music, it's the difference between playing all the notes flawlessly while showing great technical command of one's instrument, and pouring one's heart and soul into interpreting the spirit of a musical composition with great sensitivity to emotional feelings of oneself and others.[5] Craftsmanship is not exhibited in *what* one thinks but in *how* one thinks. It's not about what one is expected to perceive as reality but in how one perceives reality for oneself. Although knowledge can be transferred to another person, it cannot be understood for that person.

Therefore, rote learning is no substitute for gaining understanding, insights, and wisdom. Obtaining a keen insight into the complex relationships between means and ends and cause and effect is like doing push-ups; no one can do them for you. No one can make you do them; you must want to do them yourself. Yes, it will be hard, but once you gain that insight, you open a door to a whole new world of possibilities and opportunities that are yours for the taking. You will have, what German psychologist and linguist Karl Bühler called, an *"aha-erlebnis"*—or what we call an "aha moment"—named appropriately after the word that is commonly uttered when new insight is gained. There is a clear difference between knowing and understanding!

PAINTING THE BIGGER-PICTURE PERSPECTIVE

Whenever you paint a bigger-picture perspective of the challenge before you, you are going to discover what the right thing to do is. Because you have discovered what is right and can articulate why it is right, doing what is right becomes easier too.

Process mapping is a wonderful method for painting bigger-picture perspectives. All you need to do is identify where the process you want to map begins and ends as well as what actors are involved (people, departments, processes, functions, computer applications, interfaces) and then take inventory of their behavior—the actual activities and tasks they perform. You will discover an unexpectedly large number of interactions between actors, with frequent interdependencies on each other for the successful completion of the tasks they were designed to perform.

Process maps demonstrate that a business system is a network of nodes and connections. They show how the success of one department is dependent on that of many others, even if they are not performed within the same building, city, state, or country, thus breaking down the walls between departments and responsible managers. I like to say that the benefit of having these maps is you can hang them above your desk because they will start conversations. After all, these maps make it possible to trace the consequences of a decision, omission, mistake, or change in specific daily activities of one department on that of one or more other departments. This explains why it is not uncommon for their effects to be experienced enterprise-wide, which is another way of saying that they are inherent to the system's design, organization or structure, implementation or operation, maintenance, and management. Process maps demonstrate why solving systemic problems demands executive sponsorship for change.

A process map's level of accuracy can range from a detail-oriented flow of data, information, documents, or objects to an aggregated rendition thereof. And I can report from personal experience that making processes visible creates common ground among all participants, even when relationships between two or more of them are polarized. When everyone identifies their own specific contribution within a mapped process, in relationship to that of anyone else, they realize they are all in the same boat. Everyone takes pride in their own work, knowing all too well that no one knows more about what goes on inside the mapped process than the ones who are actually doing all the work. From there on out, finding the root cause(s) and creating an authentic solution becomes a team effort.

Scale Preferences

General George S. Patton Jr. discussed the issue of perspective in relationship to the required scale of maps:

> Whereas most commanders demanded the most detailed, largest-scale maps they could obtain, Patton declared his "opinion that, in the High Command, small-scale maps [which show a larger territory with fewer details] are best because from that level one has to decide on general policies and determine the places, usually road centers or river lines, the capture of which will hurt the enemy most."[6]

Big-picture perspectives challenge actors to break out of the comfort zone of their own world, within their specific area of expertise, within one of the nine links of the value chain. They need to let go of a high level of detailed, analytic knowledge, and embrace more general and synthetic knowledge instead.

In his televised interview with Bill Moyers on the topic of *The Power of Myth*,[7] Joseph Campbell referred to Colin Turnbull's experience when visiting with Mbuti Pygmies, a nomadic tribe of hunters and gatherers living in the dense jungle of Zaire.[8] One day, Turnbull brought a Pygmy, who had never been out of the jungle, onto a mountaintop. The man was utterly terrified by the panoramic view of the plains below, stretching as far as the eye could see. Because the animals grazing on the plains in the distance looked so small, he believed that they were ants just across the way from where he stood. Having lived his life among the trees, he had no practice in judging perspective and distance. He literally could not see the forest for the trees. Overwhelmed by this new and unexpected experience, he rushed back to the familiarity of the forest, which was a landscape without horizon.

This shows that one cannot understand the mechanics of a business system as an integrated whole from the perspective of one of its component parts. Moreover, many people feel insecure when confronted with a different perspective on the reality of their daily routine. A common knee-jerk reaction to the experience of uncertainty is to strive for certainty, which—by means of micromanagement—tends to make processes more rigid and resistant to change. Because the world around us changes, we are changing right along with it.

Therefore, the antidote to uncertainty is adaptation to change. Reliant on practical wisdom, executive decision makers will know the right course of action, and they are thus motivated to provide their wholehearted executive sponsorship for change. And they are committed to follow through until completion.

The High Price of Gold Plating

Understanding a business system starts with the acquisition of fundamental knowledge about what a business system is. Unfortunately, the way we are educated about business is through in-depth analyses of the nine separate links that constitute the value chain. Each link is then broken up even further into narrowly defined silos of specialized knowledge. Motivated by personal performance goals and annual performance evaluations, managers within each silo develop their own doctrines and assumptions regarding the (financial) contributions of their individual silo to a business system. Moreover, numerical performance goals that encourage operational efficiency are still perceived as successful, even if they reduce effectiveness and cause difficulties for other departments further down the end-to-end process.

As Deming pointed out, when you take apart a motorcar into its component parts, you no longer have a motorcar; you have a collection of parts. Then, when you reassemble the motorcar using only the top components that the motor vehicle industry worldwide has to offer, there is neither a guarantee that all those superior parts will actually fit together properly, nor any assurance that this motorcar will actually deliver a superior performance.

Strict compartmentalization of a business system, in addition to a management approach that sets arbitrary financial or numerical goals for every silo manager with line-item responsibility, causes everyone to dance to the beat of their own drummer. Each department develops the latest and greatest in their field of expertise and promotes the implementation thereof—including its requisite tools—within the business system. They will even compete with other departments for additional budget to realize their ideas for their silo only.

For the purpose of calling attention to this unfortunate phenomenon, Colonel John R. Boyd coined the derogatory expression "gold plating," remember, an urgent reminder that rethinking the allocation of limited funds—resource management—is way overdue.

Undermining Operational Effectiveness

Boyd worked on the development of fighter aircraft that had the intended purpose of gaining and maintaining air superiority.

The negative effect of gold plating is an increase in aircraft complexity, a higher all-up weight and larger size, which increases the drag ratio, wing loading, and visibility from the ground and in the air while reducing her maneuverability. This is then compensated with an even bigger engine that burns more fuel, requiring larger fuel capacity—which increases her weight even more. Because the aircraft is now bigger and heavier, she develops more drag, has a higher wingload, is more visible, and is less maneuverable. This calls for even more state-of-the-art solutions such as stealth technology, that . . . I trust you understand where this rant is going.

Not only are gold-plated aircraft more expensive to buy—they are also exponentially more expensive to operate and maintain. After all, maintenance of a gold-plated aircraft's additional specialized systems, functions, and components requires more time and increased crew training. In addition, expensive specialized replacement parts need to be kept in stock.

Consequently, to offset these cost increases, aircraft designers now develop a multipurpose aircraft, thus tapping into budgets of several service branches of the armed forces. The suggestion is for the Air Force, the Navy, and the Marine Corps to share the same airframe, albeit with some adaptations to satisfy each of their specific needs.

Because these gold-plated multipurpose aircraft require a longer turnaround time, their readiness for action is less than that of a single-purpose aircraft. Readiness is even further reduced by the smaller number of aircraft that each service branch can afford to acquire and operate.

In conclusion, aircraft designed as a compromise between the specific needs of two or more service branches—each tasked with distinctly different defense functions—results inevitably in suboptimization—an aircraft that is a jack-of-all-trades, master of none. Moreover, it is rather ironic to read about low tech, or even antiquated, technologies defeating high-tech developments. The all-too-common practice of gold plating defeats the specific purpose of a technologically advanced aircraft.

Likewise, gold plating individual processes, departments, computer platforms, silos of specialized knowledge, or value links has an equally negative effect on business system performance. The actual benefits of adding glamorous tools and advanced technology hardly ever outweigh the drawbacks of subsequent increases in system complexity and decreases in operational effectiveness at becoming the target audience's obvious choice supplier. Therefore, such change initiatives should not even make it to an executive's short list of investment proposals. Sound stewardship should act as a safeguard against this unfortunately common trend or best practice.

Creating a Common Point of Departure

That said, in order to design, build, develop, or change a business system—which includes solving systemic problems caused by complexity and events—every participant with deep domain expertise should start from the same departure point.

Although doctrines and assumptions regarding different areas of expertise are necessary, no doctrine or assumption should be allowed to dominate the conversation. Having one doctrine rule what is right risks creating false impressions that anything else must be wrong.

Executives often say conflicting ideas are wrong because they never heard them before. Therefore, decision makers must be encouraged to study, contemplate, and question unfamiliar doctrines and assumptions when they are advanced by people within various areas of expertise. After all, looking at the same challenge through the lens of different doctrines only increases one's understanding of it—*aha-erlebnis*—which in turn increases the chance of developing better hypotheses and theories that result in the creation of previously unknown and unexpected solutions.

When Boyd started the development of a new jet engine for the future McDonnell Douglas F-15 Eagle fighter aircraft, he found himself surrounded by engineers who covered a wide range of disciplines and specializations. Needless to say, every one of them understood a jet engine from a different point of view. Therefore, Boyd feared, because they already had an engine, that each engineer would just focus on identifying deficiencies one by one among those parts within their area of expertise and then come up with suggestions for improvement. Yet no individual part has an independent effect on the engine's performance. In other words, no single part can cause the engine to outperform its current capability and capacity. Consequently, performance improvement of a part—including elimination of deficiencies—should only be conducted if and when it improves performance of the system as a whole simultaneously.

Moreover, eliminating unwanted characteristics does not imply the system is now everything you would want it to be. Therefore, instead of directing attention to characteristics that are not wanted, attention should be focused on properties that are wanted. Boyd wanted those engineers to identify properties and characteristics they would want right now, not at some future date, if they could create whatever they would want to create. After all, if they cannot envision that here and now, then how could they be expected to revolutionize the jet engine in the real world where conditions constrain their abilities.

To prevent any doctrine or assumption from restricting anyone's vision for the new engine's ultimate design possibilities and performance capabilities, Boyd created a common point of departure by describing a jet engine as follows: "Cold air goes in the front door; hot air comes out the back door; it goes faster, and we call that thrust." He wanted every functional expert to measure the validity of their contribution to the new jet engine against this common departure point—major premise—as opposed to trying to justify any gold plating exercises against the doctrine of their own area of expertise. As a result, they developed an engine that exceeded everyone's expectations.

Similarly, for us to create universal understanding of the mechanics of a business system, we should define a common point of departure for all leadership positions and all areas of specialized knowledge within the nine functions of the value chain.

The reason why this is necessary becomes painfully apparent when business leaders are asked to describe what a business system is or to draw an image of what it does. Their replies range from making money to organizational charts, process maps, logos, products, and buildings. There is no consensus. Contrast this with mentioning the Statue of Liberty, the Golden Gate Bridge, or the Eiffel Tower, when instantaneously an image pops up in your mind, an image that is the same for everyone, even if you never saw any of them in real life.

With everyone judging the opinions of others—and validating their own opinions against fundamentals of areas of expertise with which they are, or are believed to be, familiar—everyone is right and wrong at the same time. Without a common point of departure, discerning which ideas, concepts, challenges, and solutions are in the best interest of the system as an integrated whole is confusing at best and catastrophic at worst.

For us to understand and communicate the fundamental principles of a business system—the business mechanics that are responsible for its behavior and performance—I designed a mental big-picture perspective, displayed in Figure 5.2, as my preferred common point of departure.

Every journey that is undertaken with an intended destination in mind requires a vehicle that is appropriate for that particular journey to that particular destination. Because the individual parts of this trinity (journey–destination–vehicle) are interdependent of each other in complex ways, changing the destination requires the journey

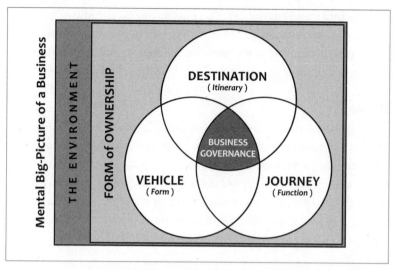

Figure 5.2: The Business Mechanics Model

In order to provide all participants with a common point of departure, the author created this business mechanics model—a mental big-picture perspective of a business as a singular, unique, integrated, and open system.

to be adjusted or changed as well. And a decision to pursue a different destination causes inevitable changes to the journey. When the journey is changed, the vehicle must be adjusted or changed accordingly because form follows function. Then, when the vehicle changes, or is proven to lack the necessary capacity and capability to continue the journey toward its destination, either the journey or the destination needs to be adapted. Shaping and adjusting of business mechanics is the unique function of business governance.

Journey

Typically, when we talk about business, we refer to commerce, doing business, or the exchange of products or services for money (income generation)—in other words, every form of interaction with members of one's intended target audience. The journey describes how the vehicle—see below—participates in and establishes its presence in the market, both physically and emotionally. These activities become tangible and visible in marketing and branding expressions, customer service, and other forms of social engagements, including sponsorship agreements, philanthropy, and demonstrations of corporate responsibility and environmental consciousness. The journey is, so to speak, the counterbalance to the supply side of the value chain.

Earlier I used the expression "forms follows function." So, if the journey is the function of a business, then the vehicle is its form.

Vehicle

Every business is a manmade system, which means it is an integrated whole that consists of two or more parts—it cannot be divided into independent parts. Furthermore, the essential properties that define such a system are properties of the whole, which none of its parts possess individually. In other words, a system is not the sum of its parts; rather, it is the product of their interactions. Therefore, when a system is taken apart—analyzed—it loses its essential properties and, so do its parts.

Parts that belong to a system share the following characteristics:

1. Each individual part has the ability to affect the behavior of the system as a whole.
2. The effect an individual part can have on the system depends ultimately on the behavior of at least one other part; all parts are interconnected—no part is isolated.
3. Each part can be taken to form a subset or sub-system. Yet, just like individual parts, no subset has an independent effect on the system as a whole.

Characteristic of such a manmade system is its purpose-built nature—it is, so to speak, a vehicle for the pursuit of a well-defined destination, following a deliberate or strategic itinerary that describes the journey ahead. Without the vehicle there can be no journey. Hence, one can tell the function of such a vehicle simply by observing its form and behavior—form follows function. Who would mistake an iconic yellow school bus for a dump truck or a taxi?

Whenever a business system—the vehicle—is said to have a purpose of its own, it's raison d'être, the system functions as an organism as opposed to a mechanism. So, what is the principal purpose of any organism? Survival. And it is necessary for the organism to develop its capability and capacity to adjust and adapt itself in order to survive the uncertainty and disruptive effect of new and unforeseen circumstances.

Now, what about the purpose of the parts of an organismic system, its organs? They don't have any. Instead, they have a function that supports the purpose of the organism of which they are an integral part. Notice the language of business becoming biological. The chief executive of a firm, or the senior manager, is generally referred to as the head. And the firm or company is now called a corporation, which is a reference to the Latin word *corpus,* or "body."

Unfortunately, not everyone has adopted an organismic perspective on business systems. Too many current decision makers are still stuck in an outdated mechanistic perspective, which suggests that the purpose of a business is not inherent to the manmade system itself; a business system has no purpose of its own, and therefore, neither do its parts. When the Chicago school of economics Professor Milton Friedman expressed his opinion that the only legitimate business of business is business, he clearly demonstrated a mechanistic perspective on business.

Following this line of thinking, as a machine or a tool, the business is just an instrument of its owners, and its only function is to maximize the monetary value it generates for those owners or shareholders. Executives—agents acting on behalf of the machine's owners or its shareholders—are said to have a fiduciary responsibility. Being a fiduciary means being bound both legally and ethically to act in the shareholders' best interests. But, what about executives' fiduciary responsibility for the interests and well-being of employees, buyers/users, the community, and the environment? Which theory justifies degrading the interests of buyers/users—the source of the money shareholders desire—to one of lesser importance?

The unrelenting pursuit of operational efficiency may suggest that the vehicle is perceived as one big cost center that is standing in the way of growing net profits. Do people believe that the way to maximize shareholder value is to minimize cost? In other words, do they believe that profits become infinite when cost is reduced to zero?

It should be evident that executive decision-making processes differ significantly with the decision maker's perspective on business as a system, and so does the outcome or effect of those decision-making processes. These differences can be explained to a decision maker but they cannot be understood for him or her. Understanding takes a willingness to learn, unlearn, and relearn—to search for the underlying principles that explain why business results, outcomes, or effects are as they are.

Destination

Merriam-Webster's Dictionary defines *destination* as "a place to which one is journeying or to which something is sent," but also as "the purpose for which something is predetermined or destined." These descriptions seem to align best with an organismic perspective on a business system, indicating that the reason for its creation and its continued existence is inherent in its purpose and its realization of that purpose.

The purpose of a vehicle refers to more than its anticipated outcome; it refers implicitly to the process by which that anticipated outcome is pursued and achieved most successfully. It raises questions regarding a decision maker's vision, values, ethics, beliefs, interests, personal background, previous experiences, and cultural traditions, as well as the system's status quo and the current geopolitical and socioeconomic situation in which it operates. Many businesses share the same purpose, for example, building family homes. Yet individual builders can distinguish themselves through their process or philosophy of building, such as tract or cookie-cutter houses, custom-built, certified net-zero or passive house, green building, fast system-built, or 3D printed. These distinctions form the basis of a competitive advantage, thus appealing to different market segments. And, in order to maintain one's competitive advantage, a business system needs to develop its capability and capacity continually in order to survive and to remain relevant to its intended target audience.

Decision makers with a mechanistic perspective on a business system think of themselves as the owners and shareholders. They make decisions based on what is best for them, what serves their own purpose for owning or investing in that business. Why, then, would they bother spending time and money on developing the system's capability and capacity, or pursue continual process improvement? If all you care about is growing the business—increasing the business's size and bottom-line results—then buying other businesses is often regarded as more efficient than developing your own existing business.

When development is regarded as an unnecessary expense, as opposed to a money-making proposition, and the business system is perceived as a machine, the modus operandi becomes "don't fix it if it ain't broke, and replace it if it can't be fixed." If executives perceive the business system just as tool, then any tool should do as long as it gets the job done, right? Then why do they expect employees to be engaged and to show passion, commitment, and loyalty? Employees rightfully ask themselves, "What's in it for me?" (other than a pay check).

A mechanistic view dehumanizes the workforce, which causes many contemporary enterprise-wide problems, such as employee disengagement and rapid turnover—both of which increase costs. Beware of the fact that employed people are human beings with purposes of their own. Also, outside groups protest the way organizations infringe on their purposes in life. So, if you don't like the effect of your decisions, the unintended consequences, then stop its cause!

Business Governance

Because a CEO possesses ultimate authority to make changes to the trinity of destination, journey, and vehicle, she or he is in effect the business system's governor.[9] Hence, business governance is the function that is ultimately responsible for the success and failure of the business system as an integrated whole.

Alas, business governance seems to occur only by happenstance. Instead, everyone focuses on their favored kind of leadership developed for different business models and under different conditions, such as international, global, strategic, agile, moral, change, charismatic, innovative, command and control, laissez-faire, pace setter, situational, transformational, and servant leadership, among others.

These different leadership approaches prescribe specific interpersonal behaviors, actions, and areas of focus, including the selection of which tools to use for different purposes, all in the name of guiding employees in the successful fulfillment of their daily activities. These are poor substitutes for proper business governance, which involves the design, organization or structure, implementation or operation, maintenance, and management of a business system. It is imperative that leaders know the why behind their decisions and actions. Also, it makes accountability a lot easier.

We must recognize the limitations of leadership as another silo of specialized knowledge. After all, different styles of leadership are no more capable of changing the character and nature of a business system than one's driving style is capable of changing the engine, drive train, and suspension-steering configuration of a motorcar.

The behavior and performance of a business system will only change in relation to the changes of its business governance: how it is designed, organized or structured, implemented or operated, maintained, and managed. It is rather unfortunate that thought leaders as well as the curricula of institutions for higher learning seem to elevate leadership studies over management studies.[10]

After all, leadership principles are not a more advanced form of, let alone a replacement for, management principles. Leadership does not solve any of its practitioners' resistance to providing executive sponsorship for change, because it does not provide a solution to executives' bewilderment when faced with system complexity and the disruptive effects of new and unforeseen events on its tightly coupled processes. That's why I wrote *The Root Cause*!

A business system cannot perform in any other way than how it was given the capability and capacity to behave. This proves that the purpose of leadership is different from that of business governance, and it is therefore no substitute for business governance—because no CEO can lead a business system without understanding its governance principles. We'll explore this further in Chapter 9, which is exclusively devoted to business governance, and Chapter 10, which discusses the role of the chief executive and the symbiotic relationship between business governance and leadership.

Form of Ownership

The character and nature of business governance is influenced by the business system's ownership structure—whether it is privately held, family owned, employee owned, or publicly traded. In addition, a business system can be funded by outside groups such as angel investors, venture capitalists, strategic capital investors, or institutional investors, all of whom become shareholders.

Shareholders sometimes express interests different from the purpose for which the business was created. By organizing their efforts—emphasizing executives' fiduciary responsibility toward them—some shareholder groups have succeeded at influencing business governance and thereby changing the function and form of a business system's destination, vehicle, and thus its journey. They have also succeeded at replacing executives of whom they don't approve.

Hence, the difference between a privately owned business and a publicly owned one is the perception of the system's destination—the system's purpose and its beneficiaries. When profits are spent on dividends and share buyback programs and are not plowed-back into the business in order to develop the system's capability and capacity, it indicates a mechanistic perspective on business, whereby satisfying shareholder financial demands is prioritized over customers' needs.

Any subsequent loss of integrity among the vehicle, the journey, the destination, and their business governance is manifested in the behavior and performance characteristics of the business system as an organic whole, and ultimately in its brand identity, profitability, and market valuation. Dueling destinations—prioritizing service to one's target audience or to one's owners/shareholders—is a major source of harmful friction and conflict.

The Environment

You cannot lead a business system, or steer it into another strategic direction if you don't understand how that business functions as a singular, unique, integrated, and open system. Attempts at changing a system you don't understand is nothing more than trial and error.

Analysis—the traditional approach to gaining understanding—is, unfortunately, not sufficient by itself. Dividing a whole into its component parts, studying each part separately, and then aggregating what you learned about the parts into an understanding of the whole just falls short. Analysis reveals the structure of a system: how it works. Hence, the product of analysis is know-how. Knowledge is what is contained in instructions, the *what* and *how*, better known as best practices. These instructions are often packaged in simple sound bites, buzzwords, and jargon. Understanding, on the other hand, creates insight, which is contained in explanations, the *why* it works as it works. Insight cannot be transferred in step-by-step instructions, sound bites, or buzzwords because each and every one of those instructions would require an explanation. Understanding is a cognitive process that is different for each and every one of us, but the end result is the same; wisdom—that is, the trait of using knowledge and experience with common sense and insight.

Understanding requires another method of thinking, synthesis, which is a reasoning from cause to effect. Explanations for the occurrence of cause-and-effect relationships are not found within separate parts but in the role or function they perform within the system as a whole. Synthesis reveals those roles and functions, which explains why a system works or behaves the way it does, as it does. While analysis produces knowledge, it is synthesis that produces understanding. Hence, it is synthetic thinking that creates understanding. And the fusion of analysis and synthesis is called *systems thinking*.

Now, if recognizing cause-and-effect relationships holds the key to understanding, we need to ask ourselves if the cause is not only necessary but also sufficient to explain why the effect occurred. For example, is a factory necessary for building cars? Yes, but is that sufficient? No. It requires raw materials; capital; a workforce that is educated, skilled, trained, and experienced; logistics to and from the factory; electricity; fuel; and so many other requirements. In other words, what is necessary for a cause to provide a sufficient explanation for the effect it creates is known as the environment.

It is the environment in which it operates—the wealth, health, education, consumer preferences, resources, and infrastructure of a country or region—where we find opportunities for a business system and its stakeholders to thrive. Note that the environment includes laws on local, regional, statewide, national, international, or supranational levels, which provide (financial and liability) protections, regulations, policies, subsidies, quotas, industry standards, work safety requirements, consumer protection, general trade practices, sanctions, morals, and ethics that cannot fail to influence decisions regarding a corporation's business governance practices. I will revisit the benefits of a well-functioning environment in Chapter 9, under "Preconditions for Success."

In conclusion, nothing can be understood independently of its environment. Every law or principle is constrained by the environment within which it applies. They're all environmentally relative, which explains the intersection between economic theory and politics. A discussion of economic theory and politics falls outside the scope of this book, although I highly recommend acquainting yourself with these topics.

WHAT HAPPENS NEXT?

Having painted a bigger-picture perspective on business mechanics, I have shown how disparate knowledge and information can be compartmentalized over a business system's journey, vehicle, and destination, in order to be *organized* and integrated into an organic whole, which is then *directed* toward the realization of its intended purpose by business governance.

Because a business system is predominantly perceived as an endless chain of buy and sell transactions, we'll start our exploration into relationships among the component parts of business mechanics by describing the journey.

CHAPTER 6

The Journey—Function

There is no foreign land; it is the traveler only
that is foreign, and now and again, by a flash of
recollection, lights up the contrasts of the ear.
—Robert Louis Stevenson
Scottish novelist, poet, essayist, and travel writer

A journey is the travel or passage from one place to another, which comes to an end when its destination is reached. And then, another one may commence.

The function of a journey is thus the pursuit of a distinct purpose; otherwise, you are just wandering around. The success of a journey is therefore tied to the clarity and precision of the purpose you envision and define for your travels.

Characteristic of a journey is the interaction with different people you meet along the way, their unique customs and habits; the immersion in new cultures; the exposure to new and unfamiliar territories, climates, and environments; and the experience of unusual, and unexpected situations and conditions.

Experiences during a journey depend heavily on one's attitude toward new and unforeseen situations as they unfold. On your journey, you'll meet fellow travelers with similar destinations, but who follow different itineraries to get there. One way is not necessarily better than another, but the journey you are following reflects who you are as a unique human being.

THE EXCHANGE

In his book *Think and Grow Rich*, Napoleon Hill called this journey "the method by which DESIRE for riches can be transmuted into its financial equivalent."[1] The first two of his six steps are precise and practical. First, fix in your mind the *exact* amount of money you desire. It is not sufficient merely to say, "I want plenty of money." Be definite as to the amount. Second, determine exactly what you intend to give in return for the money you desire. (There is no such thing as "something for nothing.")[2]

We discussed the critical success factor for the effective exchange of products and services for money in Chapter 2. (See Figure 2.5, "Creating Superior Use Value," and Figure 6.1.) Regarding the effective exchange of products and services for money, it states that "you cannot give every man more in cash market value than you take from him, but you can give him more in USE VALUE than the CASH VALUE of the thing you take from him."[3]

Cash Value = Purchasing Power of a Currency

Cash Market Value (price) = Cost of Applied Resources + Cost of Value Added

Use Value = Cost of Applied Resources + Utility

The journey is a metaphor for the exchange of products and services for money. This exchange can be described as sales, enrollment, membership, subscription, retainer, service offering, treatment, program, or curriculum. What do you call this exchange for your business?

The unique selling point that discriminates between two competing value propositions is its utility, which relates to an individual's experience as a buyer or user of the product or service and to the person's relationship with that supplier. Utility is predominantly intangible; it's an experience of one's level of satisfaction with one's choice, purchase, and usage of a product or service, and its manufacturer and supplier.

Unfortunately, some industries are dominated by an oligopoly, whose preferred business model is to take more from their clients

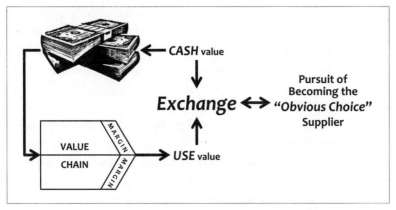

Figure 6.1: The Core Business:
Exchanging Products and Services for Money

The core principle of business is the exchange of use value for cash value. The amount of use value executives choose to create determines whether their business becomes the obvious choice supplier to their target audience or not.

in cash value than it gives them in use value. Their position of market domination makes companies in an oligopoly believe that they do not have to provide much utility at all and that they can pass on the cost of their operational inefficiencies to their clients in the form of inflated prices because of the absence of competitive forces. Their processes tend to be highly efficient when it comes to taking your money, but they make you jump through hoops for customer service, which is typically automated and outsourced to a third party who has little to no stake in satisfying your needs. As a result, their customer satisfaction rate and their brand identity rank poorly. For them, money is the highest value, higher than the value of our humanity. Nothing personal—just business.

The Electricity Metaphor

One day, when talking to a chair of an international coaching organization, it occurred to me that the journey could be made visible by using electricity as a metaphor. I realized that what brings a value chain to life, and what makes an electrical component function, depend on the same two requirements: a potential difference and a closed circuit.

The potential difference represents the level of attractiveness of a specific market for goods and services—the tension between supply and demand. The closed circuit represents the effectiveness with which a value chain is capable of exchanging goods and services for money, and its capacity to sustain the effort. Any interruptions or frayed connections cause friction or shuts down any exchange.

A Potential Difference

Within the electricity metaphor, a potential difference represents the attractiveness of a product, service, or brand within a market economy—the aggregated amount of utility members of a target audience anticipate to obtain from their purchase or investment and the use of it. Apart from the eagerness with which a product or service will be bought, it also informs us about the market's capacity—the number of units it will be able to absorb per unit of time—per month, quarter, year, season, or over the life cycle of the product.

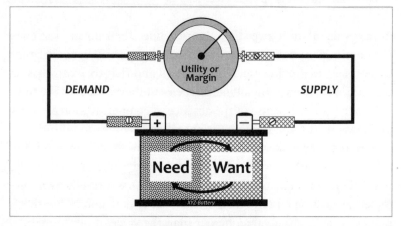

Figure 6.2: The Market Economy

The market economy is driven by demands from humans to have their needs satisfied and a supply of wants by businesses intended to satisfy that demand.

The cash market value, or price, including the profit margin per unit sold, is determined by the market forces of supply and demand and the level of industry rivalry (see Figure 6.2).

The profit potential of a market segment is determined by the utility that an individual member of a specific target audience antici-pates or experiences from buying and using that product or service. In addition, the profit potential is determined by the size of the market segment, the frequency with which members buy, the number of units they purchase at a time, and the length of time for which they will need that product or service. Because different people have different needs, the market offers competing value propositions—brands—for the satisfaction of a buyer's or user's specific need.

As Professor Philip Kotler said, "A human *need* is a state of felt deprivation in a person. . . . A *want* is a culturally defined product or service that will satisfy the need."[4]

Common human needs are satisfied with commodities, the basic goods and services that are interchangeable with other commodities of the same type (substitutes), which typically command a low profit margin. Special human needs are satisfied with specialty goods and services that are of extraordinary quality, unique, luxurious, or one of a kind, which often command superior profit margins.

Market segments with superior profit potential will entice more suppliers to enter the market in order to compete for the patronage of its potential buyers. The overall industry attractiveness can be determined with Professor Michael Porter's five forces analysis:

1. Threat of new entrants
2. Threat of substitute products or services
3. Bargaining power of buyers
4. Bargaining power of suppliers
5. Rivalry among existing competitors

The arbiters of the journey's effectiveness at satisfying human needs are the people who select one value proposition over another. The object of competition can thus be reduced to utility. In the absence of any discernible differences in utility among competing value propositions, price will decide. Similarly, price becomes an obstacle in the sales process when prospective buyers don't understand or fail to recognize the utility of the value proposition. That is why Zig Ziglar advocated that—if and when possible—salespeople should use the products they sell themselves.

A Closed Circuit

Within the electricity metaphor, a closed circuit represents the flow of products and services from their manufacturer or supplier to their buyer or user, which energizes the market. Feedback in the form of market intelligence data completes the circuit. When an individual supplier can maintain this flow—without the intention or need to liquidate or curtail the scale of its operations—we speak of a going concern.

Since all products and services demonstrate a life cycle—introduction, growth, maturity, and decline—the value chain must have the capacity to adjust and adapt this evolution according to the nature and volume of demand over the life cycle of these products and services.

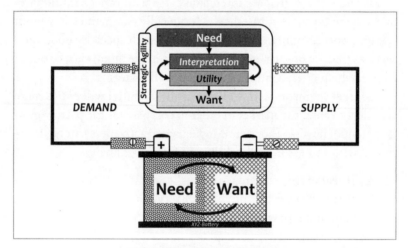

Figure 6.3: A Going Concern

Markets demonstrate needs and businesses interpret those needs into utility, which they then supply to the market in the form of wants. Because needs are subject to change, businesses need to adapt their wants with flexibility and speed—strategic agility—if they want to remain successful.

In addition, the features, advantages, and benefits of a want will be adjusted for changes in users' preferences, which evolve over time. Apart from creating different iterations or releases of existing products and services, wants will eventually have to be replaced by new products and services. Because product development takes time, this process should be initiated well ahead of the decline of existing value propositions. This period should be greater than the time-to-market (lead time) for a new product or service (see Figure 6.3).

For example, if aircraft have a life cycle of thirty years and the lead time is ten years, you'll always be working on three aircraft models, on different stages of their life cycle. This idea is well documented and explained in the growth share matrix created by Bruce Henderson, founder of the Boston Consulting Group (BCG), in 1968.

Friction and Conflict

Friction is the force that resists all action and saps energy. It makes the simple difficult and the difficult seemingly impossible.[5]

Executive management is ultimately responsible for avoiding or reducing unnecessary and foreseeable friction and conflict within the closed circuit. Forms of friction and conflict include, apart from systemic problems, mistakes in identifying and interpreting imminent and latent needs. In addition, the successful interpretation and translation of needs into utility delivering wants requires the monitoring of changes in compatibility standards for technology, personal preferences and taste, habits, fashion, commercialization, brand rivalry, alternative value propositions, wholesale and retail requirements, and legislation.

Consequently, it is not enough to just limit one's responsibility to following best practices and checking every box on a list with prescribed activities. This requires creativity and discernment that comes with critical thinking, the very nature of which cannot be captured in a fixed one-size-fits-all prescribed course of action.

The electric current (measured in amperes, or amps for short) that can pass through an electrical device per unit of time depends on the amount of resistance that it experiences. The potential difference (measured in volts) within the circuit is the pressure or speed with which a current is pushed through the circuit. Resistance (measured in ohms) is the opposition to the passage of an electric current through an electrical device or circuit. The electric current flowing through a device or circuit is calculated as follows:

$$\text{Potential difference (volts)} = \frac{\text{Current (amps)}}{\text{Internal resistance (ohms)}}$$

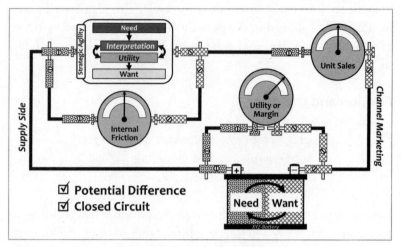

Figure 6.4: The Journey

By using electricity as a metaphor for business, we can identify
areas that require an executive's constant attention. As Tony
Robbins says, energy flows where attention goes.

Unintended Consequences

In an electric circuit, the total amount of internal resistance within
a circuit will increase with a rise in ambient temperature and load
(measured in watts [watts = volts × amps]). In addition, drawing a
current through a circuit with loose contacts or frayed wires will also
increase internal resistance because the same amount of current must
now flow through a smaller passage (reducing the circuit's capacity),
which generates excess heat—a form of wasted energy—that carries
the potential risk of starting an electrical fire.

Think of any business process with possible, figuratively speaking,
loose connections or frayed wires. When sparks are flying, the ambient temperature rises, causing internal resistance to surge. This failure
to harness all potentially available energy—entropy—increases the
risk of underperformance or even failure (see Figure 6.4).

These manifestations of systemic problems can have a wide array
of root causes for you to consider, such as: failure to solve systemic
problems, poor communication, ambiguity regarding goals, polarized relationships due to insufficient job descriptions, frustration
with equipment suitability, layout, and deferred maintenance; labor

relationships, scant employee benefits, poor work climate, toxic corporate culture, and excessive workload.

These manifestations of a systemic problem are preventable distractions from the work at hand, and they constitute the most common trigger of a chain reaction, known in the industry as human error, which is defined as a symptom of a failing system.

Employees with financial worries, with health concerns, or who fear of losing their jobs, cannot be expected to completely focus on their work—and they are more likely to make mistakes and be less effective. On the other hand, happy employees are generally engaged, alert, vigilant, motivated, creative, productive, loyal, and profitable employees.

Measures intended to raise operational efficiency have the potential of causing friction and conflict by increasing workload and heating emotional energy. People who are stressed, frustrated, and irritated are less motivated to communicate properly, causing vital information to be omitted from the work flow. In other words, most of these measures—including cutting salaries and employee benefits—tend to be obtained at the expense of operational effectiveness. Such unintended consequences are harmful because effectiveness problems are immediately noticeable to customers and will give them pause to reassess their relationship with that company. In addition, a drop in effectiveness must be compensated with a drop in efficiency in the form of an increase in waste, rework, and warranty claims. And, don't forget the need for increased expenditure on advertising and promotion to compensate for lost sales from buyers who took their business elsewhere.

However, initiatives aimed at increasing operational effectiveness go hand in hand with increasing operational efficiency because of the realization of higher process quality, employees' pride in their workmanship, job satisfaction, and ultimately in becoming a target audience's obvious choice supplier.

Unit Sales

Within the electricity metaphor, the electrical current (amps) refers to the amount of products or services that are exchanged for money, per unit of time. This is calculated as:

$$\text{Unit sales} = \frac{\text{Utility}}{\text{Friction and conflict}}$$

Therefore, the number of units sold can be influenced by:

- Reducing internal resistance within the circuit by increasing the capability and capacity of the value chain—which includes all interfaces that link the nine business functions into a value chain.
- Reducing internal resistance within the interfaces connecting your value chain to others within the value system.
- Increasing the tension between demand and supply within the circuit by creating or offering products or services that are perceived to provide superior utility in the form of unique benefits or a discount (recall Figure 2.5, "Creating Superior Use Value"). For example, the latest model iPhone, the latest book in a wildly popular series, or an annual "Black Friday" sale.[6] Due to elasticity of demand, unit sales increase when offered at a lower price. Although discounts decrease profit margins, lower prices increase unit sales—and reduce inventory—which increases revenue, generates cash, decreases inventory cost, and thus raises overall profits.

Competition

Given the fact that rivaling producers and service providers compete for the favor of buyers and users within the same demographic group, the best decision any executive leader can make is to reduce internal friction and conflict, which is well within their control. (See Chapter 2, "The Third Business Gremlin: The Means and Ends").

Colonel John R. Boyd said, "He who can handle the QUICKEST rate of change survives." By "quickest," Boyd meant the time it takes to transition a vehicle from one state to another. He even advocated doing it abruptly and violently in order to cause surprise, confusion, and even panic within his opponents. Thus, vincibility of his opponent became dependent on the amount of time they needed to recover from their disorientation and confusion, which slowed down their reaction time while increasing their vulnerability (see Figure 6.5).

Contrary to war, surviving in business does not require the defeat of one's competitor(s). Ripping the brand identity of one's opponent in an effort to enhance one's own image only creates friction and conflict within the relationship with the buyers and users one tries

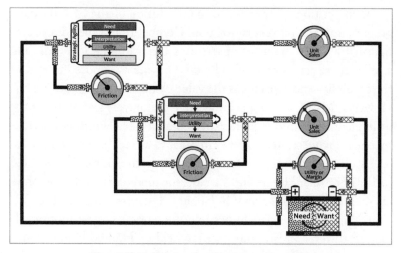

Figure 6.5: Competing Business Systems

Business system performance is limited by its capability and
capacity. Friction, conflict, and entropy reduce a system's capability
and capacity, thereby causing one's own vincibility.

to court. The logic behind a claim to be better by deriding another
as worse eludes me. In the end, it is the consumers and buyers who
decide!

Revisiting the Fifth Business Gremlin:
Interaction versus Isolation

Competing in business is about winning the patronage of a potential and qualified target audience—people with common needs and
preferences in *wants*. Since needs change and wants evolve over
time, competing is about staying relevant to one's target audience.
Any strategy aimed at becoming the obvious choice supplier to one's
intended target audience depends on the capability and capacity of
one's own value chain—the vehicle—to conduct asymmetrical fast
transients from one product or product model to the next and to conduct change initiatives at a higher tempo than one's competitors. That
is the true meaning of strategic agility, which cannot be accomplished
without sound interaction with one's potential buyers and users. Note
that no business can be agile without people who can think on their
feet and possess what Boyd identified as *Fingerspitzengefühl*—agility
of the mind—thinking with flexibility and speed.

Competition is a persistent manifestation of the fifth business gremlin: interaction versus isolation. Competition is fueled predominantly by MBO practices of setting arbitrary numerical goals and a reliance on assessment of individual people as opposed to that of the capability and capacity of the value chain as an integrated whole. However, MBO does not acknowledge that buyers and users are the ultimate umpire in the game called competition. Winning is a matter of deploying strategic agility in order to attract buyers and users.

A classic example of strategic agility is the battle that erupted in 1981 between Honda and Yamaha for supremacy in the motorcycle market, which is known in Japanese business circles as the H-Y War.[7] Yamaha intended to become the world's largest motorcycle manufacturer, a prestigious position held by Honda. Honda counterattacked with a rapidly increased rate of change in its product line, using variety to bury Yamaha and to isolate Yamaha from its target audience. Over a period of 18 months, Honda introduced or replaced 113 models, effectively turning over its entire product line twice, whereas Yamaha was able to manage only 37 changes in its product line. Offering new models in rapid succession allowed Honda to interact more closely with riders who showed their motorcycle needs with their purchase. Consequently, Honda proved to be more relevant to the motorcycle market than Yamaha.

INNOVATION

The principles that apply to a single value chain are equally applicable to an entire value system. Friction and conflict within the value system is a form of wasted energy, or entropy, the expenses of which are transferred to buyers in the price they pay for those products and services (see Figure 6.6).

Notice how industry leaders reduce the amount of friction and conflict within their markets because it facilitates the adoption and market penetration rate of their products and services.

Instead of trying to cut up the market in niches and trying to dominate the market, industry leaders endeavor to expand the potential market. Instead of exercising one's power to capture the existing potential market, why not apply it toward expanding the potential

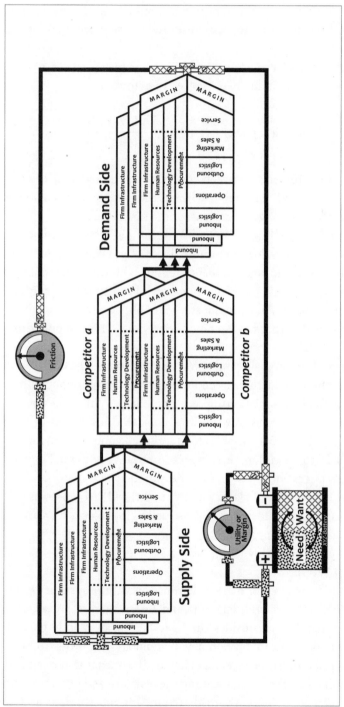

Figure 6.6: Bringing the Value System to Life

How competitors design, structure or organize, implement or operate, maintain, and manage their own value chain has an effect on the channel as a whole; backward on the supply side and forward to the demand side.

market—such as by finding new users, tapping into new market segments, increasing the frequency of use, and creating new applications for usage?

Within the electricity metaphor, power (watt) represents the force that causes an industry to evolve. Therefore:

$$\text{Innovation power (watts)} = \frac{\text{Utility (volts)}}{\text{Unit sales (amps)}}$$

Note the difference between creativity and innovation. The former refers to an ability to create, whereas the latter refers to the act of introducing something you created for the first time.

Buyers want to know, "What's in it for me?" Price becomes an objection when the value proposition does not provide the amount of utility that a specific target audience requires. However, members of a target audience who perceive a high rate of utility will happily pay the full retail price. And, an industry takes notice of any company—large and small—that has become the obvious choice supplier to a devoted clientele.

The value chain's sales and marketing function—the end-to-end process from manufacturer to end user—offers ample opportunities to reinvent a client's relationship with suppliers. Within the context of a business-to-business relationship, one can think of just-in-time delivery (JIT) of input variables to an original equipment manufacturer (OEM). In addition, there is great innovative power in knowing the OEM's treatment process of the supplied raw materials. For example, if a supplier of plastics knows that the OEM processes pellets, the supplier would not press those pellets into blocks for the ease of storing and shipping.

Cutting Waste

Competitors striving for market domination with proprietary (noncompatible) technology platforms and infrastructure are wasting resources and time. Consider the introduction of mobile phones. Given the high cost to develop new technology and infrastructure, mergers and acquisitions were inevitable. This meant that one technology won and others lost, meaning the platform and infrastructure of the losing technology was made redundant and obsolete, and its maintenance and support was discontinued. Buyers and users who invested in the losing technology—which is not necessarily the lesser technology—were forced to invest in the new platform.

The cost of developing expertise in the losing technology, and the investment in its dedicated infrastructure, was part and parcel of the valuation and the purchase price of the acquired company. Ultimately, this cost will need to be added onto the cost of the winning technology and is transferred to its buyers in the price tag of its products and services. This approach to new technology development is an attempt to become the sole supplier of a product or service that is essential for users' livelihoods, and thus, in a sense, it's an effort to take buyers and users hostage. Then, you can influence the industry because you have in fact become the industry. But, being the only choice does not mean you are the obvious choice.

From an efficiency point of view, the time, money, and expertise spent on competing technologies could have been combined to create and develop a standardized (compatible) technology. Thereafter, all parties to the development effort could have gone their separate ways and competed on the look-and-feel, features, applications, user-friendliness, security, or services.

Why would that have been in their best interest? Because a lower time to market in combination with a lower initial cost of development lowers the price-barrier for first-time buyers and increases adoption of new technology—which in turn creates a larger potential market and reduces competitive forces that typically put pressure on profit margins. However, that would have required trust and good faith among all parties, which is rare because there is always someone who will try to game the agreement and get the upper hand.

WHAT HAPPENS NEXT?

You are in business only when you are on the journey, which requires the envisioning of a well-defined destination and being in command of a vehicle that is appropriate for reaching the intended destination. This vehicle must be chosen according to a destination's itinerary, and shaped and adapted according to the anticipated strain, adversity, and duration of the journey. Therefore, the next chapter takes a closer look at the vehicle by describing its principles of business mechanics. Without a vehicle, there is no use value generated or exchanged; without a vehicle your business is just an idea—a figment of your imagination.

CHAPTER 7

The Vehicle—Form

*I see very little evidence that anyone in
management is interested in profits.*[1]
—Dr. W. Edwards Deming
America's eminent scholar, on the methods
for management of quality

Two days before their epic achievement, Wilbur and Orville Wright sent a telegram home to their father and sister, stating, *"SUCCESS ASSURED."*

During their previous visits to the sand dunes of Kill Devil Hills near the town of Kitty Hawk, North Carolina, they validated the correctness of their theories regarding lift and control. Back at home in Dayton, Ohio, they calculated the minimum amount of thrust an engine and propellers are required to produce to lift the aircraft and its pilot off the ground for a sustained and controlled flight.

The following year, when they returned to Kill Devil Hills with an engine and two propellers, they measured the actual amount of thrust they produced while still on the ground, and it exceeded the minimum requirements. That is when they knew they could not fail. And, two days later, when the weather had cleared, they proved their conviction that man was indeed capable of controlled and sustained flight in a heavier-than-air flying machine.

Wilbur and Orville had started their project because they were convinced of the idea that man was capable of flight. They saw an aircraft as a means to an end. "Making it pay came as an after-thought."[2]

FORM FOLLOWS FUNCTION

The discovery of the principles of flight serves as an inspiring analogue for developing a business system—a vehicle for being in business. Once the operative principles are known, more and better vehicles can be created and operated as long as one adheres to the concept of form follows function.

Adherence is important because form is not random; it is determined by principles that explain why, given specific conditions, a vehicle will behave a certain way, which makes the outcome of its performance predictable.

This concept of form follows function—the second business gremlin—follows the same pattern as a cookbook recipe (see Figure 7.1). Starting with the end in mind, it shows an enticing picture of the meal you want to prepare. Then it lists all the ingredients, including specifications and measurements that go into the making of that meal. Finally, the recipe describes the process by which the ingredients are combined and transformed into the final product.

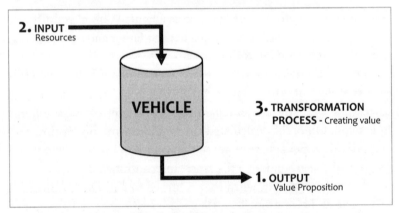

Figure 7.1: Starting with the End in Mind
Business operations is comparable to a cookbook recipe; first you envision the end result, then gather the ingredients, and finally you follow the directions for transforming input variables into output variables.

Apart from prescribing what to do step by step, the recipe suggests the appropriate tools and how to use them. Yet different cooks preparing the same meal, using the same ingredients, often obtain wildly differing results. The difference can be explained by the tools, a cook's skills, the discipline when following the recipe, and, most important of all, whether a particular cook understands the (chemical) properties of individual ingredients—why they react the way they do when diluted, blended or kneaded together, chilled, grilled, smoked, baked, heated, or sautéed.

Intellectual Curiosity

The function of a vehicle is to transform input variables into output variables. The form of this proprietary transformation process—its capacity and capability—determines the vehicle's character and nature, which is more generally experienced as its brand identity.

Capacity and capability cannot be purchased; they must be carefully developed to create products and services that deliver a consistent amount of utility to the intended target audience. Utility is derived from something intangible that promotes well-being in the form of happiness, confidence, coolness, security, safety, beauty, belonging, self-reliance, independence, and other desirable aspects. Consequently, vehicles with different functions are not interchangeable, and attempts at ranking a vehicle's level of greatness through comparison with another is an exercise in futility.

Just as the Wright brothers had to discover the principles of flight, every business leader needs to discover the principles behind producing and delivering wants that contain a consistent amount of utility to satisfy the needs of buyers and users for whom they are intended. Whereas the Wrights operated within the realm of science, business executives operate in the realm of social systems—economics, psychology, sociology, anthropology, and philosophy. This means that principles are not always set in stone; they can change over time and differ in their application in a specific industry, culture, and country.

When Orville Wright was asked about the advantages that he and his brother enjoyed over their rival aviation pioneers, he answered: "The greatest thing in our favor was growing up in a family where there was always much encouragement to have intellectual curiosity. If my father had not been the kind who encouraged his children to pursue intellectual interests without any thought of profit, our early curiosity about flying would have been nipped too early to bear fruit."[3]

The "Analytic Knife"

Speaking of intellectual curiosity, in an effort to understand a motorcycle, Robert M. Pirsig used his analytic thinking like a knife to identify the motorcycle's functions. He just drew an imaginary knife across a motorcycle according to his perception of the different functions and gave the resulting parts names. The imaginary cuts did not always correspond with a component part. After all, different engineers have different opinions regarding the form of a delivery mechanism intended to perform a specific function. That function may be performed by a mechanism consisting of a single part, or two or more parts. One mechanism is not necessarily better than another; they're just different because they were perceived and created by different people.

Likewise, a vehicle for business can be understood through the same kind of analysis of its functions, even when no two vehicles perform the same function with identical processes and activities. So, it can be argued that Michael Porter followed Pirsig's example of wielding an analytic knife when he created the value chain (see Figure 1.1, "The Value Chain Model by Michael Porter").

Allow me to wield the analytic knife myself on a more aggregated level to carve out the three component parts that I use in creating a mental image of the vehicle. They are *human beings*, a *machine* (the value chain), and the *human–machine interface(s)*.

The vehicle conducts a transformation process that, like all processes, must be perceived from end to end. It starts with a prospective buyer or user within the vehicle's intended target audience who has an unsatisfied need, and it ends when that buyer or user's need is satisfied with this vehicle's proprietary value proposition—a want (see Figure 7.2).

The purpose of a vehicle is thus to create use value (value added that represents specific utility) that is relevant to its target audience. Because a target audience's preferences and tastes change over time, different value propositions or wants will need to be created to maintain or exceed delivery of the amount of use value to which they have grown accustomed. Staying relevant to one's target audience requires continual development of the transformation process's capacity and capability (see Figure 7.3)

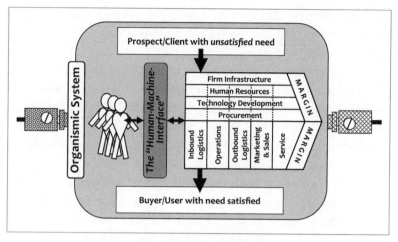

Figure 7.2: The Vehicle

The business system is a vehicle for the creation of use value
in order to satisfy specific prospect/client needs.

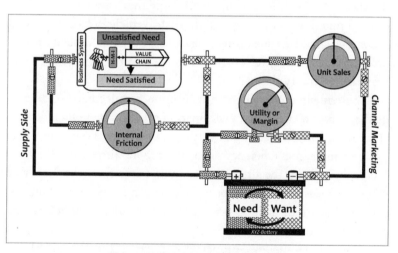

Figure 7.3: Vehicle Effectiveness

A successful vehicle is effective in generating use value and displaying
strategic agility in adapting its products and services according
to evolving needs of its prospective buyers and users.

Effectiveness

How a vehicle fulfills its intended mission—its performance in terms
of capability and capacity—is a function of quality.

Pirsig says, "Quality isn't method. It's the goal toward which
method is aimed." This goal is different for every vehicle, not because

quality is different, but because different executive leaders have different experiences of quality—they have different analogues for what constitutes good and bad quality to them.

Utility is one such experience of quality by individual members of a target audience. Quality is thus an event. It is an experience that is created with conscious forethought from inception to production, delivery, and usage of products and services. Any lack of such an event is immediately noticeable, and, nowadays, expressed and shared online.

Method refers to the craftsmanship. It is the moral skill to find out what is right in order for a buyer or user to experience the intended utility that is created during the transformation process. The moral skill reflects a craftsman's experience and interpretation of quality.

The first performance measure you need to know about a vehicle is its effectiveness (the vehicle's current capacity and capability for the successful pursuit of its mission). Note that a vehicle's effectiveness is limited by its capacity—and, what a vehicle lacks in capability is compensated by consuming more of its available capacity in the production of waste, rejects, and the need to perform rework and honoring warranty claims.

Prerequisites describe the minimum requirements—process quality—for an effective transformation process. These include specifics regarding efficiency and strategy. To use the Wright brothers as an example, fuel efficiency determines flying time, the size of the fuel tank, and thus the aircraft's maximum take-off weight. Note that efficiency measures, the sole purpose of which is to increase bottom-line results, are of little to no importance to increasing a business system's effectiveness.

These prerequisites—properties similar to the Wright Flyer's specifications for lift, control, and propulsion—need to be designed and built into the structure and organization of the vehicle itself. They are not accessories that can be added as an afterthought to spiff up its appearance. Performance is thus limited by a vehicle's capacity and capability to do what it is designed to do. Notice that *developing* a vehicle's capacity and capability is not synonymous with *growing* a business, which refers to increasing its shape and size.

What About Making Money?

I acknowledge that a large number of businesspeople believe that making money is the purpose of a business. That means that the yardstick for success is simply a measurement of one's profitability; more is better or more successful. If that were true, then all commercial enterprises would have exactly the same purpose, which makes each business a competitor of any other business.

The Bureau of Engraving and Printing—a government agency within the United States Department of the Treasury—and the United States Mint are the only two businesses in the United States of America whose purpose is to "make money" by the printing of banknotes and minting of coins. What people informally call making money refers to profit margins: income minus cost. Making money is thus a function of increasing income and/or reducing cost. Unfortunately, most efforts toward making money focus exclusively on increasing operational efficiency by cutting cost, thereby ignoring any opportunities to reallocate money for processes that use the money more effectively to generate additional income or to reduce cost. As a result, decision makers show surprisingly little interest in investments to increase income (grow bottom-line results), other than through merger and acquisition transactions.

Income can be increased by either raising the number of units sold or by increasing the price. Both options depend on how the target audience perceives the use value of those goods and services. Creating more use value, adding more utility, is a matter of improving the quality of the transformation process through continual development of the vehicle's capacity and capability. Incidentally, a higher quality transformation process increases employee engagement and productivity, pride of workmanship, and work satisfaction while reducing employee turnover, warranty claims, waste, rework, and other undesirable work situations. This shows that income and cost are not separate and independent entities, but that they are interdependent of each other.

The Effect of Mental Programming

Decision makers show a bias toward solutions that promise immediate contributions to bottom-line results. This bias toward operational efficiency measures is evident from their willingness to discount the cost of predatory cultivation on a vehicle's transformation process.

Furthermore, the significant differences between the purpose of a business (creating use value) and a prerequisite for sustaining a business (charging a profit margin) cannot be dismissed by claiming that they are just a matter of semantics. Those differences are real, with real-world consequences.

Taking more in cash value than giving in use value (making money by hook or by crook) is the purpose of a scam business. The difference between a scam and a legitimate business is contained in their vision for the business—prerequisites stipulating the necessary conditions for achieving success and enjoying personal pride. Prerequisites describe the principles for exchanging goods and services for money, such as giving more in use value than one takes in cash value. Prerequisites describe how to measure success—how well you realize the purpose for which the vehicle was created. Prerequisites will be discussed in more detail in Chapter 8.

Dysfunctional Management

Notice that making money as the purpose for being in business requires a vehicle with an entirely different structure and organization—form follows function. Trying to give as little use value as possible in exchange for as much cash value as possible is a sign of dysfunctional management. It requires creating utility from hot air, while encouraging deceitful marketing practices. In other words, this form of dysfunctionality is systemic; it is intentionally built into the system's capacity and capability. It is how some businesses are designed to operate, although responsible executives might argue that this kind of dysfunctional design is an unfortunate example of unintended consequences. Most executives, however, are reluctant to press for changes; they are either fine with the way it is or they fear damaging their career prospects.

Take for example a large car dealership that employs many service managers who act as intermediaries between the customer and the workshop. No doubt, their compensation package contains a bonus system based on performance—that is, the total dollar amount they write up in work orders per month. So, who are these managers serving? I had a personal experience with an overheating engine being diagnosed as a leaking cylinder-head gasket and an estimated $2,250 repair—which I refused to believe was true. A local mom-and-pop shop confirmed my suspicion with a \$35 test, then fixed the problem for under \$300. Six years later, that car is still running fine, and I have not set foot in that car dealership's shop again.

When it comes to strategy, there is an inordinate amount of attention to where its leadership wants to go, with insufficient awareness of a vehicle's current situation. Questions regarding the activities it is performing right now, the kind of activities it is capable of performing, and the vehicle's capacity for realizing the purpose for which it was intended go unanswered. Leaders talk about problems, but if they only have eyes for the desired state of the vehicle—which is probably just limited to growing revenue—and have little to no understanding of its current state, then what *is* the problem? "If you don't know where you are, a map will not help."[4]

ORGANIZATION AND STRUCTURE OF THE MACHINE

The transformation process includes every task, activity, process, and function a business system performs, and is visualized in the nine business functions of the value chain model, performing either a primary business process or a secondary one.

Conducting a work breakdown structure for each of these nine functions reveals, as discussed in Chapter 1, three different kinds of subprocesses for:

- Planning
- Executing
- Controlling

Interaction between these three subprocesses is known as the *cybernetic process*, which is responsible for the governance of each individual business function (see Figure Figure 1.3, "The Cybernetic Process or Governance").

Planning and controlling processes must be separated to avoid the risk of tampering with performance results by adjusting data. Also, planning and controlling processes must be conducted on a higher hierarchical level than any executing processes in order to avoid conflict regarding authority and responsibility.

Creating an organizational chart involves more than just drawing a rake-like structure with some boxes attached. Instead, based on a *work-breakdown structure*, similar tasks are organized into an activity and similar activities are organized into a job, and similar jobs are organized into departments, and similar departments are organized into a division. This was discussed in Chapter 1 (see Figure 1.4, "Translating Processes into an Organizational Chart").

Hierarchy of Objectives

The cybernetic process, or business governance, takes place on every hierarchical level of the business. The difference between hierarchical levels is the scope and the amount of detail in their everyday work. Although each hierarchical level is responsible for conducting its own cybernetic process, they receive their assignment from the next highest hierarchical level. This structure is known as a hierarchy of objectives; everyone makes their own unique contribution to the realization of the purpose of the business as an integrated whole (see Figure 7.4). This underscores the notion that a business is an organism and not a mechanism, as discussed in Chapter 4.

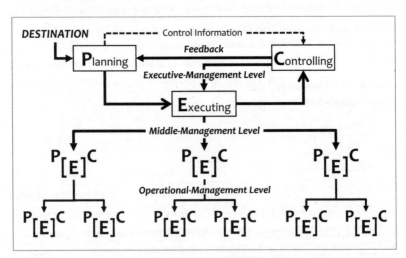

Figure 7.4: Hierarchy of Objectives

Each management level is responsible for realizing its own objectives. Objectives of one level are specifically chosen for their support of realizing objectives on the next higher management level. This principle integrates all activities and the people performing them, which supports the organismic nature of a business system.

The hierarchy of objectives is a reminder of the importance of executives warning line managers against optimizing and gold plating their particular processes. Departments that pursue their own goals separate from the purpose of the business as an organic whole—see the fourth business gremlin, wholeness versus separateness—are like a malignant cancer. When cancer is not contained, it spreads throughout the body. Therefore, it behooves executives not to incentivize line managers to increase the contribution margin of their individual department.

No wonder Colonel John R. Boyd defined leadership as, "The art of inspiring people to enthusiastically take action toward the achievement of uncommon goals." He meant that each cybernetic process is designed to develop or generate specific deliverables: a physical product, an information product or document, or a service. And, during the transformation process, these deliverables contribute to the making of a final product or the provision of a service.

Because creating a product or service must occur in a specific sequence, requiring the interaction of different processes—sometimes performed on different hierarchical levels using shared resources with different throughput times—each process does not start and end at the same time. Hence, the sequence of process execution is either sequential, cascade, or simultaneous (see Figure 7.5).

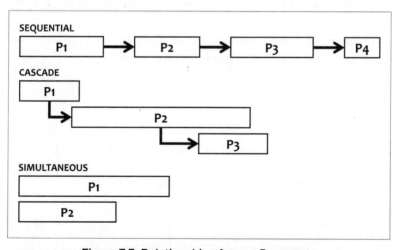

Figure 7.5: Relationships Among Processes

Work flow, resource allocation, and manpower determine when a process can be started at the earliest possible time and when it should be completed at the latest. Hence, time is what keeps everything from happening at once.[5]

Even though the objective of individual processes is to develop or generate the deliverables for which they are responsible, each of these objectives must serve the objective of the next process within the transformation process as a whole. This form of interdependency among processes is characteristic of a hierarchy of objectives; a lower-ranking process or one performed earlier caters to the needs of a higher-ranking process or one that is performed later on. However, no activity or function is more important than any other, regardless of its position within the hierarchy of objectives.

Defensible Competitive Advantage

The heart and soul of competition is found in the capacity and capability of one's vehicle to create superior utility for its intended target audience. Creating unique use value is thus dependent on having a quality transformation process, which is thus the secret to a defensible competitive advantage.

Many airlines tried to emulate the success of Southwest Airlines (SWA). With their mental programming set toward increasing operational efficiency, they seized on Southwest's idea of doing away with handing out traditional boarding passes and meals. Their efforts to copy the processes developed by SWA failed because it is nearly impossible to succeed at copying every single process with 100 percent accuracy.

Here is why. Suppose there are only five processes to copy and your rate of success at copying each process is as high as 95 percent, which is not bad at all. This translates to an overall success rate of 77 percent:

Process 1		Process 2		Process 3		Process 4		Process 5		Overall Success Rate
95%	×	95%	×	95%	×	95%	×	95%	×	77%

What those copycats failed to recognize was the reason why SWA did not hand out traditional boarding passes and meals. Their true objective was not to just cut cost, but to reduce their turnaround time because that translates to more flights per day and that's where the money is. Traditional boarding passes have assigned seats, which increases boarding time, whereas serving meals creates dependency on a supplier's on-time delivery. Any prolonged wait time can delay departure. By confusing means and ends, those copycats forgot to implement key processes geared toward accelerating their turn-around time.

Interaction with One's Environment

The fact that there is a hierarchy of objectives explains why the vehicle must operate as an open system, which means that the vehicle as a whole, and each constituting process, must have the ability to interact with the environment in which it operates.

Earlier, we spoke about the importance of interfaces between processes as a form of communication. Communication happens on four incremental levels:

1. **Content.** *What* to do.
2. **Process.** *How* to do step-by-step.
3. **Cooperation.** Pursuing the same objective(s) *together.*
4. **Interaction.** Exchanging ideas and concepts regarding *why* the pursuit of specific objectives are right in order to determine *what* needs to be done *when, why,* and by *whom.*

Colonel John R. Boyd identified interaction—the most advanced form of communication—as the antidote to friction:

- Friction is generated and magnified by menace, ambiguity, deception, rapidity, uncertainty, mistrust, and so on.[6]
- Friction is diminished by implicit understanding, trust, cooperation, simplicity, focus, and more.[7]

He argued that interaction provides:

- Focus and direction toward harmony of effort and initiative for vigorous effort[8]
- Adaptability to cope with changing and unforeseen circumstances[9]

However, adaptability without harmony and initiative leads to confusion, disorder, and ultimately to chaos. And harmony and initiative without adaptability lead to (rigid) uniformity, including standardization, and ultimately to nonadaptability. Therefore, we must uncover those interactions that foster harmony and initiative—yet do not destroy adaptability.

Consequently, Boyd defined interaction as "a many-sided implicit cross-referencing process of projection, empathy, correlation, and rejection."[10]

Using Stewardship and Craftsmanship for Guidance

Unfortunately, as is the case too often in deciding on a management approach, executives keep following their mental programming rather than demonstrating their stewardship and craftsmanship. Setting arbitrary numerical targets for every department individually (MBO) and holding each hierarchical manager personally accountable for attaining those targets creates friction and conflict among departments and managers.

Numerical targets become arbitrary when they bear no direct relationship to the purpose and performance of the vehicle as a singular, unique, integrated, and open system. Dr. W. Edwards Deming called this approach a "deadly disease" because it lacks constancy of purpose—instead of doing what is right for the entire vehicle, it encourages individual managers to pursue what is best for their own department, and their personal annual performance review, and thus their bonus payment.

Alternatively, giving every manager the same target of reducing cost by x percent causes friction and conflict between the successive departments within an end-to-end process. When there is no interaction or dialogue between departments regarding where to cut, what to cut, and by how much, performance of the business as an organic whole suffers. After all, the output variables of one department are the input variables of the next, and so on. Simply asking why cutting cost is necessary and what decision makers intend to achieve might trigger a creative approach to offset cost cutting with revenue generation. Reallocating funds to a department where those funds can be used more effectively reduces cost and creates more use value for buyers and users of your products or services.

A management approach that treats departments as separate and independent segments in the work flow of the transformation process is de facto promotion of a closed system, which is susceptible to entropy and thus ultimately to collapse (see the fifth business gremlin, interaction versus isolation).

Influencing Performance

The most obvious limitation to a vehicle's performance is the capacity of its individual component parts. This could be, for example, limited availability of a critical shared resource (such as a tool), bandwidth, processing time, or an individual's expertise. Capacity can thus be viewed as the diameter of a pipe which determines the maximum amount of work flow that can pass through that pipe per unit of time.

Therefore, increasing the capacity of a single component part—gold plating—will only improve a vehicle's capability if and when the capacity of that part formed a bottleneck to enhancing vehicle output performance. Otherwise, it just adds weight and initial cost while increasing vehicle complexity and maintenance cost, to name but a few drawbacks. The image I see in my mind's eye is of a large-bore, multi-barrel carburetor placed on a gas-powered lawnmower. It floods the engine and it will not start at all.

In addition, vehicle performance is also limited by its capability to transform input variables into output variables. Capability-limiting performance refers to the incidence of systemic problems due to, for example, outdated equipment, poor organizational climate, inappropriate quality of raw materials, high employee turnover rates, and a disengaged workforce of insufficient skills and no pride of workmanship.

Consequently, there will always be a gap between the potential maximum output and the actual output, which is determined by the level of output beyond which the average cost of production—the marginal cost—begins to rise, which ultimately leads to an increase in unit costs. Therefore, a vehicle can only benefit from economies of scale when there is excess capacity and when increasing output does not increase unit cost.

Because a transformation process is limited by its capability and capacity, its output and unit price are not steplessly scalable when prompted by increased sales. Therefore, increasing capacity with an additional machine, or with a higher-capacity replacement machine, might result in large—albeit temporary—excess capacity, or under-utilization, which drives up the average cost of production and thus unit costs.

Furthermore, vehicle performance is also influenced by seasonal effects, such as fluctuations in demand and supply, and the cost of raw materials.

Measuring Variation

Dr. Walter Shewhart, the father of statistical quality control, developed a methodology to distinguish between common-cause variation (noise) and special-cause variation (signals), which he called statistical process control (SPC). Any attempt at explaining SPC in a few paragraphs would be an injustice to this unique way of thinking and its tools. I refer you to books on this topic by Deming and Dr. Donald J. Wheeler. Hence, I will restrict myself to discussing variation.

Random variation is the statistical description of natural fluctuations in output variables caused by many irregular and erratic (and individually unimportant) fluctuations or chance factors that (in practical terms) cannot be anticipated, detected, identified, or eliminated (see Figure 7.6).

Unfortunately, too many leaders cannot accept the nature and character of a system—that it is what it is. They tend to overreact when monthly performance charts show a sawtooth pattern where they (unrealistically) expected to see a more linear pattern. This made Timothy Fuller[11] conclude that "management has taken a major step forward when they stop asking you to explain random variation."

Interpreting business performance data for the purpose of proper business governance requires a sound understanding of variation in performance measurements and the sources of their volatility.[12] Variation is caused by:

1. **Common causes**. This source of variation is systemic, which means that it is inherent to the system's design, organization or structure, implementation or operation, maintenance, and management. In statistical terms, these results fall within the bandwidth of plus and minus three times the standard deviation ($\pm3\sigma$)—which explains the origin of the term Six Sigma as a methodology.

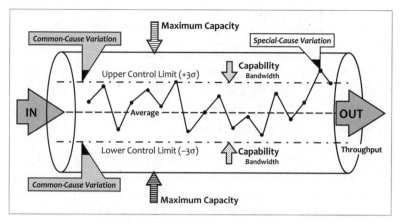

Figure 7.6: Capacity versus Capability

Capability is a measure of quality—how well a unit of work is completed. Capacity is a measure of throughput—a ratio expressing how many units of work can be completed per unit of time.

Characteristics of common-cause variation:[13]

- Phenomena are constantly active within the system.
- Variation is predictable (probabilistically).
- Irregular variation falling within a historical experience base.
- Lack of significance in individual high or low values.

As a result, system performance demonstrates a natural pattern in its outcomes, similar to those of a perfectly balanced roulette wheel. Common-cause variation is the *noise* within the system.

Examples of common-cause variation are:[14]

- Inappropriate procedures
- Poor design
- Poor structure and organization
- Poor implementation and personnel training
- Poor maintenance of machines
- Lack of clearly defined standard operating procedures
- Poor working conditions, such as poor lighting, loud noises, dirt, extreme temperature, and poor ventilation
- Substandard raw materials

- Measurement error
- Quality control error
- Vibration in industrial processes
- Ambient temperature and humidity
- Normal wear and tear
- Variability in settings
- Computer response time

2. **Special causes**. This source of variation always arrives as a surprise and is attributable to a single machine, component part, tool, individual person, or group of people. In statistical terms, these results fall outside the bandwidth of plus or minus three times the standard deviation ($\pm 3\sigma$).

Characteristics of special-cause variation are:[15]

- New, unanticipated, emergent, or previously neglected phenomena within the system
- Variation that is inherently unpredictable, even probabilistically
- Variation falling outside the historical experience base
- Evidence of some inherent change in the system or our knowledge of it

As a result, system performance demonstrates an unnatural pattern in its outcomes, which is the *signal* within a system that something has changed.

Examples of special-cause variation are:[16]

- Poor adjustment of equipment
- Poor system ergonomics
- Operator falling asleep
- Faulty controllers
- Machine malfunction
- Fall of ground
- Computer crash
- Poor batch of raw material
- Power surges
- High healthcare demand from elderly people
- Broken part
- Abnormal traffic on web ads

- Extremely long lab testing turnover time due to switching to a new computer system
- Operator absent

It is important to realize that special-cause variation can also be the result of a single individual's successful initiative to cut cost, which should be applauded and encouraged. For example, the person responsible for removing the protective plastic coating from brand new cars upon arrival from Sweden at Volvo Car Nederland B.V. in the Netherlands decided to experiment with the water-to-cleaner ratio. He kept dialing it back until it was no longer sufficient to take the coating off the cars and then he dialed it back up a notch. His initiative was only noticed by the finance department as variation in their successive monthly profit and loss statements. Strangely enough, his managers needed convincing that the man responsible for this cost reduction should be recognized and awarded with a bonus payment.

By eliminating special-cause variation and then reducing common-cause variation, a vehicle's output is more stable and predictable, which makes it more capable. In other words, leaders who understand how to decrease waste and reduce or eliminate the need for rework, warranty claims, emergency maintenance, and overtime work because of the goal to avoid mistakes, errors, and violations, make a vehicle more effective—capable—in the utilization of its overall capacity.[17] That is what Deming meant when he said doing more with less.

Tampering with Results

Unfortunately, instead of managing the vehicle's capability, best practices emphasize analyzing outcome data by comparing results from week to week, month to month, quarter to quarter, and year to year, and then by comparing that period with the same period of a previous year. The differences are measured as a percentage of change, and only the largest percentage of change is set aside for further scrutiny.

This best practice fails to make any distinction between signals and noise. As a result, decision makers risk making one of the following two mistakes:

1. **Interpreting noise as if it were a signal, or, more specifically, interpreting routine variation as a meaningful departure from the past.** A system without any special-cause variation—signals—is a stable system. Based on past experience, management can describe how that system will behave in the future. This behavior will still produce intended and unintended results. Lowering the number of unintended results is achieved by continual process improvement, aimed at improving uniformity of the results and thus reducing output volatility. A vehicle with less volatility is more capable than a vehicle with higher volatility. Any changes to a stable system (other than continual system improvement) reduces its quality, capability, and productivity. Deming called such decisions tampering with a stable system. The negative effects of tampering—correcting corrections within a stable system that make results progressively worse—were proven by statistician Lloyd S. Nelson and his funnel experiment.[18]

2. **Failing to detect a signal when it is present, or more specifically, not recognizing when the underlying process changes, especially when the results are still within the specification limits.** A system with special-cause variation—signals—is an unstable system. Therefore, management cannot describe how that system will behave in the future; its behavior is unpredictable and full of surprises. The first step toward a stable system is to eliminate, or at least explain, special-cause variation. Any change initiative that fails to address special-cause variation risks making the first mistake.

NO VEHICLE SUCCEEDS WITHOUT HUMAN BEINGS

Despite the fact that management theory classifies people as assets, it is a common management practice to treat people as a liability when it comes to protecting profitability.

Based on a pervasive belief that money is the highest of all values, dominant management theories stress the importance of operational efficiency as a means to grow bottom-line results. However, profitability of the vehicle as an integrated whole is undermined by decisions that erode a workforce's capability and capacity. Examples can be found in the all-too-common practices of hiring talent at the lowest possible expense, and then withholding proper training—in anticipation of their leaving and start working for a competitor—or firing them at will in an effort to polish up financial statements. It was Sir Richard Branson who said, "Train people well enough so they can leave, treat them well enough so they don't want to."

Moreover, the fact that personnel is a major line item on a profit and loss statement does not make it a form of special-cause variation that needs to be addressed with operational efficiency measures. Any attempt at increasing efficiency by eroding effectiveness is an example of the first mistake: "Interpreting noise as if it were a signal."

Tampering with a stable system creates friction and conflict while opening the door to surprises and unpredictable behavior. Trying to counteract the unintended and unwanted results from tampering with more and better tampering measures only destabilizes or aggravates an already unstable vehicle.

Making Performance Predictable

Better financial performance is the result of a stable vehicle that has a predictable outcome. Stable refers to operating within the limits—plus and minus three times the standard deviation ($\pm 3\sigma$)—of the vehicle's capacity and capability. Stable vehicles are thus still subject to common-cause variation, resulting in intended and unintended outcomes.

The next step in reducing volatility in common-cause variation is to make performance outcome more uniform. In other words, improve the vehicle's capacity and capability. This idea is a common-sense principle in operating a Formula One (F1), NASCAR, or Indy 500 racing vehicle. High-performing racing teams neither buy the cheapest gas, oil, tires, brakes, replacement parts, or tools, nor do they hire the cheapest mechanics or drivers, as a (best practice) measure to improve performance. They buy and hire those who are right for their intended purpose and who are the best they can afford. Performance—that what keeps you in the race so to speak—is the result of effectiveness of your vehicle, not its efficiency.

The life force behind any vehicle originates from people. Yet strategic decisions made by many executives show an intention to reduce a vehicle's dependency on people, by reducing their influence on the transformation process, and by replacing them with machines and other automated computerized robotic systems with or without artificial intelligence (AI). Apart from the "ironies of automation,"[19] which states that the more we automate the more dependent we become on people, automation tends to standardize processes and procedures that make the vehicle more rigid, which requires more time and effort to satisfy a customer's evolving needs, which makes a vehicle less agile in the production of relevant use value.

Flexibility and Speed

Agility refers to a vehicle's flexibility to adjust to new and unforeseen circumstances and to the speed—the amount of time it takes—with which it can complete a transition from one state to another. This notion of agility is similar to what the pioneers of aviation called "control." Because control was the hardest invention of the discovery of human flight, pioneers concentrated on creating stable flying machines with the same characteristics as the stability that a sailboat provides by its self-righting properties. They believed that control could be added after they had conquered the challenges posed by lift and propulsion, allowing them to fly in a straight line only.

Contrary to their peers, the Wright brothers were not interested in making their Flyer inherently stable. As bicycle mechanics, they were familiar with unstable vehicles. Instead of researching self-righting properties, they knew from experience that stability had to come from people interacting with the vehicle, just like a bicyclist with a bicycle. The influence of turbulence—up and down drafts—and crosswinds on the vehicle must be counteracted by people interacting with that vehicle. The vehicle's inherent instability made it maneuverable—able to transition from one state to the next—and the control function had to be designed into the Flyer's structure as an integral part; not as an afterthought. Form follows function.

Once Wilbur and Orville Wright figured out the principle of control—pitch, yaw, and roll—they started to improve the vehicle's control capabilities to make the vehicle more responsive to the control inputs provided by the pilot. In other words, they made the outcome of the control process more reliable and thus predictable. In essence, agility is a mental talent; an ability to change one's perception or understanding with flexibility and speed when trying to make sense of one's environment. The impetus for changing the vehicle will have to come from our creative thoughts about ways of improving the vehicle—the vehicle will not do that on its own accord. And, a vehicle will not start behaving with greater agility if the person in control of that vehicle cannot conceive of a new, different, or better exercise of that vehicle's business governance.

The Human-Error Phenomenon

Management likes to believe that success happens when everyone is doing their job, while failure happens when they are not. However, the same system that produces the successes also produces the failures in exactly the same way. Special-cause variation accounts for only 6 percent of all results, which includes individuals or groups of people not doing their job causing mistakes and errors, as well as those individuals or groups of people going above and beyond the call of duty, which accounts for unexpected successes.

As a matter of fact, it is not uncommon for a business system to experience a major, persisting, and recurring problem, the existence of which no one denies, and yet, everyone is just doing their job. This phenomenon is characteristic of a systemic problem.

A vehicle can thus operate within its specification limits and produce both intended and unintended results, which is also known as common-cause variation, or noise. The level of predictability of producing intended and wanted results of this otherwise stable system must be improved by lowering the number of incidences of unintended and unwanted results, in order to create more uniform results. Note that the bandwidth of a stable system with either a high or a low incidence of unintended and unwanted results is always plus and minus three times the standard deviation ($\pm 3\sigma$). Higher levels of uniformity correspond to less volatility within the bandwidth—results are clustered more closely around the mean (making the shape of the bell curve taller and steeper, while making its base narrower).

The experience of everyone just doing what they are supposed to do while encountering major problems is rather disconcerting to most managers. It makes everyone suspicious of everyone else and results in casting blame, which risks polarizing relationships among people, between employees and their managers, and different departments. When people become frustrated with their leaders' occupational incompetence due to the Peter Principle, and they are no longer willing to put up with a blame game and have given up on changing the status quo, the active and latent systemic problems are free to wreak havoc.

The vehicle has now entered the realm of human error, a phenomenon researched extensively by British psychologist James Reason.[20] Reason's studies found that 75 to 96 percent of all incidents—accidents and near misses—involve human error. He concluded: (1) "Human error is not the cause of failure but a symptom of a failing system." (2) "Although we cannot change the human condition [human fallibility], we can change the conditions under which humans work." Because the majority of all employees have no authority to make changes to the system, people are set up to fail. Solving systemic problems and reducing the incidence of human error is exclusively an executive responsibility.

Personal Beliefs About People

Believing that the *right* people—those who bring their A game—will outperform the capacity and capability of the system is an illusion! It is equally illusory to believe that a single rank-and-file employee with very limited authority to make any significant changes to the value chain can destabilize the entire business system (i.e., apart from deliberate violations, sabotage, or fraud). Yet, those with ultimate authority to change the system's business governance can do this even when acting with the best of intentions.

Therefore, quality and productivity are not increased by assembling a so-called high-performing team but through continual improvement of a vehicle's capacity and capability, which accounts for 94 percent of all results, including successes and failures. Let's say you had $100,000 in your budget to spend on performance improvement. Where would your money promise the highest return on investment: hiring A players and creating high-performing teams or improving the system's capability?

Similarly, exhortations, slogans, individual performance bonuses, awards, employee-of-the-month contests, zero-tolerance policies, holding everyone accountable for their actions, and threats of punishment cannot make employees outperform the vehicle. Their best efforts are limited by the vehicle's capacity and capabilities, which is subject to random variation that shows up in their performance despite people giving their best efforts every single day. Should there be, nonetheless, a noticeable change in statistics, one should remind oneself that there are lies, damn lies, and statistics—numbers can be manipulated to fit one's needs by incorporating the so-called F-factor (F stands for "fiddle").

Management Theories

The illusion that people can outperform the capabilities of a vehicle is reinforced by management theories that tie human behavior and motivation to maximizing quality and productivity. Well-known proponents of such theories are Douglas McGregor's Theory X and Theory Y, and Abraham Maslow's hierarchy of needs.

Theory X and Theory Y are generalizations of the type of employees that managers may encounter in the workplace. These theories are used to prepare tactics and protocols on how to deal with employees for the purpose of maximizing production and profits.

Managers who believe that individuals are inherently lazy and unhappy with their jobs (Theory X) rely heavily on the threat of punishment to gain employee compliance. On the other hand, managers who believe that employees can be ambitious and self-motivated and that they possess creative problem-solving abilities (Theory Y) will challenge them to aim for a job or position that satisfies a higher order of human psychological needs when their talents are underused.

Maslow believed that employees have a strong desire to realize their full potential, or what he termed reaching a level of "self-actualization." Self-actualized people are driven by innate forces beyond their basic needs to maximize quality and productivity. This drive—intrinsic motivation—can be traced back to an individual's personality (see Recognizing Our Dominant Mental Programming in Chapter 2).

Modern management theories now include behavior characteristics for baby boomers, Generation X, Generation Y (a.k.a. millennials), and Generation Z (boomlets).

Specs for Human Beings

The process for hiring employees seems to be derived from the procurement process for any other input variable. Candidates are expected to "hit the ground running" as there is no on-the-job learning. Therefore, every job and position is analyzed to determine its exact specifications. These specs are then used as a checklist in evaluating a candidate's suitability for a job or position. However, this analysis almost always excludes a candidate's personality, which happens to be a major consideration in assessing the premium for Directors and Officers Liability insurance.[21] The past president and CEO of Porsche Peter Schutz is credited with the well-known quote: "Hire character. Train skill."

Deming said, "Modern management has stolen and smothered intrinsic motivation and dignity. It has removed joy in work and in learning." Deming described intrinsic motivation as "a person's innate dignity and self-esteem, and his natural esteem for other people. One is born with a natural inclination to learn and to be innovative." Unfortunately, it is being replaced with competitiveness, selfishness, assertiveness, greed, self-defense, fear, indifference, fecklessness, and extrinsic motivation—money, power, and prestige.

Executives who trade-off humanity for profits are exercising the life force's dark side. Their perception of employees as a fungible commodity, combined with the belief that squeezing cost is a source of competitive advantage is an unsustainable practice. Denying people the ability to self-actualize—developing and giving their greatest gifts—is a major source of friction and conflict—causing disengagement, indifference, a war for talent, and so forth. Reducing a vehicle's capability and capacity has a negative effect on quality and productivity.

Reductions in quality and productivity due to an executive's systematic reliance on the dark side of the life force is an example of common-cause variation. And firing employees in order to "set an example," and hiring new employees to take their places, is testimony of poor leadership. Such decisions allow systemic problems to perpetuate themselves until the vehicle is changed—that is, collapsed or gained sound business governance. These decision makers require a mind shift in order to embrace the light side of the life force.

Employees Just Want to Be Heard

Employees are a great source of information and solution alternatives because nobody knows more about an activity than the person who is performing it on a daily basis. And yet few managers ask for their opinions because they care little for beliefs or suggestions that are not their own. In my practice, I have interviewed many employees as part of a root-cause analysis and, on many occasions, they explained to me blow by blow what was wrong with the process. When I asked them, "Did you tell management?" they answered me in an exasperated tone of voice, "Yes, but they don't listen; they don't want to hear about it."

Most employees take pride in their jobs, and they just want to experience the joy of being successful at what they do best—the feeling of being alive.

In a worst-case scenario, frustrated employees might retaliate against their employer. The story about "feeding the hog"[22] is a sad example. The "hog" is a machine for shredding wood. Whenever employees of a sawmill became disgruntled about the way they were treated by management, they would throw perfectly good sheets of plywood into the hog, hence feeding the hog. By destroying raw materials, they reduced a manager's performance numbers, hoping that it would get the person into trouble. This form of sabotage is not overt, and thus failure to detect this special-cause variation or signal is an example of the previously mentioned second mistake: not recognizing when the underlying process changes, especially when the results are still within the specification limits.

In conclusion, having the right person for the job is important. However, employees who answer to the descriptions of McGregor's Theory Y and Maslow's self-actualization can only thrive within a vehicle that is perceived as an organismic system, governed by the light side of the life force, which gives it the capability of shaping and adapting itself to new and unforeseen circumstances as they unfold.

This section on people is not intended to be exhaustive. I trust that self-actualized leaders do not need to be prescribed what to think or do, or how to think and do. I trust that they will rely on their moral skill—craftsmanship—to figure out which decisions will enhance the conditions under which humans work as a means to increasing quality and productivity. Once they have figured out the right course of action, I trust that they will exercise their moral will—stewardship—to then do what is right.

THE HUMAN–MACHINE INTERFACE

As we learned from the Wright brothers, a vehicle's predictable behavior is the result of interaction between humans and the machine. This interaction is known as the human–machine interface (HMI). The "machine" in the HMI is the value chain (the methodology used to organize a business system's activities into a work flow, so that it can be directed toward the realization of its intended purpose).

The value chain is brought to life by humans who perform these activities and are the life force behind any work flow. Humans and machine exchange information across the HMI. The HMI is a shared boundary across which humans provide control input for the machine to accept, implement, and perform. In return, the machine offers feedback regarding the state of its individual processes to its operator(s).

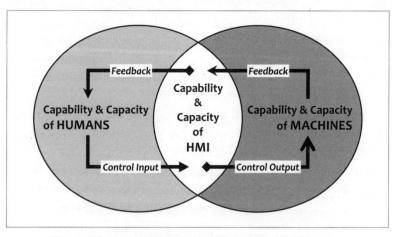

Figure 7.7: Shared Boundaries of Humans and Machine

People performing their everyday job by interacting with the machine cannot be assessed accurately without considering the design, structure or organization, implementation or operation, maintenance and management of the machine and the human–machine interface; and vice versa.

Humans use a wide variety of mechanical and electronic devices to provide control inputs to the system—for example, keyboards, keypads, touch screens, mice, joysticks, steering wheels, yokes, foot pedals, levers, toggle switches, radio buttons, and push buttons.

Machines are given an equally wide variety of mechanical and electronic devices to provide feedback to its operator(s): gauges, lights, bells, whistles, buzzers, monitoring screens, graphic user interfaces, printers, text message to mobile devices, and stick-shakers.

Compatibility Mismatches

The success of the HMI is thus dependent on the level of compatibility of humans and the machine. This is the realm of ergonomics: the study of designing equipment and devices that fit the human body and its cognitive abilities. Ergonomics draws on many disciplines in its study of humans and their environments, including anthropometry, biomechanics, mechanical engineering, industrial engineering, industrial design, information design, kinesiology, physiology, cognitive psychology, and industrial and organizational psychology.

Unfortunately, compatibility mismatches are a rich source of frequent mistakes and incidents—accidents and near misses. The occurrence of mismatches and the subsequent experience of unintended consequences, stress, and frustration rises exponentially with the automation of work processes. This makes the value chain ever more complex. Such unintended consequences are generally ascribed to human error, which is, according to James Reason, "not the cause of failure but a symptom of a failing system."[23]

Automating Human Activity

Automation is generally defined as "the execution by a machine agent (usually a computer) of a function that was previously carried out by a human."[24] The activities that humans perform are:

- **Physical.** Manual operations
- **Cognitive.** Decision making, creating, planning, and critical thinking

Automating human activity causes the relationships among the individual links of the value chain to become more complex in their interdependence. In addition, a need for cost-efficiency may demand the sharing of resources—such as computer software and hardware—which results in tight coupling of work processes. The sharing of resources reduces redundancies, which increases the adverse effects of events such as human error, equipment failure, computer viruses, breaches in cyber security, accidents, and fires.

Innovating Automation

Automation is more appropriate in the execution of some business functions than others, such as dangerous and dirty jobs, and it can be phased in gradually rather than all at once. Therefore, we recognize a scale of degrees of automation:[25]

1. The computer offers no assistance; the human must do it all.
2. The computer suggests alternative ways to do the task.
3. The computer selects one way to do the task and . . .
4. The computer executes that suggestion if the human approves, or . . .
5. The computer allows the human a restricted time to veto before automatic execution, or . . .
6. The computer executes the suggestion automatically and then necessarily informs the human, or . . .
7. The computer executes the suggestion automatically and then informs the human only if asked.
8. The computer selects the method, executes the task, and ignores the human.

Automation is thus not an all-or-nothing proposition but a continuum of options that ranges from full human or manual control to full machine or automatic control. When a business function that used to be performed manually by humans is fully reallocated to a machine, that function is then called a machine operation.

Furthermore, automation can challenge executive decision makers' forbearance when it malfunctions or does not function as intended—or when it is functional but the HMI confuses, frustrates, and aggravates the operator(s). These challenges are detrimental to workplace satisfaction, performance, and, in some cases, safety.

As computers keep decreasing in size and cost, and increasing in power, speed, and intelligence, we can anticipate a continual drive toward increased automation in the workplace. The human–machine interface will become an even more critical node within a business network that is the vehicle.

Human Factors

Automation must be designed to work in conjunction with the humans who control or otherwise interact with the machine. Unfortunately, the Bigger, Higher, Faster, Farther Syndrome causes engineers to design automation according to what is technically feasible—opting to deploy the latest and greatest—while expecting humans to accommodate any challenge that high tech throws their way. In addition, automation training is often absent or inadequate. Calling your system "intuitive" is a creative way to blame users for not understanding the engineers' line of thinking. Making human satisfaction, performance, and safety subordinate to the needs of machines (a prime example of the dark side of the force of life at work) is a recipe for disaster.

Moreover, complexities of the operational environment and limitations of individual human operators may cause automation to be used differently from what was intended by its designers, supervisors, managers, and regulators. "This necessarily means that any human error associated with the use of automation can include the human operator, the designer, or even management error."[26]

Human-Centered Automation

The discussion to determine which activity should be relegated to the human and which to automation is a classic problem, and the debate about the criteria to determine if automation is appropriately *human centered* has not yet been settled.

Some criteria of human-centered automation (and reasons to question them) are:

- Allocate to the human the tasks best suited to the human, and allocate to the automation the tasks best suited to it. (Unfortunately, there is no consensus on how to do this, nor is the allocation policy necessarily fixed, but may depend on context.)
- Keep the human operator in the decision-and-control loop. (This is good only for intermediate-bandwidth tasks. The

human is too slow for high bandwidth and may fall asleep if bandwidth is too low.)
- Maintain the human operator as the final authority over the automation. (Humans are poor monitors, and in some decisions it is better not to trust them; they are also poor decision makers when under time pressure and in complex situations.)
- Make the human operator's job easier, more enjoyable, or more satisfying through friendly automation. (Operator ease, enjoyment, and satisfaction may be less important than system performance.)
- Empower or enhance the human operator to the greatest extent possible through automation. (Power corrupts.)
- Support trust by the human operator. (The human may come to over trust the system.)
- Give the operator computer-based advice about everything the person should want to know. (The amount and complexity of information is likely to overwhelm the operator at exactly the worst time.)
- Engineer the automation to reduce the risk of human error and minimize response variability. (A built-in margin for human error and experimentation helps the human learn and not become a robot.)
- Make the operator a supervisor of subordinate automatic control systems. (Sometimes straight manual control is better than supervisory control.)
- Achieve the best combination of human and automatic control, where best is defined by explicit system objectives. (Rarely does a mathematical objective function exist.)[27, 28]

Employee Training Needs

As the interactions between humans and machine have become increasingly important and intimate, the boundaries between automation and operators have started to blur. Therefore, executives who approve investment in automation should demand designers of automation to engineer the relationship between humans and machine—the human–machine interface—and not just the technology itself.

In addition to formal education and skills training, employees should also receive adequate training on the use of automation, including an explanation of how their interactions with the machine influence the actual work process for which they are responsible (similarly, the Wright brothers recognized the need for learning to fly).

WHAT HAPPENS NEXT

Without a vehicle, there is no journey. And you can brag about closing the best and most enviable deals for the most sought-after and coolest products or services in the world, but your journey ends then and there if the vehicle cannot deliver on your promises.

In addition, people care about the road you choose to travel, the footprints you leave behind, and how you choose to overcome obstacles and adversity. Therefore, the next chapter describes the importance of envisioning a well-defined destination, including an itinerary for arriving at that destination. Itinerary and destination serve as guides for creating utility, brand identity, and developing a vehicle that has the actual capacity and capability to complete the journey on its own terms. They are your benchmarks for success.

CHAPTER 8

The Destination— Itinerary for Arrival

If we are always arriving and departing, it is also true that we are eternally anchored. One's destination is never a place but rather a new way of looking at things.

—Henry Miller
American author; from *Big Sur and the Oranges of Hieronymus Bosch*

Perhaps the most fundamental questions to ask a CEO about entrepreneurship are:

Why would you want to be in charge of leading a commercial enterprise—to be in business for yourself?

What motivates you to pursue the creation of a specific kind of use value?

Which conditions must be fulfilled for you to have peace of mind; to experience satisfaction and happiness with what you do?

The answer to the first question is usually not surprising. Entrepreneurial people just don't like working for someone else and having someone telling them what to do. And they also like to make money.

The answers to the second and third questions tend to be much more interesting and revealing of an entrepreneur's personal nature, history, or circumstances. They reveal the passion, intrinsic motivation, drive, determination, tenacity, and endurance for an individual's pursuit of a specific business idea or concept. These answers describe the journey's destination, and they dictate indirectly the vehicle's specs—form follows function—as well as the most appropriate itinerary for a successful journey ahead.

Because entrepreneurs cannot resist the stimulus that the environment continually puts upon them to create a better world and a higher standard of living, they are constantly innovating use value in accordance with their vision. So, in this way, Wilbur Wright got the idea for a flying machine because he envisioned that "flight is possible to man."

The business idea of a client of mine was to develop mobility devices because she envisioned people living independently of others should they become incapacitated. And I wrote *The Root Cause* because seeing executive decision makers struggle to learn vital change management skills through osmosis makes me cringe—the idea of being expected to demonstrate change management skills when instruction on these skills is absent from most formal education in business administration and executive development is flat-out absurd. For some unjustifiable reason, business schools and executive training programs fail to teach solving stubborn systemic problems and adapting the business system for unfolding new and unforeseen circumstances to their students—some of whom are CEOs and others who will become CEOs. Moreover, they fail "to teach their students HOW TO ORGANIZE AND USE KNOWLEDGE AFTER THEY ACQUIRE IT," which was identified by Napoleon Hill as "the missing link in all systems of education known to civilization today."

People who cannot diagnose a root cause cannot be expected to recognize an authentic solution, even when it is staring them in the face. This spells mediocrity, marked by experiences of unnecessary friction and conflict, which is disadvantageous for all concerned.

Needless to say, embracing the inspiration to create the world in which we live is the reason why entrepreneurs' enthusiasm is so infectious. For them, financing a business and being profitable are just means to an end. Unfortunately, their enthusiasm is often smothered by the so-called bean counters because it is in their nature to confuse means and ends. Once they make their mark on the business, every problem becomes a financial one, for which they only seek a financial solution—a typical example of Maslow's hammer at work.

THE VEHICLE'S PURPOSE

Every vehicle has a purpose; its raison d'être. After all, who would invest time, money, and effort in something that serves no purpose at all?

Having a definitive description of a vehicle's intended purpose—its destination—informs us about the vehicle's business governance requirements for its design, organization or structure, implementation or operation, maintenance, and management. After all, a vehicle performs best when its utilization is in alignment with its purpose. The extent to which this alignment is successful is the ultimate touchstone for measuring CEO effectiveness.

Destinations are not set in stone. They may have to be adapted or redefined as new insights and experiences influence and clarify one's vision. A destination may even be replaced by a different one as prompted by a changing journey—such as evolving consumer preferences and demands; an evolution in collective consciousness regarding ecology, economy, or humanity; changes to the vehicle, such as mechanization, automation, and digitalization; and when businesses merge or are taken over by businesses with a different purpose.

This shows the importance of constant (re)alignment between the destination and the journey, and the destination and the vehicle, and the vehicle and its journey—form must follow function in order for the system to maintain its integrity. Realignment facilitates efforts to dissipate entropy.

Benchmark for Measuring Success

The destination of a vehicle is thus comparable to the objective of a game or sport. The objective of hockey (ice and field), soccer, lacrosse, and similar games is to maneuver the ball or puck into the opponent's goal. In addition to the objective of a sport, there are rules describing the principles by which the sport is played. Violation of those rules can get a player and the team penalized, disqualified, or have a goal annulled by the umpire. Therefore, winning is not just the result of scoring more goals than one's opponent, but also of adhering to the rules of the sport—making sure the goal is counted. Note that the rules are also subject to change if and when warranted—for example, the introduction of the tiebreaker in tennis and allowing a larger size club head for a driver in golf.

However, the rules of business are more extensive and complex than those of any sport. Apart from local, state, federal, international, and supranational legislation and treaties, there are behavioral norms and standards regarding ethics, morality, humanity, cultural sensitivities, social responsibility, and environmental consciousness. In addition, management teams are expected to define critical success factors, prerequisites, policies, procedures, specifications, guidelines, strategies, and tactics for managing the business processes and the products and services they produce and deliver. In general, rules provide a benchmark against which to measure the level of success with which executives provide business governance and leadership for the pursuit of the vehicle's intended purpose. Success is thus a ratio between the vehicle's outcome and its aim (see Figure 9.1). Therefore, a vehicle's level of success is influenced by changes in either or both its current state and its desired state, which would indicate if there is a problem or not (see Figure 9.2).

Note that organizations such as consumer advocacy groups, environmentalists, trade unions, trade associations, chambers of commerce, and lobbyists exercise their influence to the best of their abilities to change the rules of business in their favor. That said, it should be noted also, although the game of business is played with multiple umpires (stakeholders), that the ultimate umpire is and will always be the public, even in cases where they have no direct relationships with the business itself. This note is especially valid in the age of social media when a message—true or false—can go viral on a moment's notice.

Benchmark for Diagnosing Systemic Problems

Destination is not only a crucial benchmark for success. It is also critical in identifying and quantifying problems and assessing the validity of an authentic solution. As explained in Chapter 1, a problem is defined as a discrepancy, or misalignment, between the current state and the desired state of a vehicle. Likewise, attempting to determine success or failure without knowledge of and agreement on the measurement for either the current or the desired state, or both, is simply impossible. That is why an executive's insistence on defining and sharing a concise definition of the business's destination is of paramount importance to CEO effectiveness. After all, the mere presence of net profits does not automatically constitute successful leadership, and the mere absence of profits does not automatically constitute failure.

Moreover, the earnings per share ratio contains no information regarding a vehicle's capacity, capability, effectiveness, efficiency, sustainability, employee engagement, or brand identity. The history of Amazon's stock valuations serves as an interesting example. It raised so much money by selling stock in the mid-1990s that it had $2,000,000,000 in the bank. Every year, Amazon spent more money than they made, so their yearly profit was negative. But because it had so much money saved up, it could afford to make up the difference out of its bank account. The big stock market cash inflows made up for the continual losses. Only after a decade did Amazon actually start making a profit. During those 10 years, investors believed Amazon would become profitable because it had a great cash flow.

However, poor public opinion regarding a company's social responsibility, environmental consciousness, and status as a good or bad workplace can be reflected in a company's earnings per share ratio, and thus in its share price. Buyers may choose substitute products or brands and investors may decide to eliminate certain stocks from their investment portfolio. Violations of rules that govern the functioning and operating of a vehicle are either sanctioned by law, rebuked by unions, called to attention by whistleblowers, or condemned by buyers, employees, and shareholders who "vote with their feet."

In short, destination is a business system's mental programming, which shapes the system's personality and morality—in other words, the thought patterns and behavior that are reflected in its brand identity. However, since business systems are human-made (through the vehicle's business governance), a business system's mental programming is closely correlated with the collective mental programming of its executive leadership team and the process by which they reach their decisions.

Therefore, blaming the (computer) system for mishaps that are encountered on the journey makes for poor excuses since executives are ultimately responsible when it comes to making decisions that influence the business governance of a vehicle—and this includes approval of the functional design of all computerized programs and systems. To be clear, nobody expects a decision maker to create the actual functional design or programming. However, the decision maker is expected to provide or approve a description of critical success factors for the final product—the look and feel of it and thus the experience that you want it to provide to buyers and users, which should be stipulated in a request for proposal (RFP).

BRAND IDENTITY AS AN INTEGRAL PART OF USE VALUE

The mental image that clients, prospects, vendors, and the general public create from their perception of your vehicle and interaction with it—including the products and services it produces and delivers—becomes your brand identity. Hopefully, that image corresponds with the image you wanted to create for your brand. Your brand identity has integrity when people's experience of your behavior in the world is in alignment with the way you say you want to be perceived and who you claim to be.

Brand identity is part of the use value that is exchanged for cash value during the journey. This shows that use value extends far beyond the physical properties and usefulness of the product or service; it encompasses the entire relationship between buyer, user, and seller. It even extends to the general public, suppliers, regulators, competitors, and shareholders on issues such as buyers' protection, workers' rights, social responsibility, and environmental consciousness.

A company that makes a decision that is perceived as a poor judgment by large groups of people can lead to a sudden change in public opinion regarding all aspects of the company. Thus, a product or service can gain and lose use value even without changing anything to the product or service itself. Let me remind you of the law of cause and effect, how thoughts create form on some level. If you want to change stakeholders' perception, you'll have to change your level of thinking.

Thus, the idea behind brand identity is for a target audience to resonate with a company's chosen destination. Executives want to attract an audience of people who believe what they themselves believe. That is how a brand becomes the obvious choice for individual members of that target audience. Any mismatches between the vehicle's destination and its behavior on its journey are easily perceived as inauthentic or dysfunctional, which erodes trust in the company and damages its brand identity.

Therefore, the concept of brand identity hinges on what executives believe should be the destination's highest value. Is it making money and profits or developing a quality vehicle, which produces high-quality products and services with inherently high use value that make it easy for the intended target audience to designate that business as their obvious choice supplier? It is not enough to talk the marketing talk; you'll have to walk the walk—your word is your bond.

Money as the Destination's Highest Value

As discussed before, quantifying everything and anything in monetary equivalents has many advantages. Not only does it eliminate any qualitative values from one's considerations, it also allows decision makers to dispassionately compare the contribution margins of different component parts, tools, individuals, departments, concepts, products, or services within their own organization and among other (rival) organizations and industries over different periods of time.

As a result, making hard trade-off decisions becomes more effortless when the pros and cons of mutually exclusive alternatives have been reduced to a single quantifiable factor. The winner is always the alternative with the highest anticipated amount of short-term profit or the lowest net present value.

However, there are serious drawbacks to reducing every quantifiable performance aspect to monetary equivalents. Apart from portraying a rather insular perspective of operational processes, these monetary values are compiled after the processes they are intended to measure are finished. Therefore, Dr. W. Edwards Deming equated this practice of management by results to driving a car by looking in the rearview mirror. Yet this historical data—which represents just symptoms or effects of a specific course of action—are oftentimes perceived erroneously as the cause(s) of success or failure and subsequently used as the starting point for developing new policies, tactics, or strategies. And that is how these symptoms or effects—historical data—take on a life of their own.

Beware of Tampering

This common practice of initiating managerial action solely based on variation in financial data between successive reporting periods is called tampering. Financial data is like readouts from an odometer and trip counter on the dashboard of a motorized vehicle. They count the number of miles a vehicle has traveled, which provides no information regarding the vehicle's actual performance—such as speed, payload, fuel consumption or kilowatt-hours (kWh) consumption, hours of idling, horsepower, torque, reliability, and dependability. The unintended consequences of this all-too-common practice is treating symptoms rather than root causes. Here are some examples of such popular all too common quick fix solutions:

- Automation—computers (including replacing people by machines)
- New machines—gadgets (including [mobile] software applications)
- Gold plating (the Bigger, Higher, Faster, Farther Syndrome)
- Operational efficiency (the Black Knight Syndrome)
- Zero defects or tolerance policies (ignoring random variation)
- Working smarter not harder (used as an exhortation)
- Doing more with less (used as an exhortation)
- Management by Objectives (setting arbitrary numerical goals)
- Making everyone accountable (ignoring the disruptive effect of systemic problems on system integrity)
- Cultivating A players and A teams (belief that some people can outperform the system)
- Delegation of quality to quality controllers (belief in creating quality through inspection)

- Merit system to determine eligibility for promotion (increasing entropy)
- Incentive pay (inviting questionable forms of creativity)

Whatever a vehicle lacks in capability (as demonstrated by excess waste[1] that increases common-cause variation in the outcome of operational processes) cannot be fixed with solutions whose objective it is to increase the capacity—including operational efficiency measures—of one or more of the vehicle's component parts. Note that reducing common-cause variation increases system capacity.

As demonstrated by the funnel experiment designed by Lloyd Nelson, letting outcomes, effects, or results decide the need for corrective actions (intended to make production processes more stable and the outcomes more predictable) has the opposite effect. This unfortunate and widespread (best) practice of tampering introduces even more variation (waste) into production processes, while reducing the predictability of performance outcomes, which makes those processes more unstable than before. Please search the internet for a video demonstration of the Nelson (or Deming) funnel experiment. Watch it!

Opportunism Conflicts with Stewardship

Alternatively, reliance on quantifiable performance data expressed in monetary equivalents might sway decision makers to pursue only the most profitable, most efficient, or least expensive options. Unfortunately, this approach sometimes leads to opportunism. Whenever an opportunity presents itself—an offer that cannot be refused based on its projected short-term financial reward—and you act on impulse with little or no regard for its consequences for reaching your destination, you effectively choose to follow a different itinerary toward either the same but more likely a different destination.

For example, a medical-mobility devices manufacturer that positioned itself as the Cadillac of the industry, seized an opportunity to close a deal with a new client for a large quantity of products for immediate delivery at a deeply discounted price, and paid in cash. Although it gave the seller's cash position a short-term boost, it also undercut her pricing policy because this new client sold these devices on the internet far below the manufacturer-suggested retail prices. This one transaction undermined the manufacturer's credibility regarding adherence to a strict pricing policy based on its product's uniqueness and exclusivity, which caused confusion among the company's exclusive retailers, and its past and prospective buyers.

For all good intents and purposes, there is nothing wrong with choosing a different itinerary in order to take the vehicle into a different strategic direction, as long as one acknowledges and accepts the consequences. Steering a new course toward a different destination is confusing to any target audience because it conflicts with their perception of your brand. It requires an explanation.

Failing to Understand Variation

The reason decision makers feel compelled to tamper with outcomes or (financial) results of otherwise stable systems can be found in their lack of understanding of variation. When decision makers fail to comprehend variation, they just fall back on their mental programming with its wide range of theories, ideologies, principles, rules, (best) practices, values, and benchmarks for growing bottom-line results. Here are some inherent risks associated with a leader's lack of understanding variation:

- Seeing a trend where there is none
- Failing to recognize a trend—such as seasonal variation— when there is one
- Mistaking outcomes, effects, and results for root causes
- Attributing systemic problems to individuals or groups of people (judging and blaming)
- Failing to understand past performance and using past performance to predict future performance
- Failing to appreciate what a system does, how it does it, and why it does it
- Failing to recognize a system's capabilities and vulnerabilities, and if and when it needs to be changed, improved, or replaced

Decision makers who are incapable, or unwilling to learn, unlearn, and relearn will suffer from entropy—they will just maintain the status quo. When unsuccessful at growing the bottom-line results of their current business system, they will resort to merger and acquisition transactions—adding the bottom-line results of another existing and profitable business system to their tally. Soon enough, the same problems will occur; they begin to misinterpret variation and start tampering with a stable system. Then what? It takes a mind shift to reprogram one's mind to generate different outcomes.

Quality as the Destination's Highest Value

The previous chapter quotes Robert M. Pirsig's book *Zen and the Art of Motorcycle Maintenance*, defining quality as "the goal at which methodology is aimed." This methodology for realizing the purpose of your business is called planning, which needs to be done with the end in mind. And, according to Pirsig, the goal—quality—of this planning process is "the continuing stimulus which our environment puts upon us to create the world in which we live."

Let's then explore the various means and ends that require planning and why it makes sense to do this with the end in mind (see Figure 8.1).

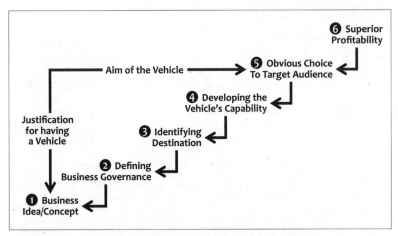

Figure 8.1: Planning with the End in Mind

Superior profitability is not the purpose of a business system but the applause for a job well done. That job needs to enfold with constancy and executed methodically as demonstrated with steps 1 to 5. In other words, if position 6 is the end you want to achieve, you'll need to pursue position 5 as the path to arrive there, and so on.

6. Superior Profitability

Napoleon Hill made a clear link between the amount of cash value that one desires to earn and the amount of use value that one plans to give in return. Figure 2.5 explains that use value (price) is equal to applied resources (cost) plus utility (profit margin). In other words, superior profitability is a function of one's ability to create superior use value.

5. Obvious Choice to Target Audience

The price buyers are willing to pay for a product or service depends on their perception of the amount of use value it contains. Therefore, members of the qualified available market for a certain category of product or service will resonate with only some brands, to the exclusion of other brands. As a result, each brand has its own target audience (see Figure 8.2).

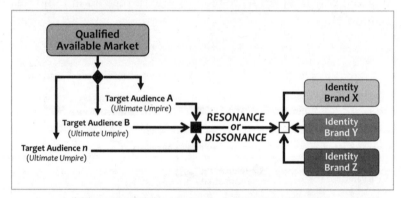

Figure 8.2: Different Strokes for Different Folks

Successful marketing relies on identifying one's preferred target audience among all members of a qualified available market and targeting one's marketing efforts specifically toward those buyers and users. This form of marketing—branding— is based on one's belief that the identified target audience will resonate with what your brand identity represents and will choose to become loyal clients.

Brands, apart from being a known entity in the industry and on the market, have their own distinct identities. That means that brand identity is more encompassing than their branded value proposition. In other words, the reason for buying the product or service of a specific brand can be influenced by either its physical properties, its intangible benefits, or the brand's reputation—it's personality, behavior, and attitude toward cultural, social, environmental, and political issues.

Therefore, the fact that competitors, each with their own brand identity, appeal to different target audiences does not imply that one brand is better or worse than the other; they just differ in their appeal—use value—to different demographics of the population.

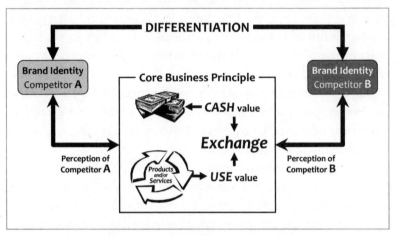

Figure 8.3: Competing Brand Identities

Buyers and users make their purchasing decisions based on quality—their analogues of previous experiences. These analogues can extend well beyond experiences with the specific product or service under consideration, or any of their suppliers.

Remember how Pirsig explained that there are no different kinds of quality—people just have different prior experiences or analogues for what they perceive as good or poor quality?

Once members of a target audience have expressed their brand preference, they no longer feel compelled to purchase any other brands or from any other suppliers. They perceive no additional use value from purchasing a lower priced brand (see Figure 8.3). Being the obvious choice supplier to your ideal target audience is more profitable than being a supplier of everything to anybody. So, who is your intended target audience and what is the kind of use value that will make you their obvious choice supplier?

4. Developing the Vehicle's Capability

Capability refers to a vehicle's potentiality, its aptitude or suitability for realizing its intended purpose. Therefore, we need to focus on the system's competence, and proficiency. In other words, we need to measure variation, which we discussed in the previous chapter.

I've said it before and I will say it again: a business is a singular, unique, integrated, and open system—a network of component parts and their intricately interdependent connections. That means, the suitability of a component part is determined by its characteristics or specs—how well it interacts with other component parts. Unfortunately, silo management and over-ambitious efficiency-improvement initiatives tend to degrade the required specification of component parts, which causes friction and conflict in interactions with other parts, and increases variation, or even causing the system to become instable—unpredictable.

This system's thinking approach seems self-evident in many situations. For instance, as discussed earlier, with a racing vehicle, it is simply unimaginable that team owners would make decisions like the ones that represent the current dominant level of thinking of business vehicle owners or their agents—the CEOs. How do you think the following solutions would affect a racing vehicle's full operational capability, winning a race, and eventually winning the championship?

- Increasing operational efficiency with across-the-board cost-cutting measures
- Minimizing use value of goods or services while maintaining the price, in order to maximize cash value
- Outsourcing labor-intensive processes to low-wage countries in order to cut cost
- Hiring people based on their willingness to accept the lowest possible wage with the least amount of employee benefits, rather than their competence
- Holding everyone accountable—except those decision makers with ultimate authority to make a real difference in vehicle performance
- Pursuing a strategy—including a mission statement—aimed at destroying competitors

- Giving in to one's urge for being recognized as an innovator by giving in to the Bigger, Higher, Faster, Farther Syndrome; increasing the capacity of component parts just because their latest-and-greatest iteration became available
- Procuring products and services only from the lowest price supplier
- Buying more cars and racing teams and merging them to realize advantages of scale

3. Identifying Destination

The choice of destination determines how you want to play the game of business—how you define winning because there are many ways of conducting business and being profitable. This requires absolute clarity regarding your brand identity: how you want to be known to potential buyers and users of your products and services; how you want to be perceived in general; what you want your legacy to be. After all, a prospective buyer's decision to purchase and use a brand's products or services may well be influenced by that brand's corporate behavior, and its leaders' personalities, public conduct, social media postings, and media articles or interviews. While these expressions may serve as an explanation for past and present behavior, they may well be used to predict future behavior.

Needless to say, properly identifying one's destination is of vital importance in choosing a vehicle, especially with regard to its capacity to reach the destination and successfully complete the journey.

2. Defining Business Governance

Business governance is the means by which you give expression to a vehicle's design, its destination, and the journey you intend to undertake. This is an iterative process because changes in the definition of one aspect of business mechanics are likely to have an effect on one or two other aspects. Therefore, proper alignment between the journey, vehicle, and destination is the main characteristic of good business governance. The validity of this statement is borne out by statistical evidence showing that 94 percent of all results are systemic in nature—they are the result of (mis)alignment between the journey, vehicle, and destination.

1. Business Idea or Concept

Every business was once just an idea for a product, a service, or the realization of an ideal in combination with a business model for its commercialization. And having a concrete concept for a business—the exchange of products and services for money, or the journey—justifies spending time, money, and effort on business governance—a vehicle's design, organization or structure, implementation or operation, maintenance, and management. You should explore the feasibility of your idea or concept before you take the plunge.

Money or Quality?

It should be abundantly clear that what executives choose collectively as the highest value for their vehicle—making money or pursuing quality—has a significant effect on the brand identity of their vehicle. To create long-term use value for your target audience or to generate short-term cash value for shareholders—that is a serious question for you to answer.

Each choice has a great number of arguments, theories, and beliefs both in their favor and against. Whereas a money-orientation tends to erode a vehicle's capability, which hurts a target audience, a quality-orientation improves a vehicle's capability (by making a business system's outcome more stable and thus predictable), which benefits a target audience and also employees, management, shareholders, and the community in which it operates.

Nonetheless, it all boils down to an individual executive's perception of the role of businesses in society. Does she or he believe that humanity should be sacrificed if demanded by a business system to safeguard some arbitrarily chosen short-term financial outcomes? That is, I believe, what is implied in Milton Friedman's doctrine, which states the business of business is business.[2] Alternatively, does the executive believe that systems are tools for the enhancement of humanity—their quality of life? How much influence does one believe to be appropriate for providers of risk capital to have—in the form of shareholder activism—in deciding on the question of what to choose as highest value?

The answer to these questions is the core topic of this book, as discussed in Chapter 4. Sooner or later, every executive will reach a fork in the road where they will receive the call to the hero's journey. Faced with a moral decision that cannot be rationalized with an impersonal cost–benefit analysis, that individual knows there are consequences attached to accepting and rejecting the call. This is their moment of truth because what hangs in the balance is nothing less than the integrity of their authentic Self. For what price are you willing to sell your soul to Mephistopheles?[3] Know that he seems to have a no-return policy.

Allocation of Profits

Profits can be allocated to the following eight line items on the balance sheet and the statement of cash flows:

- Accounts receivable (vendor-funding)
- Investment in capability and capacity
- Inventory
- Taxes (current and deferred)
- Debt repayment
- Compensation (bonuses and dividends)
- Retained earnings (savings)
- Share buyback program

Executives' decisions regarding the allocation of profits are influenced by their choice of quality or money as the highest value for the destination of their business system.

Where quality is the highest value, profits are more likely to be allocated for debt repayment, savings, or investments intended to increase the vehicle's capability of producing and delivering more use value. A more capable system is more stable and produces results that are more predictable, while being respectful of humanity. As a result, its level of profitability is more sustainable during good as well as bad economic times. And profits can be applied to invest in additional capacity.

Executives who believe that money is the highest of all values are more likely to allocate profits toward bonus and dividend payments or a stock buyback program. Alternatively, they could spend the money on a merger and acquisition transaction in an effort to increase bottom-line results. Note that raising the bottom line is also regarded as a valid excuse for increasing executive compensation packages, which increases (overhead) cost.

A stock buyback or share repurchase program is a scheme in which a company buys back a significant number of its own stock on the open market. Reducing the total number of outstanding shares increases earnings per share and tends to elevate the market value of the remaining shares. This decision is typically justified in a press release with the statement: "We find no better investment than our own company."

However, that investment money is tied up in the purchase of those shares. Therefore, it is not available for improving the company's capability to produce more use value that could have been exchanged for more cash value. Moreover, unforeseen liquidity needs may well have to be financed by taking on additional debt, which reduces the company's financial health. Failure to improve or even to maintain the current level of use value reflects poorly on the brand, which is readily recognized by members of the target audience and the uncommitted members of the qualified available market. This change in brand identity may well incentivize them to start looking for a new supplier. Have you noticed the disjuncture between a business's share price and its capability to create use value?

It is worrisome when executives believe that engaging in stock market transactions is the most sensible allocation of profits. Acting on this belief implies the choice of an additional or alternative journey (shuffling money around) that would cause unnecessary friction and conflict with the vehicle's current destination and capability. Also, it implies the intentional choice of an alternative target audience (shareholders) instead of the vehicle's original intended target audience—people who actually buy and use what you produce.

CHARTING AN ITINERARY TOWARD YOUR DESTINATION

An itinerary is a travel document that outlines a proposed route for the purpose of guiding travelers as they journey toward their chosen destination. Although different journeys can lead to the same destination, not every journey follows the same itinerary.

The difference between itineraries is the sensation, emotion, satisfaction, and happiness the traveler wants to experience, which may determine the choice of their mode of transportation—the vehicle. In addition, some itineraries require a vehicle to be personalized to better suit their needs or to be customized to accommodate specific conditions they anticipate to encounter on the journey. Alternatively, their preferred vehicle may be unsuitable for a journey to their chosen destination. Also, the destination and vehicle of choice may preclude the undertaking of certain journeys—they may prove to be ill-suited for each other.

Because an itinerary describes the journey from the current location to an intended destination, it can be considered a strategy, which Colonel John R. Boyd defined as "a mental tapestry of changing intentions for harmonizing and focusing our efforts as a basis for realizing some aim or purpose in an unfolding and often unforeseen world of many bewildering events and many contending interests."[4]

Creating an itinerary is necessarily an iterative process. And the destination serves as a constant factor; it's true north. As an analogy, think of a sailboat moored with her bow attached to an anchor point in a harbor or a bay. Regardless of the direction from which the wind blows, she is always facing the anchor point, pointing her bow into the wind, thus prevented from drifting aimlessly.

The Never-Ending Quest for "Mojo"

Mojo is good for business because it reduces friction and conflict, and increases productivity. But what is it?

Mojo has many characteristics in common with quality. It is hard to define definitively and yet everyone knows what you mean—we recognize it when we see it. It is the "magic sauce," or "it," or what the French call the *je ne sais quoi* (I don't know what). In short, mojo is not a thing but an experience, something that can only be described with personal anecdotes of real events that happened to real people.

Mojo is not a cause; it's an effect. However, there is no recipe or best practice for creating mojo. Mojo occurs naturally when a returning hero CEO, a master of two worlds, is knitting together principles of the spiritual world—advancing humanity—with those of the economic world.

Examples of this radically different mindset become abundantly clear when reading books such as *Small Giants: Companies That Choose to Be Great Instead of Big*, by Bo Burlingham, *Nuts!: Southwest Airlines' Crazy Recipe for Business and Personal Success*, by Kevin and Jackie Freiberg, and *The Great Game of Business*, by Jack Stack. These books exemplify the priceless benefits of treating people as unique human beings as opposed to fungible human resources. For the executive leaders profiled in these books, this is not a trick or a cheap ploy to placate people with the expectation that it will make them work harder. No, for them it is a demonstration of dignity and respect, a way they want to live their lives—don't ask of others what you would not want to do yourself.

Inevitably, how executives want to interact with their employees, and how they want employees to interact with clients and vendors and participate with the community in which they live and work as representatives of the company, colors the itinerary. This will be different for every entrepreneur, founder, and CEO because they all have a different vision and belief system, and thus a different perception of the world, as discussed in Chapter 4. These leaders dance to the beat of their own drummer—they are unafraid to buck conventional wisdom. That's what it means to be inspired!

Decision makers who think differently obtain different results because they make choices that align with their different mindset—their analogues of quality and success are experiences different from just making money. Consequently, they are willing to forgo lucrative opportunities when they go against their beliefs, values, and vision for the world in which they want to live. Instead of growing the business, they develop the business, aiming for it to become the best possible version of itself. That's how they sustain and enjoy mojo, which is good for business, including bottom-line results. After all, members of their target audience resonate with mojo, which is fundamental to becoming their obvious choice supplier.

Template for Charting an Itinerary

The process for charting an itinerary is very similar to the one for creating a project plan. Therefore, both processes can use the same template as an outline for the creation of their respective information products: an itinerary and a project plan (see Figure 8.4).

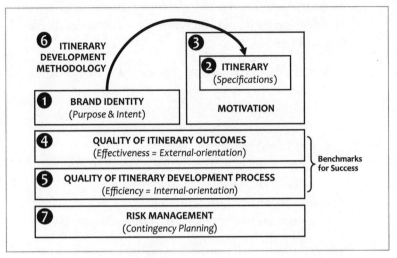

Figure 8.4: Template for Charting an Itinerary (Strategy)

Using this template is comparable to painting-by-numbers. The template offers a clear delineation of separate areas of interest and suggests what kind of information should be contained in each box. Using this template focuses the mind, prompting decision makers to think through every step of the way, from start to finish—it's a vital "look before you leap" kind of exercise.

Step 1: Brand Identity

This step is about nurturing a vehicle's brand identity. What executives need to accomplish with this step is threefold:

1. Identifying where the vehicle is located right now with regard to its destination. This is comparable to consulting a city map and looking for the bright red arrow with the text "You Are Here." This is known as assessing the current state of the vehicle. The current state is defined by people's experiences of friction, conflict, frustration, and dissatisfaction because a vehicle produces unintended and unwanted effects, especially when their root causes linger, persist, and recur.

2. Identifying the exact situation, conditions, and circumstances that make a vehicle the obvious choice for its intended target audience. This is known as defining the desired state of the vehicle. This definition must be written by executives and cannot be left to chance or to the opinion expressed by a consultant or to the actions of competitors. Failure to define

the desired state creates an indifference as was expressed in the following segment from Lewis Carroll's famous book *Alice in Wonderland*:

> ALICE: Would you tell me, please, which way I ought to go from here?
> THE CHESHIRE CAT: That depends a good deal on where you want to get to.
> ALICE: I don't much care where.
> THE CHESHIRE CAT: Then it doesn't much matter which way you go.
> ALICE: So long as I get somewhere.
> THE CHESHIRE CAT: Oh, you're sure to do that, if only you walk long enough.

Note how little direction employees receive when "making money" is chosen as the destination. So, anything goes—no questions asked, as long as you don't get caught doing something immoral or illegal. Note that any regrets refer to getting caught.

3. Describing the problem—the difference between the desired state and the current state of the vehicle, including the problem's severity, growth rate, and urgency (see Chapter 1, "Identifying Systemic Problems"). This requires knowledge of the current state and the desired state. If any of these descriptions are unknown, finding the missing piece of information must be the first order of business in Step 6: Itinerary Development Methodology. After all, it is impossible to diagnose any shortcomings in a vehicle's brand identity without knowledge of both pieces of information, which form the common point of departure for the planning of a successful itinerary.

In defining the brand's desired state, it is of paramount importance to recognize that the pursuit of becoming the obvious choice supplier—establishing a mutually respectful relationship with a target audience—is a form of courtship.

It is to be expected that target audiences face a choice of competing value propositions from rival suppliers—suitors. This is particularly true in market segments that are characterized by high profit margins. Note that a prospective buyer is not some princess whose favor is won based on the outcome of a duel among rivaling suitors. Prospective buyers are no trophy or prize to be won in a fight, but they are the ultimate umpire of the game of business. They give their patronage based on their assessment and comparison of rivaling brand identities.

Keep in mind that buyers can have relationships with more than one supplier to satisfy different needs. Therefore, a brand that tarnishes a rival brand can and will undermine its own brand identity in the eyes of the buyers it is courting.

The only aspect over which each competitor has full control is its own brand and its expression during their courtship of their target audience and thereafter. This requires the continual development of the capability of one's vehicle. Remember Sun Tzu, who said, "Thus the skilled can make themselves invincible." Consequently, itineraries must be created based on a vehicle's capability instead of an executive's arbitrarily chosen (financial) goals.

Step 2: Itinerary Specifications

The purpose of this step is to describe in detail *what* the solution must do—its look and feel—to solve the problem to the satisfaction of the commissioning principal. In other words, this is *not* a description of the solution itself—product name, model number, brand, and other particulars. What is expected is a checklist to provide focus and direction to the problem-solving process, while stating a prospective solution's features, advantages, and benefits, including a form of ranking according to their level of importance, such as must-have, should-have, and nice-to-have. Basically, everything you would ask for in a request for proposal (RFP) from prospective suppliers.

Here are some examples of items—values—that such a checklist could contain:

- Definition of success
- Beliefs regarding the measurement of success
- Beliefs regarding the allocation and distribution of net profits
- Analogues for quality that you aspire to pursue or even surpass

- Strategic direction; system development vs. business growth
- Beliefs regarding competition and cooperation, and your role within the value system
- Beliefs regarding moral leverage—ethics, trust, equality, reliability, dependability
- Beliefs regarding people and technology, and their roles within your business system
- Beliefs regarding environmental consciousness—the scale of your carbon footprint
- Beliefs regarding social responsibility, and your role within the community
- Beliefs regarding the sourcing and procurement of raw materials and other resources
- How your products or services should be used and by whom
- The format by which your products or services are made available
- How you want to interact with stakeholders—your public image
- How you want to be perceived by stakeholders—your brand identity

These questions need answers before starting the process of developing an itinerary because, just as in project management, the secret to successful (information) product development is the art of managing the expectations of one's commissioning principal.

Step 3: Motivation for Creating an Itinerary

The purpose of this step is for executives to communicate with everyone involved in the development process what they expect from a new itinerary: *why* they need one, and *why* they need it now.

The obvious answer is the need for solving the problem as described in Step 1. The motivation can be more specific when the problem's severity, growth rate, and urgency are known, including the consequences for the capability and capacity of the vehicle. Knowing why you defined the itinerary specifications as you did will guide people's thought process and assessment of possible and probable solution alternatives.

The most pragmatic answer is that executives prefer planning the journey ahead instead of hoping for a favorable outcome from future reflex actions when new and unforeseen events unfold.

Motivation calls for leadership, which was defined by Colonel John R. Boyd as "the art of inspiring people to enthusiastically take action toward the achievement of uncommon goals."

Step 4: Quality of Itinerary Outcomes

The purpose of this step is to list all factors that are critical to the success of a specific itinerary—the *critical success factors*—at guiding a vehicle toward its destination. Hence, itinerary outcomes refer to the way buyers and the public in general experience the vehicle's conduct while on its journey—what it means to a buyer or user to be associated with that brand. This requires executives to describe exactly what they intend to provide in use value in return for the amount of cash value they desire. (There is no such reality as "something for nothing.")[5]

The methodology you choose in creating use value should be aimed at the achievement of quality. Note that individual people will experience the quality of itinerary outcomes differently because they themselves differ from each other—they have different analogues of what constitutes quality to them.

The quality—or goals—of an itinerary outcome are threefold:

- To maintain obvious choice status with current members of the target audience
- To attract the uncommitted members of the qualified available market
- To discourage competitors from attempting to peel away current target audience members

Regardless of the fact that the goals are threefold, the methodology for developing an itinerary does not differentiate between the committed members within the target audience and uncommitted members within the qualified available market, or the target audience of marauding competitors. The use value you provide will attract buyers and users that resonate with your analogues of quality. That is why giving you their patronage is an obvious choice.

Step 5: Quality of the Itinerary Development Process

The purpose of this step is to describe the prerequisites for producing and delivering the intended itinerary outcomes effectively, efficiently, sustainably, profitably, and with respect for humanity. This is where you define the conditions[6] under which you want people to work, because these experiential qualities create an organizational climate and produce your own unique mojo. In plain English, this means that if you don't create a quality production and delivery process you cannot expect buyers and users to perceive your products and services as a quality brand. "You can fool all the people part of the time, or you can fool some people all the time, but you cannot fool all people all the time."[7]

Therefore, it is with this step that executives need to declare what they regard as their highest value: either making money or pursuing quality and becoming the obvious choice supplier to their intended target audience.

Step 6: Itinerary Development Methodology

The purpose of this step is to identify the significant activities and accomplishments necessary in order to complete the journey successfully. Typically, it describes the sequence in which you propose to realize specific deliverables and milestones.

The level of success with which the deliverables and milestones must be created is measured against the goals that are described in Steps 4 and 5.

Consequently, this step demonstrates executives' intent regarding the realization of the vehicle's purpose, and their commitment toward adjusting or changing the vehicle's resource management, organizational climate, and organizational processes, if and when necessary. In other words, this step is testimony to the crucial need for proper executive sponsorship for change.

Step 7: Risk Management

The purpose of this step is trying to foresee possible risks and to anticipate probable mitigating measures for each of those eventualities, should they occur.

THE DESTINATION—ITINERARY FOR ARRIVAL

GPS SIGNAL LOST . . .

When we moved to an unfamiliar neighborhood, I was able to drive around with the confidence of a long-time resident thanks to the Global Positioning System (GPS) on my mobile phone. The GPS knew exactly where I was. All I needed to do was type in my destination and Bob's your uncle. A friendly female voice tells me when to turn and where to get in a lane, and declares, "Your destination is on the right." That's absolutely brilliant! However, I'm less exuberant when this female voice declares in the same upbeat tone of voice, "GPS signal lost"! Now what? I don't know where I am, I don't know how to get to my destination, and directions on road signs are meaningless to me because I'm still on unfamiliar terrain.

From time to time, business leaders will find themselves in a similar situation. Something happened and they know it did because they are experiencing friction and conflict, unwanted outcomes or results, and unintended consequences. Employees will look to their leaders asking them for guidance and direction. If that were you, what would you tell them?

When You Come to a Fork in the Road

A fork in the road is a metaphor for a pivotal moment in your career that requires you to make a major decision because you are stuck. The only available option for getting unstuck is choosing which way you want to go. And so, the significance of this deciding moment in time is not that it forces you to find alternative courses of action. No, there is no shortage of alternative choices, and they are readily available. In addition, neither are any of the best choices a secret waiting to be discovered by you. Instead, the significance of having come to a fork in the road is that it forces you to make a decision, any decision that will move you away from this fork in the road—to put you back on track.

Standing at the fork in the road is a determining event, one that Robert M. Pirsig would have described as quality. He writes, "Quality is not a *thing*. It is an *event*."[8] And he expounds, "Quality is the event at which awareness of both subject and object is made possible."[9]

There should be no doubt in anyone's mind that quality—the continuing stimulus that our environment puts upon us to create the world in which we live[10]—is drawing ample awareness to the relationship between you, the subject standing on the fork in the road, and the business, the object experiencing unintended and unwanted effects. You are being watched in great anticipation of your decision by all stakeholders. So, what is your vision for the world our environment encourages you to create?

To decide is a form of eliminating alternative courses of action, by weighing the pros and cons of each option against the business system's destination. As was explained in Chapter 1, not obtaining your intended (financial) result is just a symptom or effect of an underlying root cause.

Just as you would do in the example of losing the GPS signal while driving, first you figure out your current position, and then search for your desired destination relative to where you are now, and only then choose the best route for arriving at your intended destination. There are many roads from which to choose, ranging from highways to country lanes, from the fast direct route to the meandering scenic drive. There is nothing inherently wrong with any of those choices. All that really counts is that your chosen route directs you to your destination. This approach to the decision-making process is rather straightforward. Nonetheless, it is not a common practice among decision makers.

Instead, the widespread approach for getting off a fork in the road is shopping for popular solutions, such as cool electronic tools and software applications, leadership best practices, and investment in capitalizing on the latest craze in the use of buzzwords such as "agility," "disruption," and "onboarding." Unfortunately, the guiding principle for choosing a course of action seems to boil down to money and whether it will increase bottom-line results. Despite its wide acceptance and adoption, the chance of these solutions solving any root causes, and re-aligning the business with its purpose—restoring system integrity—is rather slim. And the chance of these solutions contributing to underperformance of the business, and by extension of the executive decision maker, is much larger. Underperformance is the result of undermining the business system's capability and capacity, which increases cost and reduces net profits (see Figure 8.5). Hence, shopping for a solution that promises the largest contribution to bottom-line results is habitually counterproductive to solving systemic problems.

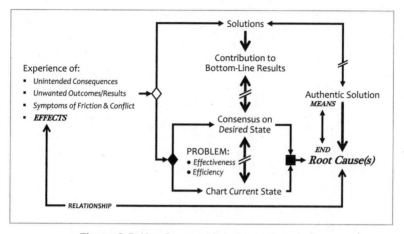

Figure 8.5: Key Source of Underperformance

Successful business performance is based on adherence to simple principles explaining relationships between cause and effect and means and ends. If you don't know the business's current state as well as its desired state, you cannot assess the problem. Without problem assessment, you cannot diagnose the problem's root cause(s). Without knowing the root cause(s), you cannot restore system integrity. Chances of restoring system integrity are equally slim if your chosen desired state conflicts with the purpose for which the system was built.

I cannot stress enough the importance of the business system's destination, including a compatible itinerary, for operating any business successfully. Every time you read about a great business—as opposed to a large one—it is their decision makers' devotion to pursuing the system's destination relentlessly that makes all the difference.

WHAT HAPPENS NEXT

Imagine that responsibility for the design, organization or structure, implementation or operation, maintenance, and management of a business system is assigned to three people: one for the journey, one for the vehicle, and one for the destination. Then who will be responsible and accountable for integrating these separate parts into a singular, unique, integrated, and open system? The answer is the person who is responsible for business governance, which is the topic of the next chapter.

CHAPTER 9

Business Governance

A superior pilot is he who stays out of trouble by using his superior judgment to avoid situations, which might require the use of his superior skill.

—Paul Brickhill
Australian World War II fighter pilot, prisoner of war,
and author; from *Reach for the Sky: The Story of
Douglas Bader, Legless Ace of the Battle of Briton*

Business governance is conducted at the intersection between a CEO's right to exercise ultimate authority to change the business system and his or her obligation to assume ultimate responsibility for the system's success and failure. It is at this intersection where the CEO dilemma, a phenomenon discussed in Chapter 1, presents itself. In the career of any CEO, business governance is where the rubber meets the road. Questions regarding one's interactions and relationships with people when conducting business governance belongs to the realm of leadership. Hence, business governance and leadership are two sides of the same coin called executive management.

Business governance is the requisite occupational competence for promotion to the chief executive position. Current CEOs who admit to being befuddled and bewildered by stubborn systemic problems, and the disruptive effect of new and unforeseen circumstances on system integrity have, de facto, fallen victim to the Peter

Principle—they have reached their level of incompetence. People can escape this predicament when they gain insight into complexity. There are no shortcuts, quick fixes, or tools that can do the understanding for you—to learn, unlearn, and relearn—because only you can change your own perspective.

Chief executive officers who have fallen victim to the Peter Principle and who are unwilling or incapable of conducting a mind shift are facing a catch-22 situation. That means whenever they feel compelled to do something, they are forced to choose between:

1. Providing executive sponsorship for change, *regardless* of their bewilderment. Because that decision would be irresponsible, they should refuse to lead the change initiative.
2. Declining to provide executive sponsorship for change *because* of their bewilderment. Because this decision demonstrates their ability to act responsibly, which is regarded as a sign of a qualified leader, they should lead that change initiative nonetheless.

There is no escape from this paradoxical situation because:

- Justifying one's decision to act by arguing that something needed to be done, despite one's confusion, is admission of one's incompetence, which justifies their dismissal.
- Justifying one's decision *not* to act by arguing that one is perplexed by complexity and events is also admission of one's incompetence, which equally justifies their dismissal.

Regardless of this catch-22 situation, everyone is looking toward the CEO for guidance in restoring integrity to the business system. And whether the chosen course of action is responsible or irresponsible, employees are most likely to comply with the executive's decision—you are the boss, boss.

The lesson to be learned from this catch-22 situation is that one cannot provide leadership in situations that paralyze one's ability to think clearly and critically. This paralysis can only be lifted by gaining insight into the complex relationships between a business system's constituent parts and understanding the relevant principles of cause and effect and means and ends that facilitate a business to function as a singular, unique, integrated, and open system.

Acquiring more of the same specialized analytic skills or gaining more advanced or new leadership skills will not make any difference. Neither gold plating systems with the latest and greatest in advanced technology nor investing in another round of operational efficiency measures will succeed in restoring an executive's occupational competence. The suggestion of creativity as the antidote of choice, as proposed in the aforementioned IBM report, is also just another leadership myth—business gremlins run amok. Unfortunately, these myths seem to represent our current dominant level of thinking. I repeat what US Army General George Patton once said: "If everyone is thinking alike, then somebody isn't thinking." That somebody would better be not you.

WORKING ON THE BUSINESS

Michael Gerber raised awareness of the difference between working *on* a business and working *in* a business with his book *The E-Myth*. Business governance—a business system's design, organization or structure, implementation or operation, maintenance, and management—refers to working *on* a business. It is rather unfortunate that too many leaders fall short when it comes to organizing people, ideas, and hardware into a force—a business system—and directing that force toward the realization of the purpose for which it was intended. We have come to know this omission as *the missing link in the value chain*.

In addition to analytic skills, a leader will also need synthetic skills—an aptitude for creating synthesis—to generate synergy among the available people, ideas, and hardware. This is not a trick or best practice, but insight into relationships of means and ends and cause and effect.

Structure Is Key

These relationships of cause and effect and means and ends form the connections—or interfaces—between a business system's people, ideas, and hardware. Therefore, a business system's capability—and thereby its capacity—depends on the quality of these relationships. The pattern in all these relationships is called structure.

Taking music as an example, Clotaire Rapaille[1] gave a wonderful explanation of structure in his book *The Culture Code: An Ingenious Way to Understand Why People Around the World Buy and Live as They Do* when he wrote: "It is very interesting this notion of structure: music is not made of notes; music is the space between the notes. You can play different notes on a piano with your left or right hand, or on different instruments, but the only thing that you must respect is the space in between." The space in between successive notes is determined by differences in their pitch or frequencies, duration, tempo, and volume; it bridges the gap between successive notes in order to create rhythm, dynamics, melody, and harmony.

Likewise, the character and nature of a business system is defined by the space in between its component parts—interfaces that are the connections or interactions between the nodes that constitute a system. And the behavior of a value chain is determined by interfaces between its nine business functions. Business mechanics depends on interfaces between its journey, vehicle, and destination. The vehicle's capability and capacity is determined by the interactions between humans, machine, and the human–machine interface. The space in between has variation. This implies that, for example, success is the space in between an outcome and an aim, and that a problem is the space in between a current and a desired state (see Figures 9.1 and 9.2). Therefore, I call those words defined by the space in between *bridge words*.

Similarly, an authentic solution is the space in between root causes and a vehicle's intended purpose. Capability is the space in between the frequency of an occurrence and its volume. Employee engagement is the space in between a job description and pride of workmanship. Business performance is the space in between a certain quantity and a unit of time. Integrity is the space in between who you claim to be as a brand and your actual behavior as it is experienced by stakeholders. And, when something goes wrong, we say it fell through the cracks—something or someone is unintentionally neglected or ignored because the structure failed.

Character and Nature

The space in between contains the purpose of the relationship between elements on either side of the space in between: what it does, what it is used for, or why it is important to the organic whole to

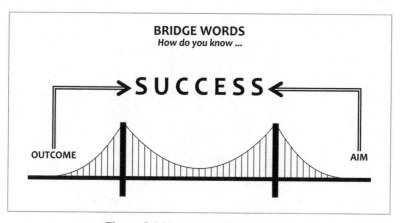

Figure 9.1: Understanding Success

Success is a structure that bridges the space in between
outcome and aim. The significance of this structure is determined
by the variation between outcome and aim.

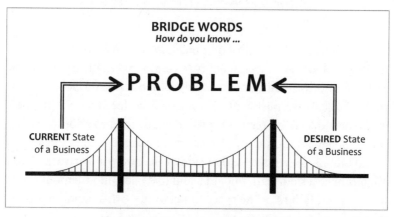

Figure 9.2: Understanding Problem

Problem is a structure that bridges the space in between current state
and desired state. The significance of this structure is determined
by the variation between current state and desired state.

which it belongs. Therefore, the space in between dictates the design, organization or structure, implementation or operation, maintenance, and management of a system, and thus the required trade-off decisions to be made for elements on either side of the space in between. Consequently, business systems derive their character and nature— brand identity—from their structure; not from gold plating an individual link in the value chain (see Figure 9.3).

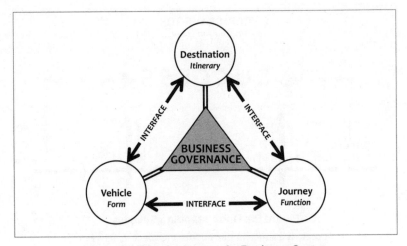

Figure 9.3: The Structure of a Business System

Interfaces are structures bridging the space in between
elements on either side of the space in between.

In addition, the quality of a business system's structure determines its robustness—its capability to continue operating even as new
and unforeseen circumstances unfold, both in good and bad economic
times. Executives must assume responsibility for system robustness
with their decisions regarding the design, organization or structure, implementation or operation, maintenance, and management
of individual elements on either side of the space in between. After
all, business systems fail, implode, and fold back into themselves due
to structural failure of the space in between—when adjoining parts
become unglued.

Providing Stability

The characteristics of an ideal or optimal vehicle are expressed in
terms of that vehicle's capacity to realize its intended purpose. This
requires that the vehicle is stable, which means that the outcome of its
processes is predictable—that it has no special-cause variation.

However, the fact that a vehicle is stable—that it only has
common-cause variation—does not imply that it has reached its
potential capability. It does not mean that it operates without creating any waste such as defects, overproduction, excessive inventory,

overprocessing, unnecessary process steps, wait-time for upstream processes, and confusion or waste of human potential.

The next step is thus to make the outcome of its processes more uniform, which implies an endeavor to create results that are consistently much closer to the specifications' average value—to narrow the bandwidth between upper and lower control limits (see Figure 7.6, "Capacity vs. Capability").

Given the fact that a business system needs to be agile—capable of adapting with flexibility and speed to new and unforeseen circumstances as they unfold—stability cannot be achieved by standardizing processes, adherence to strict procedures, and zero-tolerance policies because it renders a vehicle more rigid. Remember, people who believe that this is the way to create stability will have to change their level of thinking first before the system can start behaving with agility. After all, stability must be achieved through the interaction between people and the vehicle they operate. This principle was proven to be successful by the Wright brothers, who, instead of making their vehicle inherently stable—similar to the self-righting properties of a sailboat—relied on a pilot's basic stick-and-rudder skills to stabilize an inherently agile vehicle.

Key to Success

Here are some remarks by the Wright brothers from their published writings:

> The favorable results which have been obtained have been due to improvements in flying quality resulting from more scientific design and to improved methods of balancing and steering. The motor and machinery possess no extraordinary qualities. The best dividends on the labor invested have invariably come from seeking more knowledge rather than more power.
>
> Skill comes by the constant repetition of familiar feats rather than by a few over-bold attempts at feats for which the performer is yet poorly prepared.[2]

The footnote in their published writings regarding their skill reads:

> The Wrights understood that learning to fly was just as important as building the airplane itself. They recognized that an airplane is not a single device but a system of discrete mechanical and structural entities that all had to work in proper unison to achieve flight, with no one element more important than another. Realizing that the pilot is a part of this system, they devoted as much attention to learning to fly their aircraft as they did to designing and building them.[3]

The structure that makes this kind of interaction between operator and vehicle possible and successful—the human–machine interface—must be designed, built, and implemented right into the business system itself, so that it can be maintained and managed through a process of continual improvement by its leaders.

The function dedicated to structuring a business system is business governance,[4] a unique leadership responsibility aimed at keeping the outcome of a business system's processes nearly uniform, notwithstanding variations in market forces or internal friction and conflict. That is what working *on* the business means! Business governance is not only the missing link in the value chain; it is also the missing link in practically all curricula of business education, especially executive development.

BASIC STICK-AND-RUDDER SKILLS

The Wright brothers' approach to discovering the basic principles of flight—lift, control, and propulsion—gave birth to the scientific field of aeronautics. As a result of this discovery, the world of aviation evolved rapidly and dramatically. The cockpit of a modern aircraft has become a veritable control center for many complex manual and (semi-)automated systems. Hence the many gauges, dials, buttons, toggle switches, screens, displays, and aircraft warning systems such as lights, buzzers, and computer-generated voices (a.k.a. Bitching Betty, Barking Bob, or Hank the Yank). These systems vie for attention from the captain and first officer, which is the source of a wide range of distractions that have proven to be imminent causes of mistakes, errors, and violations. This, as will be discussed later, is an example of human error.

From the earliest days of flight training—regardless of the simplicity or complexity of the aircraft—pilots are instructed to follow the A-N-C axiom, a common approach to prioritizing one's attention during all flying situations, especially emergency conditions:

Aviate. Maintain control of the aircraft.

Navigate. Know where you are and where you intend to go.

Communicate. Let someone know your plans and needs.

Aviation studies have found that pilots get so focused on an activity or solving a problem that they sometimes forget to fly the aircraft. In one accident, the pilots became so distracted by a burned-out indicator light in the cockpit that they actually flew the aircraft into the ground. In another incident, the pilots were distracted by obsessing over the many features of their new GPS receiver that they accidentally flew straight through the terminal control area (TCA), as it is known in the United States (it is termed the terminal maneuvering area, TMA, in Europe)—the controlled airspace surrounding a major airport with a high volume of traffic. In other words, distractions often interfere with a pilot's basic stick-and-rudder skills—the art of flying.

Similarly, business leaders become so overly invested in implementing the latest version of another operational efficiency measure that they lose sight of the very purpose for which the business system was created in the first place—creating use value for members of their intended target audience.

For all intents and purposes, I am by no means suggesting that executives should not spend their precious time, money, and efforts on subjects such as efficiency, strategy, branding, leadership skills, social media, advanced technology, or restoring system integrity. As a matter of fact, I am a vocal advocate for executives' sponsorship for change. I am merely saying that the CEO of a business—equivalent to the pilot in command aboard an aircraft—should never waver in his or her commitment to the business system's core principle: giving buyers and users more in use value than taking from them in cash value. To be more specific, I'm warning against initiatives and investments that distract a CEO's attention from the core business function—in other words, the perfection of means and the confusion of ends. Decisions aimed at improving financial performance without improving the system's capability, or gold plating of (personally favored) component parts without creating more use value, are all too common examples of such distractions.

Slips and Lapses

The Human Factors Analysis and Classification System (HFACS) developed by Dr. Scott Shappell and Dr. Doug Wiegmann shows that too many accidents happen as a result of slips and lapses in a pilot's basic stick-and-rudder skills (see Figure 9.4): "Slips relate to observable actions and are commonly associated with attentional or perceptual failures. Lapses are more internal events and generally involve failures of memory."[5] Slips and lapses are skill-based errors, that refer to the performance of "routine, highly-practiced tasks in a largely automatic fashion with occasional conscious checks on progress. This is what people are very good at most of the time."[6]

Statistics of human error show that skill-based errors are the major contributor to unsafe acts and oftentimes they are seminal in causing accidents and near misses (see Figure 9.5).

Skill-based errors are often induced by distractions caused by the workplace environment, such as stress, fatigue, pressure to perform, dissatisfaction, attempts at doing more with less, worrying about the health and welfare of loved ones, financial worries, and fear of losing one's job.

Consequently, British psychologist James Reason—author of a seminal study of human error that formed the foundation for the HFACS model—concluded, "Although we cannot change the human condition [human fallibility] we can change the conditions under which humans work."[7] That includes decisions regarding employee benefits. Human resource managers and executives should consider how providing and withholding certain employee benefits affect employees' ability to keep their mind on the job, especially when execution of that job is critical to the vehicle's capability to create exceptional use value for its intended target audience. What is the fair market price of employees who are attentive to their environment because they deeply care about their job and colleagues, and who are committed to doing what is right when the business is in dire straits?

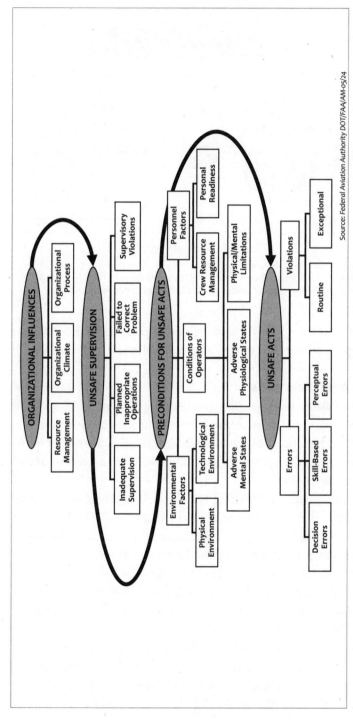

Figure 9.4: The HFACS Framework

Source: Federal Aviation Authority DOT/FAA/AM-05/24

The Human Factors Analysis and Classification System (HFACS) is a comprehensive human error framework, which folded the "Swiss cheese" model of human error (see Figure 9.6) into the applied setting, defining nineteen causal categories within four levels of human failure.

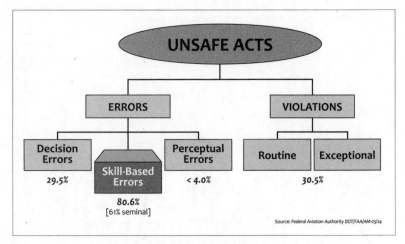

Figure 9.5: Unsafe Acts
Most errors and violations are committed by frontline operators—people who do the actual work—when they find themselves at the receiving end of poor business governance—an exclusive executive responsibility.

Then, what is your priority? Cutting cost or creating work conditions that engage, attract, and retain talented employees?

Errors and Violations

Errors are either made in *commission* (doing something that should not have been done) or by *omission* (not doing something that should have been done). Because it is much harder to correct errors of omission, these errors are generally more likely to cause an organization's decline or demise.

Violations refer to breaking the rules. A violation plus an error is frequently a formula for disaster in hazardous work. A violation is not in itself sufficient to cause an accident or near miss. However, it reduces the margin for tolerating a subsequent error considerably, which makes the error less likely to be forgiven.

Hence, an unsafe act is either a single error or violation, or combinations thereof, committed by people in operational positions whose jobs are, for instance, to fly aircraft, drive cars and trucks, perform maintenance, prepare food, sell goods and services, control (air, water, rail, and road) traffic, and enforce the law. In other words, these are people who find themselves at a vehicle's human–machine interface—the front line or sharp end—where errors and violations almost always have an immediate adverse effect on the capability and safety of the vehicle itself and that of others in the vicinity.

As much as those responsible for vehicle performance like to point fingers at a single individual, and designate the person as the proverbial rotten apple that spoiled the barrel, frontline operators cannot be held responsible for active failures that are induced by business governance, which is an exclusive executive responsibility. After all, frontline operators have no authority to decide any issues regarding the design, organization or structure, implementation or operation, maintenance, and management of the vehicle, which implies that they are oftentimes, in a sense, set up to fail. Therefore, scapegoating one or more employees whose job happened to be on the sharp end of the vehicle and replacing them with new recruits does not prevent human error from happening again and again.

Strategic and other top-level decisions made by governments, regulators, manufacturers, industry groups, designers, and organizational managers, which result in poor design, manufacturing defects, maintenance failures, incorrect implementation, gaps in supervision, undetected unworkable procedures, clumsy automation, shortfalls in training, or less than adequate tools and equipment, create latent conditions throughout a vehicle's system defenses. "Latent conditions are to technological organizations what resident pathogens are to the human body."[8]

Latent Conditions

Latent conditions shape a distinctive corporate culture while creating error-producing factors within individual workplaces.

However, individual latent conditions are noncritical. They just puncture holes in the system defenses where they lie dormant for a time. Because latent conditions are an inevitable part of organizational life, they are present in all vehicles. James Reason made this fact visible with his Swiss cheese model (see Figure 9.6).

Although latent conditions puncture holes in system defenses, they do no particular harm until some of those holes in all four system defenses line up to create what is called a "trajectory of accident opportunity." A generally incomprehensible interaction of one or more minor active failures with local circumstances is enough to unleash a chain reaction with the uncanny ability to defeat, disable,

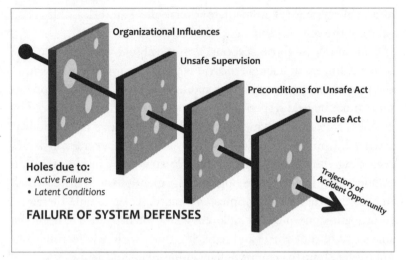

Figure 9.6: The Swiss Cheese Model (by James Reason)

Poor business governance decisions puncture holes in a business system's defenses. When holes in all system defenses line up to form a trajectory of accident opportunity, it only takes an otherwise insignificant incident to unleash a damaging chain reaction.

and bypass those system defenses, which results in a surprising vehicle failure. Consequently, James Reason concluded that "human error is not the cause of failure but a symptom of a failing system."

A Dutch study into marine incidents[9] found that:

- Seventy-five to 96 percent of all marine incidents involve human error.
- Each incident has 7 to 58 distinct causes.
- Fifty percent of those incidents have at least 23 causes.
- Each incident involves two or more people, each making two mistakes.

Many incidents of human error never result in a full-blown accident because a single link in the chain reaction was thwarted, thus preventing the entire chain reaction from running its course. Such incidents are called near misses. The Dutch study into marine incidents found there were 600 near misses for every accident.

Common-Cause Variation

Human error is an example of common-cause variation, which is particularly difficult to measure, predict, or manage. Even though there are thousands of actions or tasks that can go wrong, we have little chance of anticipating which ones will become a link in a future chain reaction. This reality is hard to accept knowing that thwarting a single link could prevent a chain reaction from taking place.

Furthermore, implementing measures to prevent anything that could possibly go wrong from actually going wrong at some future date will only grind the system to a screeching halt. For example, standardizing processes will lead to standardization of value propositions, which leads to commoditization that eliminates differentiation, which increases competitive market forces. Hiring more people to check for mistakes (quality assurance) does little for improving the performance of a vehicle as an organic whole, but a lot to increase cost and throughput time. However, improving process quality (capability), doing it right the first time around, guarantees product quality.

Therefore, creating certainty by way of micromanaging every single aspect of every process within the value chain is no antidote to worrying about uncertainty regarding anything that could go wrong, but adaptability to new and unforeseen circumstances is. This requires of any leader a sound understanding of what a vehicle is doing at any given moment in time, and what it is capable of doing.

HOW TO UNDERSTAND THE VEHICLE

American organizational theorist Myron Tribus said, "You can manage what you don't understand, but you cannot lead it." Therefore, business education, especially the leadership component within executive development programs, should instill a sound understanding and appreciation of business mechanics within the minds of its students—current and future CEOs.

After all, understanding refers to knowledge and comprehension of the many relationships between means and ends, and cause and effect that facilitate the functioning of all processes as a singular, unique, integrated, and open system. Insight into a system's character and nature (a brand's identity) leads to good discernment and foresight in decision-making processes. Appreciation refers to a sense of value and respect, which lends import to its function and form; you wouldn't harm what you value (see Figure 9.7).

On his inquiry into values, Robert M. Pirsig describes two modes of understanding systems: *romantic* understanding and *classic* understanding. Since he uses a motorcycle as a vehicle for conducting this inquiry into values, he describes romantic understanding as riding the motorcycle and classic understanding as motorcycle maintenance—hence the title of his book *Zen and the Art of Motorcycle Maintenance*.

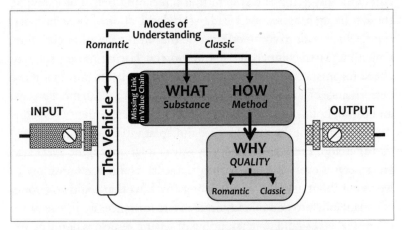

Figure 9.7: Modes of Understanding the Vehicle

A business system is not created, nor will it evolve by happenstance. In order for it to be successfully directed toward the realization of its intended purpose, its substance—component parts and their connections—will have to be organized (remember that organizing and directing form the missing link in the value chain). Decision makers organize substance according to their analogue for quality, the goal at which methodology is aimed.

Romantic Understanding of a System

In describing romantic understanding as riding a motorcycle, Pirsig referred to experiential aspects as perceived through the five traditionally recognized methods of perception, or senses: sound, sight, touch, smell, and taste. In other words, a perception of a system's look and feel, its immediate appearance on the surface. Romantic understanding is about what a business system means for its target audience and environment, which requires inspiration, imagination, creativity, intuition, vision for the utilization of its current potential, and seizing possibilities and opportunities as they unfold to improve system capability.

An observer can obtain romantic understanding of a business system from its brand identity, the use of its products and services, experience with its customer service, visiting (one of) its point(s) of sale, sophistication in the use of technology, seeing or entering its headquarter building(s), its geographical location(s), impression of its spokesperson, stories in the news, meeting with an employee, or being an employee oneself. Alternatively, an observer can consult public records to form an understanding through the names and curriculum vitae of its board members and executive team, or as a function of its past financial performance data.

Because romantic understanding is influenced by the observer's own prior knowledge of the system, personal experience, preconceived notions, opinions, or point of view, it is difficult to develop an unbiased understanding of a business system's true character and nature.

Classic Understanding of a System

In describing classic understanding as motorcycle maintenance, Pirsig referred to the meaning of the underlying form, or the purpose and function for which it is created. The underlying form of a vehicle can be perceived in terms of *what* its component parts are and *how* it functions—the substances of a vehicle and the method by which those substances are organized for their interaction with one another and to be directed toward the realization of its intended purpose.

Note that the boundaries around a substance or function exist only because that's how it was carved from the vehicle by an imaginary analytic knife. Pirsig describes this analogy as "an intellectual scalpel so swift and so sharp you sometimes don't see it moving. You get the illusion that all those parts are just there and are being named as they exist. But they can be named quite differently depending on how the knife moves." And, "It is important to see this knife for what it is and not to be fooled into thinking that motorcycles or anything else are the way they are just because the knife happened to cut it up that way. It is important to concentrate on the knife itself."[10] This knife represents our analytic thought, which accounts for the fact that different vehicles, offering similar products and services to a similar target audience, design their processes and organizational chart differently.

Breaking down a vehicle into various categories of substances and functions, and further subdividing them into ever finer and finer categories, creates a structured hierarchy of a vehicle's underlying form. The methodology for finding one's way through these hierarchies are deductive and inductive logic:

> **Deductive logic** reasons from the general (the hypothesis or theory) to the specific (the observations) or from cause to effect.

> **Inductive logic** reasons from the specific (discernment of patterns and paths among many intellectual thoughts and observations, all of which are believed true or found true most of the time) to the general (a specific conclusion, explanation, or theory).

Consequently, these forms of logic constitute opposing idea chains of analysis and synthesis. Disassembly of a comprehensive whole into its constituent substances and functions (analysis) destroys relationships that tie them together; the structure—the space in between—that makes substances and functions behave as a network or business system (see Figure 9.8).

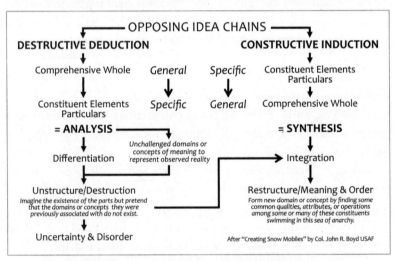

Figure 9.8: Opposing Idea Chains: Analysis and Synthesis

Decision makers call complexity their greatest source of frustration; they are overwhelmed by their experience of uncertainty and disorder. This is not surprising given the enormous emphasis on and demand for highly specialized analytic knowledge at the expense of synthetic knowledge as expressed in the missing link in the value chain.

Note that individual substances and functions can be organized into many different kinds of structures and directed toward the realization of different purposes, each causing the network to behave in distinctly different ways.

Therefore, selecting an individual substance or function on the basis of the vehicle's capability to interact with other substances and functions, instead of on the basis of that substance's or function's capacity—best in class (gold-plated edition)—is most beneficial for improving system performance. Structure—the space in between—can thus be identified as the interfaces between individual substances and functions that constitute a system.

Destructive Deduction

Therefore, analysis—removing any interfaces or structure between interconnected substances and functions—causes those substances and functions to lose the purpose or meaning which they derived from the domain to which they belonged. The resulting disorder, the lack of organization of the disassembled substances and functions and uncertainty regarding their meaning or purpose, is what baffles and bewilders executives from around the globe.

And no amount of additional highly detailed analytic knowledge of a single narrowly defined area of expertise can explain or predict the behavior of a network as an organic whole, let alone restore structural integrity to the system after disruption by new and unforeseen circumstances, which results in systemic problems that have a tendency to persist and recur.

Constructive Induction

Assembly of separate substances and functions into a comprehensive whole—a synthesis[11]—establishes structural relationships and interdependencies among those substances and functions. The ensuing network of constituent substances, functions, and relationships determines a vehicle's character and nature as experienced by its intended target audience for the duration of its journey (see Figure 9.9).

Therefore, the real vehicle is our present construction of systematic intellectual thought with which we create these substances, functions, and relationships. A vehicle is thus a system of concepts worked out in, as Colonel John R. Boyd would say, "People, Ideas, and Hardware: in that order." And executives who reject perceiving the business as a vehicle just need to change their level of thinking, which is exactly what Albert Einstein suggested when he said, "The problems that exist in the world today cannot be solved by the level of thinking that created them."

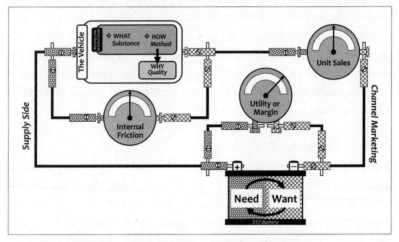

Figure 9.9: Vehicle–Environment Interactions

Business governance not only designs, structures or organizes, implements or operates, maintains, and manages the business system, it also creates authentic solutions for systemic problems, and adapts and adjusts the system when its integrity is threatened by new and unforeseen circumstances as they unfold.

Any effort to build, develop, grow, improve, change, reorganize, or reengineer a vehicle without adopting a new level of thinking will only recreate a similar vehicle that performs in a similar fashion as the one it replaces. That should not surprise anyone, and yet . . . that seems to be what best practices prescribe.

What—Substance

The best way to describe a complex assembly is to identify its substances: its subassemblies and its parts. A vehicle is such a complex assembly with constituting substances, such as its workforce, resource management, organizational culture and climate, organizational processes, organizational chart, owners, office, factory, warehouse, computer platform, motor pool, furniture, inventory, tools, intellectual property, brand, business plan, income projections, strategic plan, budget, and financial statements.

Note that this structured hierarchy expresses no value judgment—the words "good" and "bad" and all their synonyms are completely absent. This laundry list of substances is insufficient for gaining any significant understanding of the vehicle's character and nature unless one already knows how the vehicle operates.

How—Method

In addition to identifying substances, a vehicle can also be perceived as a structured hierarchy of line and staff functions, as captured in the value chain model—inbound logistics, operations, outbound logistics, marketing and sales, service, procurement, human resources, technology development, firm infrastructure.

The structural conceptual relationships between functions are sustained by methods that explain, predict, and account for how functions collaborate with one another within a vehicle. Without this knowledge, functions lose all meaning and purpose, causing employees to think that the jobs they perform are totally meaningless.

Methods establish countless interrelated patterns and paths within and among functional structural hierarchies that are so complex and extensive that no one person can understand more than a small part of them in a lifetime (see Figure 9.10).

Moreover, these methods keep developing as time goes by, and have resulted in vehicle complexity that consists of its own hierarchy in three major structures:

- **Professor Michael Porter's Value Chain.** The vehicle is divided into primary and support processes, which are subdivided into nine generic processes. Each of those generic processes can be further subdivided into finer subprocesses.
- **C H A F P I L O T Centralized Organizational Facilities.** All processes in the value chain outsource their activities, tasks, and processes for **C**ommerce, **H**ousing, **A**dministrative Organization, **F**inance, **P**ersonnel, **I**nformation, **L**egal, **O**rganization, and **T**ools and Technology to a dedicated specialized department.
- **Governance Aspects of a Vehicle.** Each process must be planned, executed, and controlled, which includes responsibility for the choice and deployment of a vehicle's

substances. The fact that these are often shared by multiple departments, processes, or business functions creates further interdependencies that increases the potential risk of reducing a vehicle's capability and capacity.

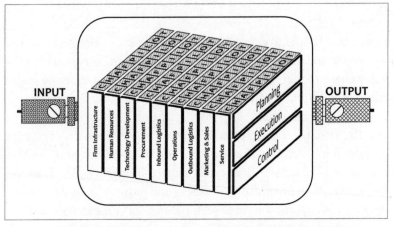

Figure 9.10: Three Sources of Vehicle Complexity

Three methods—templates—for organizing knowledge into a system in order to be directed successfully toward the realization of the purpose for which the system was created. Recognize the organizing and directing part, which we have come to know as the missing link in the value chain.

And yet the success of a vehicle's capability, sustainability, competitive advantage, brand identity, and profitability depends on the choice of methods for organizing substances into functions and directing functions toward the realization of a vehicle's intended purpose (see Figure 9.11). Remember, this organizing and directing is the missing link in the value chain.

Note that business governance aimed at the reduction of friction and conflict is synonymous with improving vehicle capability and capacity, which is an exclusive executive responsibility.

Why—Quality

The challenge before executives is deciding on the right method, which is no easy task given the fact that there is absolutely no shortage of methods—means to ends—available on the market from which to choose. Each method is defined by its own set

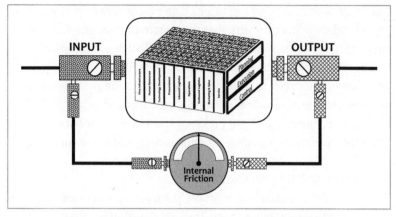

Figure 9.11: Resistance to Change inside a Vehicle

The extent to which one structures and organizes knowledge into a singular, unique, integrated, and open system, thereby controlling the level of internal friction and conflict to a minimum, determines the system's capability and thereby its de facto capacity for creating use value.

of characteristic properties, and they are all promoted as superior to competing alternatives.

As discussed before, selecting a method is not a matter of comparing features, advantages, and benefits among rivaling methods. Besides, a gold-plated version is often times just a "bigger, higher, faster, farther" version of the current method that failed at organizing substances into functions and directing those functions toward the realization of that vehicle's intended purpose. What counts is how well a particular method suits the specific needs and requirements of an individual vehicle at a given time and place on its life cycle. In other words, the kind of structural integrity it creates.

The concept that reveals suitability, if and when a method is the right choice, is called quality. Robert M. Pirsig says quality is "the goal toward which method is aimed." To illustrate this point, he writes: "If one builds a house using the plumb-line and spirit-level methods he does so because a straight vertical wall is less likely to collapse and thus has higher quality than a crooked one."

Whereas the goal of building a quality house is to prevent walls from collapsing by making them straight vertical, the goal of governing a quality business system is to prevent the value chain from collapsing into itself by maximizing the value chain's capability to perform as an organic whole—making sure that the system has integrity. Therefore, the goal toward which method is aimed is a vehicle's destination.

So, the question regarding which method is right can be restated as: "How will a decision maker recognize the amount of quality contained within an individual method given the need of a vehicle?" To answer that question, Pirsig picks up the analytic knife once again and splits quality into a classic understanding and a romantic one.

Understanding Classic Quality

This form of understanding relies on a rational and analytic approach to discover the underlying form. The first question involves an objective definition of quality. English dictionaries describe quality as a characteristic property that defines the apparent nature of something or someone, something that can be noticed as a part of a person or thing, a high level of value or excellence, and how good or bad something is.

The second question involves identifiable aspects that constitute quality. Here are some examples: capability, productivity, sustainability, profitability, durability, reliability, dependability, effectiveness, efficiency, capacity, user-friendliness, complexity, lead time, availability, flexibility, adaptability, compliance with regulations, future proof.

Methods, such as process behavior charts, Lean, Six Sigma, Management by Objectives (MBO), annual or merit ratings, and many other theories and best practices are just devices (means) to satisfy the requirements (ends) as stated by aspects of quality.

However, in the absence of a clear, well-defined, and shared goal of quality, aspects of quality are reduced to mere prescriptions, rules, techniques, gimmicks, or tricks—a set of building blocks that serve other purposes than that of the vehicle as an organic whole, such as indulging in gold plating and the thrill people derive from empowering the Bigger, Higher, Faster, Farther Syndrome.

When checking-off prescribed aspects of quality from a list becomes more important than satisfying the goal of quality, the underlying form is robbed of its value, thus becoming quality-free. The main concern of a quality-free business system—driven by the dark side of the force of life—is preserving the system for itself and by itself, thus becoming more efficient at making money, even if that requires sacrificing its capability to create use value, serve humanity, or enhance the culture. Then, methods are selected on the basis of their ability to increase bottom-line results, which is in conflict with the purpose for which the vehicle was intended. This misalignment—confusing means and ends—is a proven source of friction and conflict.

Similarly, people who obtain an academic degree by learning only to pass the required tests do not satisfy the goal of a quality education. By silencing their curiosity and forsaking their critical thinking skills, they dull their mind and kill their creativity.

The ubiquitous phenomenon of gold plating is the result of decision makers losing sight of the goal of quality. They have forgotten *why* they needed a method. They need a method because competitive advantage is found in the process whereby input variables are transformed into output variables (see Figure 2.6, "How to Succeed in a Competitive Market"). Method contains the proprietary recipe for creating the amount of use value that makes you the obvious choice supplier to your target audience. Who would care about the extent of a vehicle's capacity for being busy if it lacks capability of producing and delivering high use value?

Understanding Romantic Quality

This perception of quality is correlated with an individual's instantaneous impressions of something or someone. These impressions are nonrational value judgments—pairs of opposites—such as good or bad, right or wrong, worthy or unworthy, excellent or inferior, perfection or imperfection, goodness or evil. They are undistorted by any prescribed conscious thought structures. Who knows what records of past experiences, memories, and cultural heritage the nonconscious mind is playing in the background, thus influencing our emotions, intuition, or gut feeling?

Because this form of quality is understood before it is being chopped up into words in an attempt to define something or someone intellectually, it's a *you'll recognize it when you see it* kind of understanding. A decision maker just knows intuitively if a proposed method adds or subtracts from the goal of quality.

Every decision has consequences that determine if a decision is right or wrong—whether it agrees or disagrees with a decision maker's own conscience. In other words, there is no objective universal measure for right and wrong, or appropriate and inappropriate. And demanding to express romantic quality in terms of an objective and universally valid quantitative goal is defeating its purpose. Moreover, the individual who cannot tell if a method adds or subtracts from the goal of quality is generally seen as incompetent or not qualified to judge or to make a decision on the topic at hand.

People who perceive a vehicle from a romantic quality perspective (which seems to be the majority of business leaders), experience a death-force effect from vehicle complexity, which causes them to run away from anything that has to do with a vehicle's underlying form. The validity of this statement was confirmed by IBM in their aforementioned report "Capitalizing on Complexity."

On the other hand, there will always be people who rebuff romantic understanding of quality on the basis that it makes no "sense" to them. It makes no sense to them because they try to capture its meaning by means of traditional thought patterns. They extrapolate classic quality to arrive at romantic quality despite the fact that the latter is no extension of the former. Therefore, the source of their confusion does not originate from quality as a concept but from their own obsession with making *sense* through analysis. This makes them feel overwhelmed, bewildered, and befuddled. They are stuck.

Pirsig says that "stuckness is the psychic predecessor of all real understanding." This is similar to what Einstein said: "It's not that I'm so smart, it's just that I stay with problems longer." The longer you stay with a problem—stuck in your own opinions and traditional knowledge—the sooner you will recognize the "quality-reality" that gets you unstuck.

In other words, we need to change our perception of reality in response to quality because reality isn't static. Rather, it's made up, in part, of ideas that are expected to develop. Hence, reality is dynamic, which we experience as our rational understanding of an underlying form is modified from minute to minute when we work on it and see that a new and different rational understanding or explanation has more quality—that it is better; a gut feeling about what is right.

An age-old method for getting unstuck is meditation: the emptying of the mind to be free to receive inspiration from the universe. Romantic quality appears as a "lightbulb moment"—a sudden insight that cannot be explained rationally and is therefore described as "something clicked" or "getting it." This transcendence of stuckness provides decision makers with a sense of identity with the very problem that caused their becoming stuck.

Consequently, stuckness provides decision makers with experience in handling new and unforeseen circumstances, which is the difference between being self-taught and being institutionally trained. After all, theoretical knowledge always needs to be translated into a practical application. It is this translation where consulting, training, or education leave its students and clients to their own devices—expecting them to learn how to perform this translation through osmosis. Have you ever asked yourself from whom this knowledge and experience is supposed to rub off onto a decision maker?

The Goal of Quality

Instead of prescribing the various aspects that constitute quality, Pirsig chose to describe quality as "the continuing stimulus which our environment puts upon us to create the world in which we live." Decision makers become acutely aware of this stimulus every time they are signing off on a mission-critical decision with consequences for the business's future state.

This continuing stimulus is the goal of quality; it's an executive's vision of the future state of something or someone. A vision should be bold and audacious while appealing to the heart as opposed to the mind. A vision is created from infinite future possibilities as opposed to obstacles created by our current level of thinking about what is real and practical.

Vision is about one's firm belief in the future—faith.

Whereas Wilbur Wright held a firm belief in man's ability to fly, his contemporaries were convinced of the opposite:

Heavier-than-air flying machines are impossible.

—Lord Kelvin
British mathematician, physicist, and president
of the British Royal Society, circa 1895

Aircraft are interesting toys but of no military value.

—Maréchal Ferdinand Foch
professor of strategy at and commandant
of Supérieure de Guerre, 1911

These examples show that the environment stimulates differ-ent people in different ways, which does not imply that there are different kinds of quality. There are only differences in people's personal life experiences, which they use as analogues for assessing the meaning of new and unforeseen circumstances, addressing systemic problems, and predicting the future state of something or someone. Consequently, people with identical a priori analogues will see quality identically every time. Therefore, decision makers define themselves with their personal perception of quality.

RESPONDING TO EVENTS FROM OUR ENVIRONMENT

It's hard to deny that the human race has come a long way since the eviction of Adam and Eve from the Garden of Eden. Experiences with phenomena, such as those caused by the natural world, the universe, and the human condition,[12] have caused us to ask questions, discover explanations, and find solutions. Phenomena that we used to attribute to the gods are now explained by scientific laws, which has even prompted us to believe that we can predict, influence, and control many of nature's powerful forces. Consequently, adversity is no longer punishment from an irate god, but the result of our own decision or indecision; it is an opportunity to learn, often from our own mistakes.

Challenges regarding coexistence, cooperation, and interac-tion among people of different nationalities, ethnicities, religions, socioeconomic backgrounds, and social standings (which includes organizational hierarchies) often originate from differences in people's mental programming because of different personal experiences, edu-cation, culture, and individual preferences. These differences become formidable challenges to overcome when the decision maker on one or both sides of the argument solely identifies with ego, which makes any agreement on a possible solution impossible to achieve. Despite the fact that there are no universal laws for human relations, apart from the Golden Rule,[13] we have made great strides in this realm too.

And so, decision makers keep being challenged by the environ-ment on many aspects such as automation, technology, exploration, organization, direction, leadership, capability, human factors, capacity, social responsibility, environmental consciousness, human rights, labor rights, antitrust laws, privacy, and international treaties. Whereas some challenges result from a natural progression of events, many more are of our own making. Furthermore, every aspect comes with its own set of consequences that hit different businesses, industries, or countries differently and at different points in time.

Quality as an Event

After Adam and Eve ate the apple from the forbidden Tree of Knowledge of Good and Evil, they felt ashamed. This was the first moment in human history where mankind became aware of good and evil. Thereafter, we were conscious of our ability to choose to be or to do good or bad. This inborn pre-intellectual awareness is what we now know as quality. This means that quality makes us aware of the world around us.

Pirsig writes: "Quality is not a thing but an event. It's the event at which the subject becomes aware of the object." Events take place at the leading edge where the present meets the future—the first time a decision maker is confronted with new and unforeseen circumstances as they unfold.

It is at this event that decision makers get to choose between listening to their inner voice or rationalizing their response by asking themselves what others would do in their position or what stakeholders would expect of them. However, the leading edge is neither the time nor the place for intellectual thought because a mental subdivision of the vehicle into hierarchical structures would bring it to a standstill, which interrupts the journey.

Pirsig calls the absence of intellectual thought "pure quality," which will confuse and bewilder any chief decision maker. Being on this leading edge, in the present moment, gives anyone the feeling of being alive, which was described by Victor Frankl[14] as the purpose of life. This is the moment for a decision maker's authenticity to shine through—or it's when and where an individual is found out to be inauthentic because his or her ego identification is more concerned with what others think or might say or with emulating an image that was portrayed by some authority on leadership issues.

The Risk of Amoral Behavior—Doing Whatever It Takes

Actions that are justified on the basis of rational intellectual thought can only be legal or illegal. Moreover, such actions can be amoral or immoral and still be legal. In other words, decision makers who only rely on classic quality to the exclusion of romantic quality risk pushing their conscience beyond shame. People who are beyond shame reject the common frame of reference regarding values such as the rule of law, respect, humility, decency, kindness, or courtesy that bonds all of humanity.

Without any common ground—a frame of reference—among people, there no longer is any basis for reconciliation of conflicts. A convenient disguise for this dichotomy in values within the world of business is the all-too-common expression "Don't take this personally, this is business," as if "personal" and "business" are alternate universes governed by different sets of law, ethics, and mores.

Using financial modeling and calculation methods as the sole rationale for making so-called tough decisions is an example of excluding romantic quality from the decision-making process. Romantic quality is eliminated when money is perceived as the highest value and when everything has been given an arbitrary price tag, including human beings, clean water, clean air, liberty, freedom, and animals' natural habitats. As a result, calling for a trade-off decision between pleasing providers of risk capital—the shareholders, which include many decision makers themselves—and protecting the rights of employees has become a perfectly rational and therefore valid request. This is but an amoral excuse for absolving oneself as the ultimate decision maker.

However, employees are neither freely interchangeable commodities with academic degrees, vocational education and training, skills, and experience for resource specs; nor are they assets that turn into liabilities the minute profitability is squeezed. The fact that such trade-off decisions are regarded as a best practice by some executives and management consultants does not make this morally justified. Ascribing a higher value to money than to humanity is a failure to recognize that financial investments can only be transformed into productivity and capability if there are sufficient work opportunities for people. Please be reminded of Thornton Wilder's insightful quote:

"Money is like manure; it's not worth a thing unless it's spread around encouraging young things to grow."[15]

Stimulation that Makes Us Create the World in Which We Live

Psychologists have undertaken many rational analyses of what people want from life to determine what they need and what makes them pursue the realization of those needs.

In his 1943 paper "A Theory of Human Motivation," Abraham Maslow introduced his concept of a hierarchy of needs. He described the highest level of human needs in the following way:

> What a man can be, he must be. This need we may call self-actualization. It refers to the desire for self-fulfillment, namely, to the tendency for him to become actualized in what he is potentially. This tendency might be phrased as the desire to become more and more what one is, to become everything that one is capable of becoming.

The drive compelling us to engage in behavior that contributes to our self-actualization is called intrinsic motivation. When we engage with life in the pursuit of individual needs that are intrinsically rewarding, we will feel alive. We can only truly feel alive when we live in the present moment—the frontier between present and future. Time appears to stand still when the past and the future recede, when the only time is *now*.

On the frontier between present and future there is only romantic understanding of new and unforeseen circumstances, which provide leadership opportunities for those people who assume personal responsibility for delivering a timely and adequate response. It was Sir Winston Churchill who said, "The price of greatness is responsibility." Great leaders help develop the world in which we live, for us as human beings, as a business, as a nation, and as a species to evolve and become everything we are capable of becoming.

"Motherhood" Position

A business leader can only respond in a timely and adequate manner to an unfolding event if she or he has a clear vision of the future state of a vehicle, as opposed to the result of a cost–benefit analysis. This should be a unifying vision that "is rooted in human nature so noble, so attractive that it not only attracts the uncommitted and magnifies the spirit and strength of its adherents, but also undermines the dedication and determination of any competitors or adversaries."[16] Boyd called this a "motherhood" position, meaning a position to which no one can object, like the mythical "motherhood, apple pie, and the American way."[17]

The goal of a motherhood position is to improve one's capacity for independent action by building support for and attracting the uncommitted to one's cause. After all, national and local governments and the public are more likely to facilitate and support the development of commercial endeavors that help create the world in which we live rather than those with detrimental effects on humanity and on communities in which we live and raise our children.

This means delivering use value that "represents the cultural codes of conduct or standards of behavior that constrain, as well as sustain and focus, our emotional and intellectual responses."[18] In other words, to demonstrate moral behavior in our interactions with the environment.

According to Boyd:[19]

- We **interact morally** with others by avoiding mismatches between what we say we are, what we are, and the world we have to deal with, as well as by abiding by those other cultural codes or standards that we are expected to uphold.
- We **interact mentally** by selecting information from a variety of sources or channels that allow us to generate mental images or impressions that match up with the world of events or happenings that we are trying to understand and cope with.
- We **interact physically** by opening up and maintaining many channels of communication with the outside world, hence with others out there, that we depend upon for sustenance, nourishment, or support.

Mismatches between "what we say we are, what we are, and the world we have to deal with" brings relationships to the verge of mental and moral collapse. This is how Colonel John R. Boyd described the consequences of moral-mental-physical conflict:[20]

Unless such menacing pressure is relieved, adversary[sic] will experience various combinations of uncertainty, doubt, confusion, self-deception, indecision, fear, panic, discouragement, despair, etc., which will further:

Disorient or twist his mental images/impressions of what's happening:

Thereby, disrupt his mental/physical maneuvers for dealing with such a menace;

Thereby, overload his mental/physical capacity to adapt or endure; and

Thereby, collapse his ability to carry on.[21]

Morality plays a vital role in understanding romantic quality (determining whether a decision is good or bad). Morality determines trust and credibility, and no one is immune to menace from amoral or immoral behavior. A breakdown in moral behavior is at the root of many problems within the internal and external environment. Here are some common examples that people frequently complain about: employee engagement, employee loyalty, the war for talent, wasteful behavior, productivity, the right to organize, employee benefits, bait-and-switch, brand loyalty, warranty, customer service, marketing hype, cooking-the-books, embezzlement, fraud, social responsibility, environmental consciousness, and breakdown in trust.

This is how Boyd describes some of the worst breakdowns in moral behavior:

- **Evil** occurs when individuals or groups embrace codes of conduct or standards of behavior for their own personal well-being and social approval, yet violate those very same codes or standards to undermine the personal well-being and social approval of others.
- **Corruption** occurs when individuals or groups, for their own benefit, violate codes of conduct or standards of behavior that they profess, or are expected, to uphold.[22]

In conclusion: There are many methods available for organizing substance and directing them toward the realization of the vehicle's purpose. "In each case there is a beautiful way of doing it and an ugly way of doing it, and arriving at the high-quality, beautiful way of doing it, both an ability to see what 'looks good' and an ability to understand the underlying methods to arrive at that 'good' are needed," writes Robert M. Pirsig in his inquiry into values.

Once leaders understand and appreciate the vehicle—show gratitude for people's craftsmanship, ingenuity, resourcefulness, and dedication to doing their job to the best of their abilities—they will make the right decisions unselfconsciously. Any decision that detracts from quality violates their sense of integrity. This is a trait often associated with craftsmen who experience pride of workmanship when they are solidly engaged, completely absorbed, in solving stubborn systemic problems.

EXECUTIVE DEVELOPMENT POLICY

Most business schools have a department or center for executive development. The word "development" often refers to an academic policy or advocacy, a curriculum concerning core executive leadership capabilities that is promulgated by faculty thought leaders.

The word "executive" suggests that the program is designed for current and future executives, whose job relates to execution or the carrying into effect *something* about which there seems to be little consensus. As a result, it has been shrouded in a veil of mystique and vagueness. Consequently, I have defined that something as business governance—which is a unique executive leadership responsibility aimed at keeping the outcome of a business system's processes nearly uniform, notwithstanding variations in market forces or internal friction and conflict.

The Office of Continuous Learning and Career Management of the US Department of Labor identified an executive's job with a "Summary of the Executive Core Qualifications (ECQs) and Related Leadership Competencies."[23] It identifies the following:

Fundamental Competencies	and	Executive Core Qualifications
• Interpersonal Skills		ECQ #1: Leading Change
• Oral Communication		ECQ #2: Leading People
• Integrity and Honesty		ECQ #3: Results Driven
• Written Communication		ECQ #4: Business Acumen
• Continual Learning		ECQ #5: Building Coalitions
• Public Service Motivation		

The US Office of Continuous Learning and Career Management says this about business acumen: "This core qualification involves the ability to manage human, financial, and information resources strategically." It provides the following elaboration:

Financial Management. Understands the organization's financial processes. Prepares, justifies, and administers the program budget. Oversees procurement and contracting to achieve desired results. Monitors expenditures and uses cost–benefit thinking to set priorities.

Human Capital Management. Builds and manages the workforce based on organizational goals, budget considerations, and staffing needs. Ensures that employees are appropriately selected, appraised, and rewarded; takes action to address performance problems. Manages a multi-sector workforce and a variety of work situations.

Technology Management. Keeps up to date on technological developments. Makes effective use of technology to achieve results. Ensures access to and security of technology systems.

Learning Through Osmosis

Pirsig would recognize the US Department of Labor's summary as "riding a motorcycle," and Orville Wright would call it "learning to fly." Apparently, they assumed that every student is already fully competent in what was called respectively by Pirsig and Wright "motorcycle maintenance" and "designing and building aircraft," even though business governance is absent from practically any curriculum for business education.

Similarly, most literature on leadership assumes that its readers are already successful, providing prescriptions for becoming even more successful. These prescriptions are nearly always geared toward helping regular employees make fewer mistakes—not improving their leaders' "motorcycle maintenance" and "designing and building aircraft" skills. Where do you think executive work is most effective and an efficient use of executive time?

However, if the primary causes of executive underperformance—the Peter Principle as evidenced in the CEO dilemma; a lack of CEO effectiveness; and resistance to providing executive sponsorship for change—were deficiencies in any of these "executive core qualifications and related leadership competencies," then the alleviation of executive underperformance depends primarily on the removal of these deficiencies. Anything else would be just another business gremlin—an excuse for not facing reality; a denial of quality.

Primary causes of executive underperformance are lack of understanding vehicle complexity and inability to adapt and adjust the business system accordingly when new and unforeseen circumstances disrupt its structural integrity. No wonder, because curricula for executive development fail to provide their students with a basic insight into vehicle structure—the space in between individual links of the value chain and between its many silos of specialized knowledge. Because of this, executive leaders have become dependent on unquestioned adherence to prescribed instructions, while showing no sign of curiosity regarding the underlying principles that explain the "why" for fear of proving not to be all-knowing. This attitude shows identification with ego—serving personal interests instead of interests of all stakeholders.

How can anyone be expected to acquire basic stick-and-rudder skills without any understanding of the basic principles underlying business governance? However, that seems to be the reality of today's executive development education. Students are expected to learn what executives are supposed to do through osmosis. And yet board members expect them to "hit the ground running" because "there's no on-the-job learning."

The Importance of Vehicle Control
Regardless of the purpose one intends to pursue in business, it can only be realized through the intervention of a vehicle—a force

consisting of people, ideas, and hardware. The suitability or effectiveness of that vehicle is determined by its capability to realize its intended purpose. Given the fact that the business environment in which the vehicle must operate is dynamic and volatile, that vehicle must be capable of adjusting and adapting to new and unforeseen circumstances with flexibility and speed. In other words, a capable vehicle must be agile, yet stable, to be able to perform predictably. Note that stability is a function of interaction between the chief executive and the vehicle under his or her leadership.

That is why business governance is defined as a unique executive leadership responsibility aimed at making and keeping the outcome of a business system's processes nearly uniform, notwithstanding variations in market forces or internal friction and conflict.

Chief Executives—Operators Skilled in Business Governance

New leadership prescriptions are proposed on a regular basis and at a rapid succession, all claiming to improve business performance. And yet I cannot think of having seen one that is actually capable of creating a more stable business system, which outcome is more predictable, or capable of solving stubborn systemic problems. These prescriptions for "riding a motorcycle" simply have no effect on a rider's understanding of "motorcycle maintenance."

In discussing the merits of agile vehicles, as opposed to the inherently stable kind, Orville Wright wrote:

> These machines possess the means of quickly recovering balance without changing the direction of travel and of maneuvering with greater dexterity when required. On the other hand, they depend to a greater extent upon the skill of the operator in keeping the equilibrium. It may be taken as a rule that the greater the dynamic efficiency of the machine and the greater its possibilities in maneuvering, the greater the knowledge and skill required of the operator.[24]

The commonality between aviation and business is the recognition that the critical issue for both is vehicle control, or more succinctly how to steer, navigate, or govern a vehicle. The meanings of these functions find their origin in the Greek words *kybernao*, meaning to steer, and *kybernetike*, which is the word for "helmsman" and the etymological basis of the word "governor" (and also what James Watt called his ingenious feedback control device that transformed the use of steam engines). Cybernetics, as in the cybernetic process, is also derived from *kybernetike*.

Aircraft can be steered, simply put, by pushing or pulling a yoke and stepping on rudder pedals, whereas the ability to steer a business vehicle relies on human interaction in the form of written and verbal and nonverbal communication, motivation, inspiration, and the sharing of a noble vision, which falls squarely within the realm of leadership studies. However, successful performance of these activities depends on the extent to which capable and suitable control functions have been implemented into the system's design, structure, and organization, and whether they have been properly maintained and managed.

Control Loops

Cybernetics, the science of control or guidance, is concerned with the communication and manipulation of information, and its use in controlling or guiding the behavior of hierarchical and complex natural and man-made systems (see Figure 9.12).

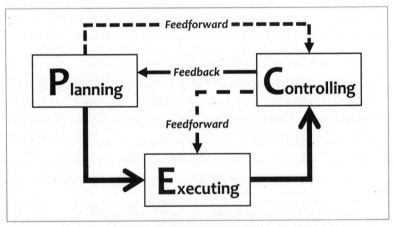

Figure 9.12: The Cybernetic Process or PEC Cycle

The cybernetic process of a business system is a methodology for humans and some machines to respond to or make adjustments to the value chain's design, organization, implementation, maintenance, and management, based upon input from their internal and external environments.

Having the ability to control the system requires:

- Communicating information on the system's desired state—how the system is supposed to perform
- Receiving information on the current state of the system—what the system is doing in real time
- Communicating information about necessary adjustments to the system

This flow of information instructing the system on what to do—feedforward—and information the system reports back—feedback—is known as the control loop. Consequently, control loops concern themselves with the following elements:

- **Standard setting.** Initiating and establishing the level of required performance.
- **Output monitoring.** Measuring the ongoing progress against the standard.
- **Comparison.** Checking for error signals; the level of divergence between the current state and the desired state of the system. Initiating corrective action if and when needed.
- **Compensation.** Taking remedial action by the device controller to reduce the error signal.
- **"Hunting."** Output "pulsates" above and below the required performance level, typically as a result of shortcomings in the governor or other speed control systems. It occurs because there is always a time lag between the detection of an error and the application of the correction. Corrections can either be applied to the execution process or to the standard or desired state of the system. Moreover, if the correction is not carefully applied it is easy to overcompensate.

Knowing Why

Orville Wright explained that flying or piloting skills cannot be separated from knowledge regarding the principles that make flight possible. In other words, the outcome of a specific control input can only be predicted when the operator knows why a specific control input will deliver the intended results, given the actual state of the vehicle and the challenge at hand. This kind of interaction between man and machine—the human–machine interface—makes a vehicle stable and behave predictably.

Whereas a pilot can reference an aircraft's flight envelope—indicating the capabilities of a specific design in terms of airspeed, wing loading (g-forces), altitude, payload, and other measurements such as maneuverability—business executives must rely on their personal sense for classic and romantic quality in order to assess the limits of their vehicle's capability.

By the way, the expression "pushing the envelope" comes from aviation, and refers to forcing the aircraft to perform maneuvers that are dangerously close to the limits of its capability or capacity—where it stalls and stops flying, enters a spin, or flaps and landing gear will be damaged if deployed. The fact that a pilot is capable of managing the flight controls in order to keep the aircraft straight and level does not imply that she or he is equally capable of coaxing the aircraft safely into a different direction, changing altitude or speed, completing takeoff or landing, or surviving an emergency situation. Indeed, piloting skills cannot be separated from knowledge regarding the principles that make flight possible.

Lack of Knowledge

Comparable to piloting an aircraft, governing a business system requires knowledge of and insight into a vehicle's capability—the principles that facilitate the creation of use value for its intended target audience. The fact that a vehicle's individual component parts have the capacity to do more, better, faster, or longer is irrelevant when the vehicle as an organic whole—people, ideas, and hardware—lacks the capability of utilizing that excess capacity, due to systemic problems, including internal friction and conflict. No motivational speeches or carrot-and-stick programs can make a vehicle perform beyond its capability limits.

Unfortunately, it seems as if executive development policies are making the same mistake as the contemporaries of the Wright brothers regarding the topic of governance. Because they were perplexed by the complex issue of control, they decided to focus all of their efforts on inventing an inherently stable vehicle. They were convinced that control could be added later as some form of accessory, comparable to attaching a rudder to a dinghy or a skiff by means of a pintle and gudgeon.

Complexity Is the Result of Evolution

Given the fact that the core business of any vehicle is to give its intended target audience more in use value than it takes from them in cash value, both a startup and an established business system need to perform the same business functions of the value chain. What is just another task for a startup requires a full-time job or even an entire department for an established mature company, for example, an IT, human resources, or procurement department. Activities that a startup performs manually is automated or even outsourced by a mature and established company. Complexity is thus the result of a startup's evolution into a mature business system, which is reflected in its organizational chart with increasing number of hierarchical layers between executive management and frontline operators.

Each link of the value chain can be perceived as *substance*, meaning the functions it contributes to the vehicle as an organic whole. The method by which these contributions are delivered is defined by a multitude of ever-changing management theories and tools. This was explained in Figure 8.7, "Modes of Understanding."

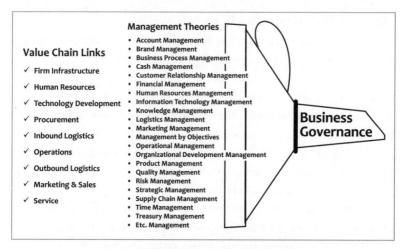

Figure 9.13: Management Integration

The value chain indicates that every business at any stage during its life cycle will have to perform the same functions as represented by the nine links in the value chain. What changes over time as the system develops and grows is the method—the use of management theories—by which those functions are organized including their size, form, and complexity. This can be accomplished using the same (paint-by-numbers) templates.

Implementing new, more, smarter, or more-efficient tools within the value chain does not change a vehicle's dependence on a pilot's basic stick-and-rudder skills for predictable, stable, and controlled performance; it just increases the number of interfaces between a value chain's component parts, while establishing more interdependencies among those parts (including tight coupling of resources), which creates more opportunities for human error, which requires management integration from its business governance (see Figure 9.13).

Uniqueness of Social Systems

Moreover, some theories and tools conflict with each other because of competing perceptions of the purpose of business governance. Most notably is the tension between making money and continual improvement of vehicle capability. This tension creates a process of *mutual poisoning*. Successful operational efficiency measures poison vehicle capability, and the resulting poor vehicle capability poisons the amount of cash value it can collect because it lacks capability of delivering the use value that it is marketing to its target audience. That's the Black Knight Syndrome in action.

The material form of vehicle capability is not an idea that springs ready-made out of any executive's mind, but it's the result of evolution. It is the ongoing discovery of basic underlying principles of vehicle control and a process characterized by learning from mistakes.

This evolution includes the discovery of new principles or laws that have made many innovative phenomena possible. This is how Orville Wright described his excitement of his own evolution: "Isn't it astonishing that all these secrets have been preserved for so many years just so we could discover them?"

Contrary to mechanical systems, business vehicles are social or organismic systems that are governed by principles that are less iron-clad than those of mathematics, physics, chemistry, or biology. Social systems are characterized by governance "of the people, by the people, for the people." The principles that determine the capability of social systems are norms and values such as laws, rules, regulations, contracts, procedures, courtesy, goodwill, respect, trust, moral rectitude, ethics, and above all, the Golden Rule: "Do unto others as you would have them do unto you."[25]

Preconditions for Success

The aforementioned process of mutual poisoning over the choice between money and humanity as the highest value should be obvious. Happy employees are engaged and have their minds on the job, which is the best prevention against human error. Decisions to cut wages and benefits, demanding that people do more with less, and instilling fear of losing their job while enforcing strict zero-tolerance policies create latent conditions for future incidents of human error when employees become distracted, dissatisfied, disengaged from their work, uncaring, or when they quit, especially when they quit at a time when you need them the most.

No wonder key talent learned to be only motivated by wages and benefits and to start hopping from one employer to the next, giving rise to high turnover and the war for talent. Therefore, schemes to reduce short-term cost can result in long-term suffering for vehicle capability. Remember, loyalty is a two-way street.

Gaining insight into vehicle capability, and more specifically its preconditions for success, is challenging for any executive because most aspects that constitute vehicle capability are, like an iceberg, invisible. These constituting parts are either material or immaterial (see Figure 9.14).

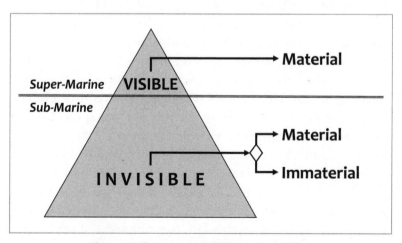

Figure 9.14: Aspects of Vehicle Capability

Just because aspects of vehicle capability are invisible, one should not assume they are therefore nonexistent or of lesser importance. In actual fact, invisible aspects of vehicle capability are the prerequisites for the creation of all its visible aspects.

During a site visit of a business system, the immensity and complexity of the arrangements that we know as supply-side and marketing and distribution channels—the value system—remain invisible. This includes public infrastructure such as roads, railways, airways, bridges, and airports, and the delivery of gas, water, electricity, and high-speed internet access without which normal operations come to a halt. Nor can visitors see the intellectual achievements behind the business governance of a vehicle, including its ability to organize substance into a force and to direct that force toward the realization of its intended purpose, through the sourcing of commodities, packaging, labeling, logistics, financing, hiring and training of personnel, legal protection of intellectual property such as trademarks and patents, research and development, quality improvement, and contractual obligations. In Chapter 5, under the heading "Creating a Common Point of Departure," we identified these elements as the environment of a business system: that what makes a cause not only necessary but also sufficient to explain an effect such as the behavior of a business system.

Education, Organization, and Discipline

The least visible of all is the educational background of all stakeholders, which extends from primary schools to universities and specialized research establishments. As a matter of fact, continuous education is the foremost precondition for the success of any business system and its vehicle, journey, and destination.

A key difference between aspects of vehicle capability is the fact that material aspects can be planned, created, ordered, borrowed, leased, or bought. Development of immaterial aspects depends on their evolution over time. Since the primary causes of executive underperformance must be found within immaterial aspects—in particular, executives' education, their ability to organize and direct (the missing link in the value chain), and discipline—then the alleviation of executive underperformance depends primarily on the removal of these deficiencies. Discipline refers to a character trait that demonstrates patience, composure, tenacity, commitment, and self-control, as opposed to spontaneity, ad hoc, or hope for the best.

In his epic book *Small Is Beautiful: Economics as if People Mattered*, E. F. Schumacher illustrates that the invisible aspects are the prerequisites for the creation of all visible aspects as follows:

Development doesn't start with goods; it starts with people and their education, organization, and discipline. Without these three, all resources remain latent, untapped, potential. There are prosperous societies with but the scantiest basis of natural wealth, and we have had plenty of opportunity to observe the primacy of the invisible factors after the war. Every country, no matter how devastated, which have a high level of education, organization, and discipline, produced an "economic miracle." In fact, these were miracles only for people whose attention is focused on the tip of the iceberg. The tip had been smashed to pieces, but the base, which is education, organization, and discipline, was still there.

Note that a miracle is often described as a change in perception, which sometimes takes a hero's journey to manifest itself.

The objective of executive development policy must be to match students' evolution in their education, ability to organize and direct, and discipline to follow through with a newly acquired mental programming, with the ongoing evolution of the invisible aspects that generate the visible aspects that improve vehicle capability. After all, creativity is a special form of vehicle development.

AUTHENTICITY AND CREATIVITY

The quality of a system's business governance is determined by the CEO's application of his or her authenticity and creative ability when structuring work processes into a singular, unique, integrated, and open business system. Therefore, no CEO will have to rely on a best practice or wait for the publication of a detailed step-by-step prescription—the *Idiot's Guide to Authenticity and Creativity*. Simply by exercising their free will to do what is right, they can improve their own value chain's capability today, starting right now. In addition, acting on one's authenticity and personal experiences with quality guarantees that the value chain's capability and capacity align with one's leadership and strategic skills. This reinforces the idea that competitive advantage is the result of good business governance.

Freedom

In the first chapter of this book, I discussed the movie *Instinct* and the interaction between the psychiatric patient Dr. Ethan Powell and his treating physician, Dr. Theo Caulder. When Powell escaped from the institution, going back to live in the wild with his gorillas, he left a farewell letter addressed to Caulder in which he writes: "You were right. Freedom is not just a dream. It's there, on the other side of those fences we build all by ourselves."

We fence ourselves in with ideals and ideologies about perfection, the pursuit of one-size-fit-all magic silver bullet solutions for doing business in bad economic times, fear of charting our own journey through uncharted territory, fear of making mistakes, fear of listening to one's intuition, fear of cooperation with competitors, and other impediments. And yet we claim to be bold, adventurous, creative, and innovative, but when an opportunity presents itself, it is subjected to a focus group in order to decide on its adoption or rejection. That's how innovation is reduced to pursuing the so-called low-hanging fruit that anyone can pick.

Occupational competence is not demonstrated by the acquisition of better, higher, and more prestigious specialized knowledge within the same area of expertise but by what one does with the knowledge and experience one already acquired up until now. As a matter of fact, this body of knowledge and experience already contains most answers you are looking for. This means whenever your peace of mind is disrupted by the countless manifestations of the same root dysfunction, you most likely already know instinctively what to do.

The trouble is that, just as in psychotherapy, you are not yet aware of it. While the right answers have been inside of you all along, you just do not know which questions to ask in order to bring them to light. Therefore, a good consultant will not force his or her solution upon a client, but will ask questions to extract it from the client. You will know if that solution has integrity and authenticity when it resonates with your personal values and beliefs. That's when you'll experience freedom—freedom from dogma and from other prescribed ways of thinking, acting, deciding, and leading.

Development from Within

Whenever the brain is used just as a repository for data and facts—rote memorization as a result of teaching to the test—we are not using the mind. Regurgitating what has been stored neither gives meaning to that knowledge nor translates theoretical knowledge into a practical application.

Have you ever experienced how some consultants or coaches explain a theory about what to do but then leave you to your own devices in order to figure out the actual practical application—all the details, the logic involved, the assumptions about what you believe you know but don't really know and what they anticipate you will do but then forget?

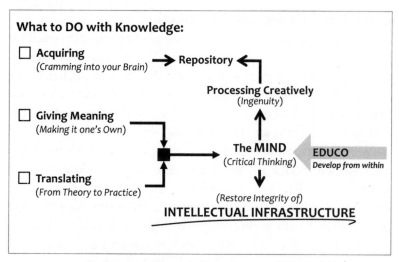

What to DO with Knowledge:

☐ **Acquiring**
(Cramming into your Brain) → **Repository**

Processing Creatively
(Ingenuity)

☐ **Giving Meaning**
(Making it one's Own)

The MIND   **EDUCO**
(Critical Thinking)   Develop from within

☐ **Translating**
(From Theory to Practice)

(Restore Integrity of)
INTELLECTUAL INFRASTRUCTURE

Figure 9.15: *Educo*: To Develop from Within

Intellectual infrastructure is the human component—knowledge, skills, and abilities—required for businesses and organizations to function effectively. This human component is developed from within when one feels intrinsically motivated to use one's mind to that effect. The mind is one's brain in action—thinking one's own thoughts.

The origin of the word "education" is the Latin *educo*, which means to develop from within through curiosity, asking questions, and running the risk of making mistakes and looking foolish! Different personal backgrounds and exposure to different environments, areas of interest, and cultures will evoke those questions that start more often than not with *Why* instead of *What* and *How*, and entice experimenting with new concepts. It shows that there are no interesting or uninteresting topics, just interested and uninterested people (see Figure 9.15).

When Colonel John R. Boyd assisted Colonel Michael Wyly USMC in creating the Amphibious Warfare School (AWS), they put together an extensive reading list. They argued that "the AWS was fundamentally an educational institution, and educational institutions are places where students consider all ideas. One of the best ways to do that is to have students read."[26] And so they now complete extensive reading lists covering a wide range of topics that enhances their judgment, which puts them in a much better position to make well-informed decisions.

Cultivating Intellectual Infrastructure

Boyd's briefings are testimony to his unrelenting efforts to teach his students how to survive on their own terms in fluid, dynamic, and ever-changing environments. His premise was that "he who can handle the quickest rate of change survives." Therefore, he took issue with anyone who would treat his body of knowledge as doctrine because he feared that "what is doctrine on day one becomes dogma forever after."[27]

Disregarding valid existing knowledge and experience because it does not fit a specific and prescribed rigid line of thinking is corrosive to the intellectual infrastructure—the human component (i.e., knowledge, skills, and abilities) required for businesses and organizations to function effectively—within any business. It causes unnecessary friction and conflict, while eroding joy and the pride of workmanship.

The problem with dogma and ideology is that they tend to be a nonthinking. Adhering to an ideology is a lot easier on the mind than formulating one's own opinions developed through critical thinking, because you already know the answer to everything and you do not have to learn anything new. Dogma and ideology are forms of absolutism that are impenetrable by new facts. The adherents do not allow for any critical discussions. Whenever you make an attempt to have one, they will slam the door on you by asking if you are in favor or against their viewpoint; it's always either one or the other, you are with them or against them and there is no middle ground. No grey tones, just black or white.

Stating that the purpose of a business is to develop the capability of its value chain instead of growing bottom-line results is met with a parry and riposte in the form of a rather rhetorical question: "Oh, so you think that money is not important, huh?"

Beware of "Incestuous Amplification"

The certainty of personal infallibility prevents any learning from mistakes. While persisting in the soundness of their own judgment, ideologues risk piling one mistake on top of the other, causing a chain effect of unwanted results, without knowing it. Because they tend to socialize only with like-minded people, they are prone to what Boyd called, "incestuous amplification"; their perception of reality is distorted by each observer's preconceived notions. As a result, their observations provide justification for those preconceived notions, which in turn validates their beliefs.

Therefore, Boyd taught his students to look for strategic opportunities in an opponent's mismatches between their observations of the outside world and their mental programming. Remember that whenever there is a mismatch between your own observations of a new and unforeseen event in the outside world and your interpretation of what is happening in real time, you will experience confusion and disorder and you will procrastinate making any decisions. Eventually, this condition can lead to panic and abandonment of one's responsibilities.

The ability to make sense out of new and unforeseen circumstances by creating mental images, one after the other, until you find a match or a mismatch, is what Boyd identified with the German word *Fingerspitzengefühl*, meaning "tip of the finger feeling." It's an intuitive form of knowing that is often correct—similar to romantic quality. It will only become intuitive when you have opened your mind to all ideas and thus question all assumptions, theories, and doctrines. Your opinions will then tend to be more broad-minded and flexible.

Remember that everything is created twice—first mentally and then in its physical form. We can only solve systemic problems—challenges that originate from the value chain's design, organization or structure, implementation or operation, maintenance, and management—by changing our current level of thinking. If you want to change the physical form, you must first change your own mental programming by allowing new ideas and points of view to enter the mind for contemplation.

New ideas will find you every day, calling you to embark on a CEO adventure. Do you have the willingness, and the courage, to answer that call this time? Why would you want to wait until you have exhausted all viable alternative options, or when you have run out of time and money, or when there is talk about your replacement? Why wait?

WHAT HAPPENS NEXT

At this point, there should no longer be any doubt that a business is a singular, unique, integrated, and open system. That means that decisions made by a chief executive officer reverberate throughout every aspect of the system's resource management, organizational climate, and organizational processes. This assertion raises the question of the role of the chief executive in solving systemic problems—what does the system require of the person with ultimate authority and ultimate responsibility in order to sustain itself?

The next chapter explores the role of the chief executive and the urgent need for business governance in addition to leadership—they are two sides of the same coin. Remember, only a different level of thinking will produce different outcomes.

CHAPTER 10

Role of the Chief Executive

There is no expedient to which a man will not resort to avoid the real labor of thinking.

—Sir Joshua Reynolds
influential eighteenth-century English painter;
from a speech addressed to the students
of the Royal Academy, December 1784

We have developed a vocabulary that equips our students with the ability to speak with authority about subjects they do not understand.

—Russell Ackoff
American organizational theorist and a pioneer
in the field of operations research, systems
thinking, and management science

B ecoming an inspired CEO—a master of two worlds—is a form of self-actualization because it appeals to a leader's id; it is an invitation to become the greatest form of who we are intended to become—our authentic Self.

Authenticity requires critical thinking—analysis and synthesis— and thinking for oneself, which requires moral fortitude. Because there is no Idiot's Guide to being authentic, a best practice prescribing an *n*-step method for you to follow, you'll need to summon the power of your conviction about what you believe is right and wrong. Yes, that can be scary!

Thought is immensely important because it will always cause the creation of form on some level. Its effect—good or bad—will make itself known somewhere in some unforeseen future situation. This is a demonstration of the most fundamental law of the universe, the law of cause and effect—thought is the cause and our life experiences are its effects.

The world of business education, consulting, coaching, and mentoring proffer prescriptions, best practices, methods, and tools for what to do and how to behave under certain circumstances to obtain success. Who doesn't want to be successful as quickly as possible, but at what price?

Yet many prescriptions for success have resulted in low-quality and ill-conceived processes and products, illegal practices, cartel formation, unsafe working conditions, stagnating wages, withholding of employee benefits, contamination of the environment, outsourcing of jobs to low-wage countries, replacing people by machines, and other negative results. If those long-term effects are the price we are supposed to pay for short-term success, then what was the problem these prescriptions for success intended to solve?

These unintended and unwanted consequences cannot be addressed and turned into successes on the level of experience or effect. As Dr. W. Edwards Deming said, "Experience by itself teaches nothing. Without theory, experience has no meaning. Without theory, one has no questions to ask. Hence, without theory, there is no learning."[1] Learning changes our thinking (cause), which cannot fail to change the outcome of our decisions and actions (effects).

Popular propositions for solving problems on the level of effect usually involve copying from others—investing in a better tool, a faster process, or a newer something. No wonder there is a convergence of value propositions among competitors. But copying from one system and implementing it into another is unlikely to work well. When it does work well, it usually involves a very simple process with few interactions with or dependencies on other processes within the containing system.

The inherent danger in attempting to solve problems on the level of effect is to mistake correlation of events for causation of them. Correlation between a decision or an action and the occurrence of an effect does not automatically imply a cause-and-effect relationship. Cause-and-effect relationships are based on theories that explain or predict a certain outcome or effect. In other words, the occurrence of unintended and unwanted consequences is a signal that what you thought would happen and what actually happened are misaligned.

As an executive decision maker, you cannot just demand different effects if you are unwilling to change your level of thinking—or resist educating yourself on new, different, and unfamiliar theories. Note that the operative word here is "willing." Are you willing to open one corner of your mind to the possibility that there might be a different way? Are you willing to learn, unlearn, and relearn? Nobody cares about your intentions but your willingness means everything.

So which theories, values, principles, and methods are you willing to embrace or reject? What kind of decisions do you think amount to "good" leadership, and what is your definition of success? Do you know the current state of your business system, and do you have absolute clarity on the system's desired state? In other words, do you know the root cause(s) of your systemic problems? Ultimately, what is your vision, or what do you envision for the business to become under your leadership? What do you want your legacy to be? Do you care? Have you given these questions any critical and independent thought?

COMMANDER'S INTENT

Colonel John R. Boyd wrote extensively about success, but not just as a prescription for winning a battle and the war but for winning "on your own terms." Success, as mere survival, is not enough! Boyd explained what he meant with "your own terms" as simple criteria—the desired state—for the prevention of disintegration and collapse. He called the following criteria prerequisites for shaping a sensible grand strategy:

- Support the national goal.
- Pump up our resolve, drain away adversary resolve, and attract the uncommitted.
- End conflict on favorable terms.
- Ensure that conflict and peace terms do not provide seeds for (unfavorable) future conflict.[2]

Boyd explained the basis for a grand strategy as "an appreciation for the underlying self-interests, critical differences of opinion, internal contradictions, frictions, obsessions, etc., that we as well as the uncommitted and any potential or real adversaries must contend with."

Whenever people are working together under stressful and uncertain situations, there is bound to be friction and conflict, and Boyd's grand strategy serves as a guide for leaders to shape the terms of conflict to their liking—to maneuver themselves in the best possible situation to not only survive but thrive. In other words, do not antagonize your workforce with fear and threats of pay and benefit reductions, layoffs, or any other measure threatening their livelihoods, because it causes them to disengage themselves from their jobs. The same principle applies to interactions with buyers, users, and vendors, and the public at large.

Please recall the devil's triangle discussed in Chapter 1, which is comprised of the MOTIQ variables money, time, and quality. These three variables form a triangle because they can be traded off against each other; less of one can be compensated by more of another, and vice versa. However, demanding employees to be more productive—generating the same or an even greater output in less time at a lower cost—can only be achieved at the expense of quality. Guess what that does to the morale in the mind of the employees? As Deming proclaimed time and again, all any worker wants is the privilege of doing a good job; they want to experience pride of workmanship and job satisfaction. Being denied the opportunity of doing a good job (encouraged to cut corners), people become disengaged, cynical, and indifferent.

Boyd said the national goal should be "to improve our fitness, as an organic whole, to shape and cope with an ever-changing environment."[3] This raises some questions. How can businesses support the national goal? Why would they support the national goal; what is in it for them? Is the national goal supported by transferring major manufacturing capability—know-how—and capacity oversees, thus making us dependent on imports from foreign countries? Is the national goal supported when profits are not ploughed back into the national economy, thus reducing tax revenue? Is the national goal supported when economic principles defeat humanitarian principles; for example, when profit motives limit people's access to health care—curative and preventative—and higher education, thus suboptimizing the workforce. Is the national goal supported by lax regulation on zoning, employee rights, and environmental protection, thus socializing the cost for unintended consequences? Is the national goal supported by unwarranted tax cuts that take away money from infrastructure maintenance and improvement, thus increasing the cost, safety, and security of transportation and communication? Is the national goal supported by concentrating wholesale and retail power in the hands of only a few (too big to fail) juggernaut conglomerates, thus privatizing profits and socializing losses? In earnest, is there any executive decision maker who does not grasp the intricate relationships between an economy that is working for every citizen, and a healthy, sustainable business climate? A rising tide lifts all boats! Note that an *ever-changing environment* thrusts upon us a continuing stimulus to create the world in which we live. So, what is your analogue for "good" quality, and what will be your response to new and unforeseen circumstances as they unfold? Will your response be in alignment with who you are—your id?

Consequently, Boyd said: "What is needed is a vision rooted in human nature so noble, so attractive that it not only attracts the uncommitted and magnifies the spirit and strength of its adherents, but also undermines the dedication and determination of any competitors or adversaries." Boyd outlined the following ingredients as essential for the pursuit of such a vision:

> **Insight.** The ability to peer into and discern the inner nature or workings of things.
>
> **Initiative.** The internal drive to think and take action without being urged.
>
> **Adaptability.** The power to adjust or change in order to cope with new or unforeseen circumstances.
>
> **Harmony.** The power to perceive or create interaction of apparently disconnected events or entities in a connected way.[4]

Chet Richards, one of Boyd's close associates during his time at the Pentagon, writes in his book *Certain to Win* that Toyota crafted their unifying vision as "Take our destiny in our own hands." This requires a different kind of leader, someone who sees himself or herself as a follower of a distant star, a vision, which is reflected in one's eyes. Other people who resonate with that light will then rise to the occasion as collaborators.

Is there any executive leader who honestly believes that making money to pay for their own exorbitant compensation packages and shareholder dividends is a unifying vision for a workforce whose own compensation packages are constantly under attack and whose job security is always threatened?[5] Remember how Boyd emphasized the importance of moral leverage.[6] Employees disengage when executive decisions violate basic codes of morality and ethics, thereby exerting menacing pressure on their livelihoods—a perfect example of cause and effect.

The other prerequisites for shaping a sensible grand strategy are based on humanitarian principles, and they should be rather self-evident. Unfortunately, economic principles seem to reign supreme in most decision-making processes at the expense of humanitarian ones. But what goes around comes around; a dispirited force—of people and their ideas—is a recipe for defeat. Remember the words of Sun Tzu, who said: "To secure ourselves against defeat lies in our own hands, but the opportunity of defeating the enemy is provided by the enemy himself." You may also recall Walt Kelly's cartoon figure Pogo, the central character of a long-running daily American comic strip, who came to the painful realization: "We have met the enemy and he is us!"

Knowing What You Are Doing

It is important to reiterate that the money executives desire to make for their business will need to come from buyers. Favorable terms for the procurement of input variables will need to come from vendors, and employee productivity will need to come from individual people. In other words, overall business performance is a matter of an executive's vision for what she or he wants to be done vis-à-vis the minds of people—vendors, employees, and buyers—and their subsequent attitude and behavior toward the business system. After all, influencing people's thinking (the level of cause) determines their behavior (the level of effect). This vision is what Boyd calls "commander's intent," which must be shared with leaders on every hierarchical level so that everyone knows their role in pursuing this vision—hierarchy of objectives—and understands their mission. How would you want people to feel, perceive, and behave in regard to the purpose for which the business system was created?

Consequently, there is no substitute for knowing what you are doing and why. And, in the words of Deming, you don't know what you're doing if you cannot explain what you do in terms of process. Process is not just about the mechanical performance of prescribed activities such as pushing buttons, entering data, answering the phone, or selling widgets. No, it's about adding value to a work flow. This requires knowledge about *why* your job is important within the value chain as an organic whole. That is why commander's intent must include the reason the added value is important to at least the next two higher hierarchical levels. Therefore, the pursuit of arbitrarily chosen numerical goals for an individual employee or a department makes no sense when the value chain as a whole is ineffective and inefficient. The pursuit of such goals is internally directed and thus prone to generating entropy, which endangers the survival of the system overall.

People who know what they are doing develop *Fingerspitzengefühl* for business processes—appreciation for what processes do in real time and what they are capable of doing. They are well aware of the four system defenses as explained by James Reason in his Swiss cheese model (see Figure 9.6, "The Swiss Cheese Model") and assure themselves that their decisions and subsequent actions will not create latent or active failures that would threaten to disrupt the system's integrity.

Such employees can decide for themselves where to focus and direct their attention. People who are generally identified as key talents are such people. They are the glue that keeps even dysfunctional systems together, preventing them from folding back into themselves, especially under chaotic and uncertain economic conditions—but not for long. They are typically the first to resign—jump ship—because they experience a lack of vision and support from their leaders up and down the hierarchy, thus giving rise to the so-called war for talent. In the absence of clear commander's intent, people do what they think is best for the business or for themselves, which makes the business vehicle appear to be rudderless and out of control.

Why and How

Systemic problems are perceived by many people to be without solution, which makes responsible leaders erroneously believe there is nothing they can do to solve them. However, allowing these serious problems to persist or recur is unsustainable.

Nothing happens by accident, which means that results, effects, or outcomes are governed by distinct cause-and-effect relationships. In addition, those results, effects, or outcomes are generated by—and originate from—distinct relationships between means and ends (see Figure 10.1).

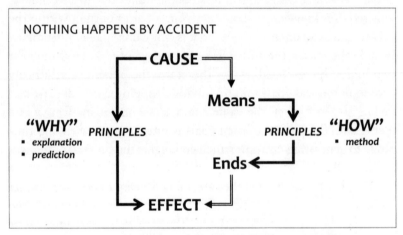

Figure 10.1: Cause and Effect versus Means and Ends

In a cause-and-effect relationship, cause represents one's thoughts and effect is one's real-life experience. An effect can be brought about by a choice of ends, each with their own means to an end. For example, once you diagnose the root cause of a systemic problem, you can create an authentic solution (= a means) that will restore system integrity (= an end).

Relationships between cause and effect are explained with principles answering the *Why* question. Relationships between means and ends are described by principles answering the *How* question—methods by which an end can be achieved. Consequently, a single effect is obtainable through a single mean or a choice of means that vary in nature and character, generating either intended or unintended consequences.

For example, there are cause-and-effect relationships between:

- Cutting cost and increasing net profits
- Increasing a system's capability and increasing net profits

In general, the end result of cutting cost is achieved by means of operational efficiency measures, which are explained through economic principles. And the end result of increasing a system's capability is achieved by means of reducing common-cause variation, which relies on methods that are derived from principles of quality—that are indicative of a unifying vision.

A decision maker's choice of a means to an end is at the heart of every decision-making process. After all—as we saw in Chapter 8, under "Charting an Itinerary Toward Your Destination"—decisions are the result of a trade-off between:

Critical Success Factors. Product quality, which determines operational effectiveness and thus how buyers and users experience a brand

Prerequisites. Process quality, which determines operational efficiency

Risk. The possibility and probability that unintended consequences will occur, combined with the estimated cost of risk mitigation

A decision maker chooses a means to an end based on the principle(s) explaining cause and effect. Therefore, if you believe in the validity of principles that explain the need for cost reduction because they increase net profits, you would never choose any means to an end that aims to reduce common-cause variation. Moreover, believers in the principles of cost reduction are more likely to perceive means to increase the system's capability as an expense, which they believe will reduce net profits.

Alternatively, if you believe in the validity of principles that explain the need for increasing a system's capability, you would never choose a means to an end for the sole aim of reducing cost. Believers in the principles of increased system capability are more likely to perceive means to increase operational efficiency as an additional source of common-cause variation, which increases cost and thereby reduces net profits.

A critical reader will argue that not all effects are created equal; some generate short-term gains whereas others build long-term value. Note that decision makers may well choose their preferred means based on criteria by which their annual performance is evaluated. A performance review based on quarterly earnings and profitability may entice decision makers to put personal interest ahead of the business's sustainability.

The Way the Cookie Crumbles

Decision makers can either reject the validity of a cause-and-effect relationship or reject the appropriateness of a proposed means to an end. However, when they reject the underlying principles, they do so at their own peril. Those principles merely describe the way things are, thus ruling—predicting—the outcome of one's endeavors no matter if one believes a principle to be true or false, or if you already discovered them or not.

Principles derive their power from their predictive value. Not only does this power apply to the material realm, it is equally applicable to the nonmaterial realm, particularly where it concerns morality, ethics, and trust. For example, employees want to believe that leaders are trustworthy, that they walk their talk. That means when leaders proclaim that the company's employees are the business's greatest assets, they should not start laying them off one by one the minute profitability drops. When people are told they are assets but their experience is that of a liability, they lose faith in their leaders. And when they can no longer believe what they are told, their mental state takes a hit, which affects their physical state; they disengage from their daily work, stop caring about their employer, and start looking for employment elsewhere. Leaders should not blame employees for learning from experience.

Principles also rule the field of mathematics. According to your country of origin you will have learned one of the following acronyms for solving equations:

USA:	**PEMDAS**	Parentheses, Exponents, Multiplication, Division, Addition, Subtraction
Canada:	**BEDMAS**	Brackets, Exponents, Division, Multiplication, Addition, Subtraction
UK:	**BODMAS**	Brackets, Orders, Division, Multiplication, Addition, Subtraction

Needless to say, you can ignore the principles of mathematics, or you can apply any interpretation of your own choosing. However, know that you do so at your own peril, whether that materializes in the form of a low test score at school, an engineering disaster, or a poor business calculation. Unintended and unwanted outcomes will persist and recur until you change your decision.

Consequently, it is the task of every leader to discover and apply the principles that make a system—natural, man-made, and social—capable of performing successfully. Systems do not adapt to your favored principles or values. Instead, you will have to embrace those principles that facilitate those cause-and-effect relationships that bring a system to life!

You either embrace principles that work *with* the system, or you embrace principles that work *against* it. When working against a system, you are either going to break the system or the system is going to break you. That's the way the cookie crumbles.

The Missing Link in the Value Chain

A business system is going to experience systemic problems—friction and conflict—and ultimately collapse when the commander's intent violates the principles that facilitate the cause-and-effect relationship for optimal business performance.

A common misconception regarding system optimization is optimizing each individual link in the value chain separately and in isolation of each other. This sounds practical because individual leaders can then be given specific goals and held accountable for delivering on those goals. These goals are nearly always arbitrary numerical goals aimed at cutting cost, increasing efficiency, and raising the department's contribution margin.

Therefore, department leaders are now competing with each other to achieve and even over-deliver on their goals in order to increase their chances of a better performance review. As a result, the space in between individual links of the value chain becomes a no-man's-land for which no one is responsible because nobody has been authorized to integrate departments on either side of the space in between. That is why work flow can fall in the crack between silos of specialized knowledge and department leaders seem to be unanimous in their opinion: Not my problem!

We saw earlier that the space in between dictates—defines the specs—how processes on either side of the space in between must be organized and directed toward realization of the purpose for which the system was created. This organizing and directing is the missing link in the value chain.

Throughout this book you will have come across principles for organizing and directing, which is a primary function of business governance. Here are some examples:

Everything is created twice Thinking is cause Experience is effect	Cybernetics (*planning, executing, controlling*) Separation between planning and controlling
People, ideas, hardware—in *that* order	Humanity Ethics vs. Economics
Moral-Mental-Physical Leverage vs. "The end justifies the means"	Golden Rule (*law of reciprocity*): "Do unto others as you would have them do unto you."
Closed systems vs. Open systems Risk of incestuous amplification and entropy	Effectiveness (*capability and capacity*) vs. Efficiency
Interaction vs. Isolation	Wholeness vs. Separateness
Predatory cultivation The Black Knight Syndrome	Gold plating The Bigger, Higher, Faster, Farther Syndrome

Give more in *use* value than you take in *cash* value	Lowest cost producer vs. Lowest price competitor
Form follows function	Obvious choice supplier
Authentic solutions	Span of control
Unity of command	Unbroken line of command

When you consistently obtain unintended and unwanted results, the system is letting you know that your thoughts about cause and effect and means and ends are flawed. In other words, it's time for a mind shift; you should relinquish old favored principles and adopt new ones. That is the essence of *The Root Cause*.

Neither is there any point to arguing the merits of one tool, method, or leadership style vis-à-vis another, nor in discussing the validity of an observation (minor premise), when you conclude that the results are unintended and unwanted. Unfortunately, that is exactly where a lot of precious time is wasted. Take the gold-plating principle as an example. Why is "bigger, higher, faster, farther," the latest and greatest state-of-the art iteration of a tool or technology, more desirable than the previous "smaller, lower, slower, closer-by" iteration? What are the appropriate assessment criteria? What are the lessons learned when they are still producing unintended and unwanted outcomes? Unfortunately, there seems to be an obsession with creating rankings by the comparison of features, such as bigger, higher, faster, and farther. However, in the absence of objective criteria for determining why a tool or technology is relevant to the case at hand, ranking is just an exercise in futility. The appropriate criteria are the ones mentioned above: critical success factors, prerequisites, and risk.

Following the principles of a syllogism—a logically correct line of reasoning—there must be something wrong with your major premise—an implied relationship between cause and effect—when the means and ends relationship does not support the cause-and-effect relationship. Here is an example:

Major Premise. *If* I raise labor productivity (= profits divided by the cost of direct labor) (= cause), then profitability will increase (= effect).

Minor premise. I increased labor productivity (= ends) by reducing the cost of direct labor through increased automation and bought-in goods and services (= means).

Conclusion. Profitability increased.

Here is the criticism of the major premise: automation requires new investment in assets and specialized labor, while outsourcing requires more staff to manage contracts, which increases total cost and overhead cost. In the end, it is questionable if labor productivity will increase, whereas profits will most definitely plummet. Moreover, clients will not receive a faster, lower-cost, or better product or service.

If you emulate your main competitors, using the same principles for the governance of your business processes and for measuring success, then don't complain when you can only compete with them on price!

Consequently, decision makers become obsessed with price, which requires them to control cost to preserve their profit margin. Control means to have power or authority to regulate, restrain, verify (usually against some standard), direct, or command. The word "control" is derived from Medieval Latin *contrarotulus*, a "counter roll" or checklist (*contra*, against plus *rotulus*, list).[7] Unfortunately, when every proposed means to an end is assessed on its merits to immediately reduce cost, all other arguments—such as reallocation of resources—become mute.

Substituting the control factor vehicle capability for cost is an example of a tail-wags-the-dog story. It demonstrates an erroneous belief in the following major premise:

If I reduce cost to zero, *then* profits will be maximized.

Now, do you still value the major premise as explained by the principle of labor productivity? If not, would you be willing to commit to a mind shift and explore the principle of reducing common-cause variation? This would create a new major premise stating that:

If I reduce common-cause variation (= cause), *then* profitability will increase (= effect).

To embrace this major premise, a decision maker will have to believe in the validity of the principle regarding common-cause variation, and that is the crux of creating authentic solutions. Different outcomes originate from different belief systems, or mindsets. Unfortunately, incestuous amplification causes many decision makers to reject unfamiliar theories off hand.

Exploring different major premises, instead of ranking solutions—such as tools, technology, and best practices—or practicing management by objectives by setting arbitrary numerical goals or appraising performance are at the heart of Deming's life work.

BUSINESS GOVERNANCE AND LEADERSHIP

Strangely enough, many firmly held principles, values, and beliefs about being successful in business are used to justify and defend the choice of major premises that, at the end of the day, undermine a business system's effectiveness. In other words, these premises require executive decision makers to sacrifice the value chain's capability and capacity in order to squeeze out one more dollar in net profits for the quarterly report. These premises are prime examples of predatory cultivation that I have called the Black Knight Syndrome. These premises create systemic problems that are, ultimately, unsustainable.

Systemic problems are symptoms of a failing system. Businesses fail due to poor design, organization or structure, implementation or operation, maintenance, and management of their systems, which undermine their performance capability and capacity.

Those symptoms will only go away once their root cause(s) are removed. Let me explain. When you have been to a movie theater, you know that you cannot eliminate any unintended and unwanted images from the screen by rubbing, painting, replacing, or even removing that screen. The only solution is to take the movie—the projected images' root cause—from the projector, and to replace it with new and different images.

Consequently, every initiative to reduce the costly effect of systemic problems fails until you reduce or eliminate its root cause(s)—the occurrence of a specific act, circumstance, or incident that you chose as a condition for achieving your intended outcome. In other words, you will need to rewrite your major premise.

After all, when experiments with different conditions for the achievement of your intended outcome fail, you will need to consider the possibility that your major premise is flawed. In other words, you will have to change your dominant-level of thinking. Within the context of our example, that means reconsidering the business system's true purpose—the specific reason for which it was created in the first place.

You will know when you are successful when the condition for achieving your revised outcome—the minor premise—produces intended and wanted consequences that enhance your revised intended outcome. Success includes the realization that, as Eckhart Tolle explained in his book *The Power of Now*, "once you understand the root of the dysfunction, you do not need to explore its countless manifestations."

Incongruent Leadership Behavior

The value chain is comparable to any other form of vehicle—on land, on and under water, in the air, or in space—in the sense that it is a means to an end. Whatever you commit yourself to doing, it can only be accomplished—be successful—with the use of the vehicle.

This implies that responsible leaders feel compelled to develop that vehicle's capability (its skill set) to perform and its capacity (throughput volume per unit of time and frequency) to deliver its products and services. Note that a more capable system is also more efficient in the use of its capacity because less capacity is taken up by creating waste.

Then which principle explains why leaders of any vehicle, except for the value chain, dedicate themselves to optimizing their vehicles as an integrated whole, whereas those leading a value chain seem ignorant, or indifferent toward sacrificing their vehicle's capability and capacity to make an extra buck? They must have different definitions of success.

Since form follows function, I can only assume that business leaders have a different perception of the function—the purpose—of their vehicle. That's the eternal dichotomy between growth and development, increasing bottom-line results or increasing the value chain's capability and capacity for realizing its purpose.

This dichotomy represents the fork in the road: a choice between following the beaten track that leads to more and better of the same results, including disengaged employees, the war for talent, and attrition price wars, or embarking on the less traveled path, which, in the end, will make all the difference.

Both system development (increasing a system's capability and capacity) and system growth (increasing a system's size and form) are functions of business governance. Whether to pursue system development or system growth is a function of leadership; the continual improvement of conditions—including interpersonal relationships—under which people work.

Executives who deliberately decide to increase operational efficiency at the expense of effectiveness by committing predatory cultivation on their value chain must not have much appreciation for the value chain. Appreciation is a function of understanding and insight into the complex, interdependent processes that the business system performs. People, thoughts, and things are liked, loved, cherished, and protected to the extent they are understood. And research[8] shows that the majority of executives are perplexed by system complexity; they don't understand the principles that facilitate the nine separate links of the value chain to work together as a singular, unique, integrated, and open system.

CEO Effectiveness

Every business starts with an idea or an ideal. Successful manifestation of that idea or ideal requires a vehicle, which is the only means to an end available. And a vehicle's effectiveness is measured against its journey and destination. Vehicle effectiveness is thus a function of its business governance, the extent to which the vehicle conforms and aligns with the intended journey and its stated destination.

It is the task of leadership to formulate descriptions of and specifications for business governance of the vehicle (form), its journey (function), and its destination (itinerary). Think of business governance as an ongoing project—the supply of capability potentiality—and of leadership as its project management, the provision of focus and direction, and the allocation of resources.

Because vehicles are composed of many processes that are complexly interdependent of each other, and because they are performed on shared resources, we simply cannot be aware of all cause-and-effect relationships that determine success and failure. In addition, vehicles operate within dynamic environments that cause a vehicle to experience new and unforeseen circumstances. Failure to adjust or adapt the vehicle will result in misalignment between the vehicle, the journey, and its destination, which causes systemic problems. Consequently, business governance is necessarily an iterative process (see Figure 10.2).

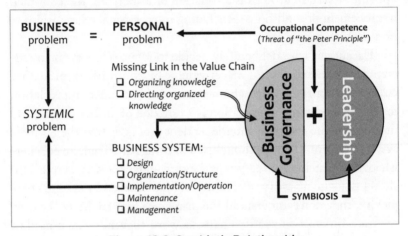

Figure 10.2: Symbiotic Relationship

Success in the role of CEO depends on one's level of occupational competence—a symbiotic relationship between business governance and leadership. Business governance is responsible for the system's capability and capacity, and leadership is responsible for interpersonal relationships among all employees as they utilize the business system's capability and capacity.

The function of a chief executive is thus to assume ultimate responsibility for keeping the vehicle, journey, and destination well aligned. Therefore, she or he received ultimate authority to change the business system's design, organization or structure, implementation or operation, maintenance, and management; in other words, to execute business governance.

Exercising ultimate authority over business governance requires skilled leadership, which was defined by Colonel John R. Boyd as "the art of inspiring people to enthusiastically take action toward the achievement of uncommon goals." Goals are uncommon because of the hierarchy of objectives; each department has its own objectives, but each departmental objective supports the purpose for which the system as an organic whole was created.

The word "executive" in the CEO title suggests responsibility for the execution of something—and I believe that something is exercising ultimate authority over business governance. This includes delegating authority to individual managers down the hierarchical chain of command. Although individual managers can be held accountable for their (in)actions, responsibility remains ultimately with the chief executive. And as organizations grow, the chain of command is extended, causing the chief executive to become further removed from operational processes. The challenge regarding exercising authority is losing influence when authority is used in an autocratic manner, as was discussed when explaining the CEO dilemma in Chapter 1. After all, people who are hired for their skills, expertise, and experience don't like being told how to do their job. This is what Steve Jobs had to say on this topic: "It doesn't make sense to hire smart people and tell them what to do; we hire smart people so they can tell us what to do."

Commander's intent is a leadership style aimed at gaining influence by explaining why an assigned mission is important to the success of a business as a whole. Consequently, commander's intent requires a sound understanding of a business as an organic whole—how a business functions as a singular, unique, integrated, and open system.

In addition, the HFACS framework[9] lists the category of *organizational influences*—which consists of organizational climate, resource management, and organizational process—as the first system defense against disintegration and collapse. And establishing good organizational climate, resource management, and organizational process requires keen insight into the functioning of a business system as an integrated whole.

It seems that successful exercise of ultimate authority over business governance should be conducted through vision—based on morality and humanity—and understanding of a business system's mechanics. And assuming ultimate responsibility for the organization of knowledge and direction of the business system toward realization of its intended purpose—the missing link in the value chain—requires proper initiation, preparation of a leader's mind, and understanding how the brain functions.

It should be evident by now that business governance needs a unifying vision for its brand identity, and leadership needs a vehicle in order to become the obvious choice supplier to its intended target audience. Therefore, CEO effectiveness depends on a symbiotic relationship between business governance and leadership.

CALLED TO CEO ADVENTURE

Leadership development should not be about filling one's tool bag with the latest-and-greatest tools, *n*-step secrets, or best practices for improving inter-personal relationships; instead, it should be about developing practical wisdom. After all, embarking on a CEO adventure is about an executive leader's human maturation.

Because human maturation is about a mind shift—changing our thoughts—*The Root Cause* is less concerned with practical actions or activities that you can implement once you are back at your desk. After all, thought is the level of cause—the theories that predict the outcome of our life experiences.

Therefore, the assignment of the returning heroic CEO, the master of two worlds, is knitting together humanitarian principles of the spiritual world with economic principles of the world of common day. For example, many systemic problems seem to be without solution because of a decision maker's firm, unquestioned beliefs or assumptions that such a solution must be based on a specific economic principle. However, the solution for a seemingly unsolvable systemic problem requires invariably the use of spiritual (path of the heart) and humanistic principles. This implies that what is often described as an economic crisis is more likely to be a moral crisis—a denial or even rejection of humanistic principles.

Consequently, the so-called take-home value of *The Root Cause* is a personal awakening, a recognition of recurring patterns of behavior, or an opening of one's heart and eyes to the power of clearly discernable relationships between cause and effect and means and ends that determine success and failure of a business as an organic whole. Personal awakening is an invisible and immaterial aspect of vehicle capability (see Figure 9.14, "Aspects of Vehicle Capability"). Personal awakening is a choice, a call to adventure.

Authentic solutions are not complex or difficult, but they are different, which requires an open mind. In her lectures, Marianne

Williamson teaches how *A Course in Miracles* interprets the well-known line from the Bible "Many are called but few are chosen" as "Everyone is called but few care to listen." Every executive leader receives the call to adventure—to examine what she or he believes or assumes implicitly to be valid and true regarding executive leadership. Note that the universe does not send you a voice or text message, an email, or tweet. Calls go out to you either because you want to go of your own volition, when you are lured away by something or someone, when you blunder into an unfamiliar situation, or when you are forced to go by an external power. Now you know; forewarned is forearmed. Are you willing to accept the call this time around?

WHAT HAPPENS NEXT?

Have you ever made a decision and known intuitively that something about that decision was not right? Have you ever heard the small, still voice of your unconscious mind telling you there must be another way? Those were calls to adventure! Yes, the suggestion of changing your dominant level of thinking might be a radical idea, but investing in more of the same tried but failed solutions, while hoping for a different outcome, is insane. Not only that, it's also bad for business, and for your career!

The good news about the need for a new level of thinking is that it opens doors to possibilities and opportunities that were previously unattainable, while it provides a rich source of creativity, innovation, and fun. More good news comes from Joseph Campbell: "Furthermore, we have not even to risk the adventure alone; for the heroes of all time have gone before us; the labyrinth is thoroughly known; we have only to follow the thread of the hero-path."[10]

The bad news is that no one can change your dominant-level of thinking for you. Hence, Colonel John R. Boyd's compelling "To Be or to Do" speech, which he concludes as follows:

> In life there is often a roll call.
> That's when you will need to make a decision.
> To Be [somebody of importance]
> or to Do [something important].
> Which way will You go?

BIBLIOGRAPHY

Axelrod, Alan. *Patton's Drive: The Making of America's Greatest General.* Guilford: The Lyons Press, 2009.

Brickhill, Paul. *Reach for the Sky: The Story of Douglas Bader, Legless Ace of the Battle of Britain.* Cutchogue: Buccaneer Books, 1954.

Briggs, John P., and David F. Peat. *Looking Glass Universe: The Emerging Science of Wholeness.* New York: Simon & Schuster, Inc., 1984.

Browne, Robert. *SYS-TAO: Western Logic ~ Eastern Flow. An Emerging Leadership Philosophy.* Oklahoma City: Millichap Books, 2015.

Burlingham, Bo. *Small Giants: Companies That Choose to Be Great Instead of Big.* New York: Portfolio/Penguin, 2005.

Campbell, Joseph. *The Hero with a Thousand Faces.* Novato: New World Library, 2008; *The Masks of God, Vol. 4: Creative Mythology.* Arkana, 1991. (USA) Inc., 1991; *The Power of Myth with Bill Moyers.* New York: Anchor Books, 1991.

Coram, Robert. *Boyd: The Fighter Pilot Who Changed the Art of War.* New York: Back Bay Books, 2002.

Dahl, Roald. *The Gremlins: The Royal Air Force Story by Flight Lieutenant Roald Dahl. The Lost Walt Disney Production.* Milwaukee: Dark Horse Comics, 2006.

Deming, W. Edwards. *Quality Productivity and Competitive Position.* Massachusetts Institute of Technology, 1982.

Diamond, Jared. *Collapse: How Societies Choose to Fail or Succeed.* New York: Penguin Group (USA) Inc., 2005.

Frankl, Viktor E. *Man's Search for Meaning: An Introduction to Logotherapy.* Boston: Beacon Press, 1963.

Freiberg, Kevin L., and Jacquelyn A. Freiberg. *Nuts!: Southwest Airlines' Crazy Recipe for Business and Personal Success*. Austin: Bard Press, Inc.

Gimian, James, and Barry Boyce. *The Rules of Victory: How to Transform Chaos and Conflict—Strategies from The Art of War*. Boston: Shambhala Publications, Inc., 2008.

Hill, Napoleon. *Think and Grow Rich*. Hollywood: Wilshire Book Company, 1999.

Jakab, Peter L., and Rick Young. *The Published Writings of Wilbur & Orville Wright*. Washington, D.C.: Smithsonian Books, 2000.

Keirsey, David. *Please Understand Me II: Temperament, Character, Intelligence*. Prometheus Nemesis Book Company, 1998.

Latzko, William J., and David M. Saunders. *Four Days with Dr. Deming: A Strategy for Modern Methods of Management*. Reading: Addison-Wesley Publishing Company, 1995.

Melman, Seymour. *Profits without Production*. New York: Alfred A. Knopf, Inc., 1983.

Murphy, Joseph. *The Power of the Subconscious Mind*. New York: Prentice Hall Press, 2008.

Neave, Henry R. *The Deming Dimension*. Knoxville: SPC Press, 1990.

Peter, Laurence J., and Raymond Hull. *The Peter Principle: Why Things Always Go Wrong*. New York: William Morrow & Company, Inc., 1969.

Pirsig, Robert M. *Zen and the Art of Motorcycle Maintenance: An Inquiry into Values*. New York: Harper Collins Publishers, 1974.

Porter, Michael E. *Competitive Advantage: Creating and Sustaining Superior Performance*. New York: The Free Press, 1985.

Rapaille, Clotaire. *The Culture Code: An Ingenious Way to Understand Why People Around the World Live and Buy as They Do*. New York: Broadway Books, 2006.

Reason, James. *Human Error*. Cambridge: Cambridge University Press, 1990; *Managing the Risks of Organizational Accidents*. Aldershot, England: Ashgate Publishing Limited, 1997.

Richards, Chet. *Certain to Win: The Strategy of John Boyd, Applied to Business*. Bloomington: Xlibris Corporation, 2004.

Schucman, Helen (scribe). *A Course in Miracles*. Mill Valley: The Foundation for Inner Peace, 1976.

Schumacher, Ernst F. *Small Is Beautiful: A Study of Economics as if People Mattered.* London: Blond & Briggs Ltd., 1973.

Sinek, Simon. *Start with Why: How Great Leaders Inspire Everyone to Take Action.* New York: Penguin Group (USA) Inc., 2009.

Stack, Jack, and Bo Burlingham. *The Great Game of Business: The Only Sensible Way to Run a Company.* New York: Crown Business, 1992.

Tieger, Paul D., Barbara Barron, and Kelly Tieger. *Do What You Are: Discover the Perfect Career for You Through the Secrets of Personality Type.* New York: Little, Brown and Company, Hachette Book Group USA, 2014.

Tolle, Eckhart. *The Power of Now: A Guide to Spiritual Enlightenment.* Novato: New World Library, 1999.

Tyreman, David. *World Famous: How to Give Your Business a Kick-Ass Brand Identity.* New York: AMACOM, 2009.

Tzu, Sun. *The Art of War: Translation, Essays, and Commentary by the Denma Translation Group.* Boston: Shambhala Publications, Inc., 2001.

US Marine Corps. *Warfighting: Marine Corps Doctrinal Publication 1.* Washington D.C.: Department of the Navy, 1997.

Wattles, Wallace D. *The Science of Getting Rich: Financial Success through Creative Thought.* New York: Barnes & Noble, Inc., 2007.

Wheeler, Donald J. *Understanding Variation: The Key to Managing Chaos.* Knoxville: SPC Press, 1993.

Wiegmann, Douglas A., and Scott A. Shappell. *A Human Error Approach to Aviation Accident Analysis—The Human Factors Analysis and Classification System.* New York: Routledge, 2016.

Williamson, Marianne. *A Return to Love.* New York: Harper Collins Publishers, 1992.

NOTES

Dedication and Introduction

1. Alfred de Musset—*Translation:* "I do not know where my road goes, but I walk better when my hand holds yours."
2. Chuck Lucier, Rob Schuyt, and Edward Tse, "CEO Succession 2004: The World's Most Prominent Temp Workers," *Strategy + Business* 39, (Booz Allen Hamilton), Summer 2005.
3. Robert Coram, *Boyd: The Fighter Pilot Who Changed the Art of War* (New York: Back Bay Books, 2002), 285.
4. From Eckhart Tolle's *The Power of Now: A Guide to Spiritual Enlightenment*, New World Library (Novato CA.) and Namaste Publishing (Vancouver, B.C. Canada), 1999, 163.
5. S. Berman and P. Korsten, "Capitalizing on Complexity, Global Chief Executive Officer Study," *IBM Institute for Business Value* (New York: Somers, 2010).
6. Matthew 5:38–40.
7. John R. Boyd, "The Strategic Game of ? and ?," *Unpublished presentation* (1987), slide # 23.
8. W. Edwards Deming, *Out of the Crisis* (MIT Press, 1982), chapter 11, "Commons Causes and Special Causes."
9. William Latzko and David Saunders, *Four Days with Dr. Deming* (New York: Pearson, 1995), chapter 9, "The Funnel."

Chapter 1

1. Laurence J. Peter and Raymond Hull, *The Peter Principle: Why Things Always Go Wrong* (publisher not identified, 1992).
2. Douglas A. Wiegmann and Scott A. Shappell, "Human Error Analysis of Commercial Aviation Accidents: Application of the Human Factors Analysis and Classification System (HFACS)," *Aviation, Space, and Environmental Medicine,* 72(11), 2001, 1006–1016.

3. Michael Patrick Lynch, *True to Life: Why Truth Matters* (Cambridge, MA: MIT Press, 2004). Lynch, a professor of philosophy at the University of Connecticut and head of the Humanities Institute there, defines intellectual integrity as "recognition of the need to be true to one's own thinking; to be consistent in the intellectual standards one applies; to hold one's self to the same rigorous standards of evidence and proof to which one holds one's antagonists; to practice what one advocates for others; and to honestly admit discrepancies and inconsistencies in one's own thought and action."

4. John R. Boyd, "A New Conception of Air-to-Air Combat," *Unpublished presentation* (1976), slide #24.

5. Modern advanced autopilots, in combination with flight management computers can do much more than maintaining heading, altitude, and airspeed.

6. Michael E. Porter is the Bishop William Lawrence University professor at the Institute for Strategy and Competitiveness, based at the Harvard Business School. He is a leading authority on competitive strategy and the competitiveness and economic development of nations, states, and regions.

7. Michael E. Porter, *Competitive Advantage: Creating and Sustaining Superior Performance* (New York: Free Press, 1985), 11–15.

8. ITIL, acronym for Information Technology Infrastructure Library, is a set of practices for IT service management that focuses on aligning IT services with the needs of business.

9. William J. Latzko and David M. Saunders. *Four Days with Dr. Deming: A Strategy for Modern Methods of Management*, (MA: Addison-Wesley, 1996), 96.

10. Napoleon Hill, *Think and Grow Rich* (Hollywood: Wilshire Book Company, 1999), 105.

11. Michael E. Porter, Jay W. Lorsch, and Nitin Nohria, "Seven surprises for new CEOs," *Harvard Business Review* 82(10), 2004, 62–75.

12. In complex aircraft, Fly-by-Wire, and Flight Management Computers, this connection is maintained through computers and electric servo engines, which makes the connection indirect.

13. S. Berman and P. Korsten, "Capitalizing on Complexity, Global Chief Executive Officer Study," *IBM Institute for Business Value* (New York: Somers, 2010).

14. Tom Baker and Sean J. Griffith, "Predicting Corporate Governance Risk: Evidence from the Directors' and Officers' Liability Insurance Market," *Chicago Law Review* 74 (2007): 487.

15. John R. Boyd, "Patterns of Conflict," *Unpublished Paper* (1986), slide #143.
16. Ibid., slide #144.

Chapter 2

1. *Wikipedia*, Carl Philipp Gottfried von Clausewitz was a Prussian general and military theorist who stressed the "moral" and political aspects of war.
2. US Marine Corps, "MCDP 1: Warfighting" *Washington, DC: United States Marine Corps*, (1997).
3. See also Sir Karl Popper on falsification/problem of induction. It is impossible, Popper argues, to ensure a theory to be true; it is more important that its falsity can be detected as easily as possible. See http://en.wikipedia.org/wiki/Karl_Popper#Falsification.2Fproblem _of_induction.
4. Marianne Deborah Williamson (born July 8, 1952) is an American spiritual teacher, author, and lecturer. She has published 10 books, including four *New York Times* number one bestsellers.
5. Marianne Williamson, *A Return to Love* (New York: HarperCollins, 1992), 52–53.
6. The few is likely a reference to Sir Winston Churchill's famous wartime speech at the conclusion of The Battle of Britain: "Never in the field of human conflict was so much owed by so many to so few."
7. Wallace D. Wattles, "How Riches Come to You," in *The Science of Getting Rich* (New York: Barnes & Noble, Inc., 2007), 24.
8. Sun Tzu, "Form," in *The Art of War: Translation, Essays, and Commentary by The Denma Translation Group* (Boston and London: Shambhala, 2001).
9. Gossen's first law of diminishing marginal utility: A law of economics relevant to decision making stating that as a person increases consumption of a product—while keeping consumption of other products constant—there is a decline in the marginal utility that person derives from consuming each additional unit of that product.

Chapter 3

1. James Gimian and Barry Boyce, "The Basic Practice," in *The Rules of Victory*, 116.
2. Lisanne Bainbridge, "Ironies of automation," *Automatica* 19(6), 1983, 775–779.

3. I use the term *machine* in order to be in alignment with the concept of a human–machine interface, even though I describe the value chain as an organism rather than a mechanism.

4. John P. Briggs and David F. Peat, "Entropy and the Paradox of Life," in *Looking Glass Universe*, 160.

5. An excellent example of converting nonproductive human energy back into productive energy can be found in the must-read book *The Great Game of Business* by Jack Stack, founder and CEO of SRC Holdings at Springfield, MO.

6. S. Berman and P. Korsten, "Capitalizing on Complexity, Global Chief Executive Officer Study," *IBM Institute for Business Value* (New York: Somers, 2010).

7. Chuck Spinney, "Iraq Invasion Anniversary: Inside the Decider's Head," March 22, 2013, http://chuckspinney.blogspot.com/search?q=incestuous.

8. Erich Jantsch, quoted in Briggs, *Looking Glass Universe*, 181.

9. Dr. Russell Lincoln Ackoff was an American organizational theorist, consultant, and Anheuser-Busch Professor Emeritus of Management Science at the Wharton School, University of Pennsylvania.

10. Joseph, Campbell, *The Hero with a Thousand Faces* (Novato: New World Library, 2008).

Chapter 4

1. Ken Olson, President of Digital Equipment Corporation, 1977.

2. *Merriam-Webster Online* defines a syllogism as "a deductive scheme of a formal argument consisting of a major and a minor premise and a conclusion."

3. *Ceteris paribus*: "all other things being equal."

4. Thomas Paine, in *The American Crisis*.

5. Aristotle.

6. Sir Karl Popper (1902–1994) was an Austrian-British philosopher who is generally regarded as one of the greatest philosophers of science of the twentieth century. His views on the scientific method favored empirical falsification: a theory in the empirical sciences can never be proven, but it can be falsified, meaning that it can and should be scrutinized by decisive experiments. If the outcome of an experiment contradicts the theory, one should refrain from ad hoc maneuvers that evade the contradiction merely by making it less falsifiable.

7. Oscar Wilde.

8. From Joseph Campbell's *The Hero with a Thousand Faces* Copyright © Joseph Campbell Foundation (jcf.org) 2008. P 48. Used with permission.

9. From Joseph Campbell's *The Hero with a Thousand Faces* Copyright © Joseph Campbell Foundation (jcf.org) 2008. P 49. Used with permission.

10. Bhagavad Gītā, 2:22–24.

11. From Johann Wolfgang von Goethe's *Freudvoll und leidvoll:*

> *Freudvoll*
> *Und leidvoll,*
> *Gedankenvoll sein,*
> *Langen*
> *Und bangen*
> *In schwebender Pein,*
> *Himmelhoch jauchzend,*
> *Zum Tode betrübt;*
> *Glücklich allein*
> *Ist die Seele, die liebt.*

12. http://www.enlightened-spirituality.org/Zen_Humor.html.

13. From Joseph Campbell's *The Hero with a Thousand Faces* Copyright © Joseph Campbell Foundation (jcf.org) 2008. P. 163. Used with permission.

14. From Joseph Campbell's *The Hero with a Thousand Faces* Copyright © Joseph Campbell Foundation (jcf.org) 2008. P 188. Used with permission.

15. Miguel de Cervantes. "I never thrust my nose into other men's porridge. It is no bread and butter of mine; every man for himself, and God for us all."

16. From Joseph Campbell's *The Hero with a Thousand Faces,* Copyright © Joseph Campbell Foundation (jcf.org) 2008. P. 188. Used with permission.

17. From Joseph Campbell's *The Hero with a Thousand Faces* Copyright © Joseph Campbell Foundation (jcf.org) 2008. P 94-95. Used with permission.

18. From Joseph Campbell's *The Hero with a Thousand Faces* Copyright © Joseph Campbell Foundation (jcf.org) 2008. P 115-116. Used with permission.

19. Prof. Barry Schwartz is an American psychologist and the Dorwin Cartwright Professor of Social Theory and Social Action at Swarthmore College.

20. Russell L. Ackoff, "On Learning and Systems That Facilitate It," *The Center for Quality of Management Journal* 5(2), Fall 1996, https://

citeseerx.ist.psu.edu/viewdoc/download?doi=10.1.1.203.758&rep=rep1 &type=pdf.

21. John Boyd would have described such a person as someone who knows more and more about less and less until she or he knows everything about nothing.

22. Ernst F. Schumacher, *Small Is Beautiful*, 33.

23. Russell L. Ackoff, "On Learning and Systems That Facilitate It."

24. From Joseph Campbell's *The Masks of God: Creative Mythology* © 1991, Digital Edition, Copyright © 2016 © Joseph Campbell Foundation (jcf.org). Used with permission.

25. William McDonough, "A Centennial Sermon," *Perspecta* 29 (1998), 78–85.

26. From Joseph Campbell's *The Hero with a Thousand Faces* Copyright © Joseph Campbell Foundation (jcf.org) 2008. P. 196. Used with permission.

27. In psychology, this form of mental stress is referred to as cognitive dissonance.

Chapter 5

1. Philip Kotler is a Professor of International Marketing at the Kellogg School of Management at Northwestern University.

2. Benjamin Franklin, *Poor Richard's Almanack*.

3. "Machines don't fight wars; people do, and they use their minds."

4. *Understanding Variation: The Key to Managing Chaos*, 2nd Ed., by Donald J. Wheeler, PhD, © 2000 by SPC Press, Knoxville, Tennessee, U.S.A. All Rights Reserved, 140.

5. Watch award-winning filmmaker Christopher Nupen's capture of the spirit of one of the greatest musicians of the twentieth century in his classic documentary, *Jacqueline du Pré and the Elgar Cello Concerto*.

6. Alan Axelrod, *Patton's Drive: The Making of America's Greatest General*. Globe Pequot, 2010, 34/5.

7. Joseph Campbell with Bill Moyers, *The Power of Myth* (1988). The PBS documentary was originally broadcast as six one-hour conversations between mythologist Joseph Campbell (1904–1987) and journalist Bill Moyers.

8. Colin Macmillan Turnbull was a British-American anthropologist who came to public attention with the popular books *The Forest People* and *The Mountain People*, and one of the first anthropologists to work in the field of ethnomusicology.

9. Physicist James Clerk Maxwell defined a governor as a part of a machine by means of which the velocity of the machine is kept nearly

uniform, notwithstanding variations in the driving power or the resistance.

10. Marshall Goldsmith, PhD, "How We Opened the World's Eyes to Coaching," (http://www.marshallgoldsmith.com/articles/how-we -opened-the-worlds-eyes-to-coaching/?utm_source=05+-+SCC+ Coaching+Is+for+Winners&utm_campaign=01+-+SCC+How+It+ Started&utm_medium=email): "Yesterday's management approach was becoming less and less relevant as we struggled to find a better way. We wholeheartedly believed and still do that way was through coaching. Back then, coaching was considered a sign that the person being coached had a 'problem'. That they had issues. Today, having a coach is a positive, prestigious thing. Today, you're a winner if you have a coach. You are someone the company is investing in because the leadership believes you are and can be an even greater leader."

Chapter 6
1. Napoleon Hill, Chapter II: "Desire," in *Think and Grow Rich*.
2. Ibid., 42.
3. Wallace D. Wattles, Chapter 6: "How Riches Come to You" in *The Science of Getting Rich*, 24.
4. Professor Philip Kotler.
5. US Marine Corps, "MCDP 1: Warfighting."
6. Black Friday: (in the US) the day after Thanksgiving, noted as the first day of traditional Christmas shopping, during high crowds of consumers are drawn to special offers by retailers.
7. George Stalk, Jr., "Time: The Next Source of Competitive Advantage," *Harvard Business Review*, July 1988.

Chapter 7
1. Rafael Aguayo, *From Dr. Deming: The American Who Taught the Japanese about Quality*.
2. Peter L. Jakab, *The Published Writings of Wilbur and Orville Wright*, 83.
3. Ibid.
4. Watts S. Humphrey (1989). *Managing the Software Process*, Addison-Wesley Professional.
5. From "The Girl in the Golden Atom" by Ray Cummings, *All-Story Weekly*, March 15, 1919, 205. Attributions to Albert Einstein and Mark Twain are unsupported.
6. John R. Boyd, "Organic Design for Command and Control," *A discourse on winning and losing* (1987), slide 8.
7. Ibid.

8. Ibid., slide #4.

9. Ibid.

10. John R. Boyd, "Organic Design for Command and Control," *A discourse on winning and losing* (1987), slide 11.

11. Timothy Fuller (1778–1835) was a US Representative from Massachusetts. He was the great-grandfather of inventor and thinker R. Buckminster Fuller.

12. Volatility is the rate at which the numeric value of a measurement increases or decreases over a given period of time. If this numeric value fluctuates rapidly in a short time span, it is termed to have high volatility. If this numeric value fluctuates slowly in a longer time span, it is termed to have low volatility.

13. Common-cause variation: https://en.wikipedia.org/wiki/Common _cause_and_special_cause_(statistics).

14. Examples of common-cause variation: https://en.wikipedia.org/wiki /Common_cause_and_special_cause_(statistics).

15. Characteristics of special-cause variation: https://en.wikipedia.org /wiki/Common_cause_and_special_cause_(statistics).

16. Examples of special-cause variation: https://en.wikipedia.org/wiki /Common_cause_and_special_cause_(statistics).

17. The difference between capacity and capability can be likened to a set of golf clubs and an individual player's skill set. Each club is specifically designed with the capacity in terms of distance and arc of the trajectory to facilitate a particular stroke, while the successful delivery of that stroke—with as little variation between strokes, under all conditions of terrain and weather—depends on the capability of each individual player. Therefore, a better set of golf clubs (rated on their specific capacity) does not improve any player's skill (= capability). Only a skillful player is capable of harnessing the benefits of clubs with a higher capacity for accuracy and distance.

18. https://deming.org/management-system/funnel-experiment.

19. Lisanne Bainbridge, "Ironies of Automation," *Automatica* 19(6), 1983, 775–779.

20. James T. Reason, PhD, is a British psychologist, author of the book *Human Error*. His principal research area has been human error and the way people and organizational processes contribute to the breakdown of complex, well-defended technologies such as commercial aviation, nuclear power generation, process plants, railways, marine operations, financial services, and healthcare institutions. His error classification

and models of system breakdown are widely used in these domains, particularly by accident investigators.

21. Tom Baker and Sean J. Griffith, "Predicting Corporate Governance Risk," 487.

22. http://www.southamconsulting.net/resources/HogHandbook.pdf.

23. James Reason, *Human Error* (Cambridge University Press, 1990), 118.

24. John D. Lee, "Review of a Pivotal Human Factors Article: 'Humans and Automation: Use, Misuse, Disuse, Abuse.'" *Human Factors: The Journal of the Human Factors and Ergonomics Society* 50(3), 2008, 404–410.

25. Thomas B. Sheridan and Raja Parasuraman, "Human-Automation Interaction," *Reviews of Human Factors and Ergonomics* 1(1), 2005, 89–129.

26. Raja Parasuraman and Thomas Riley, "Humans and Automation: Use, Misuse, Disuse, Abuse," *Human Factors: The Journal of the Human Factors and Ergonomics Society* 39(2), June 1997, 233.

27. Ibid., chapter 2, 95.

28. See Rasmussen, Pedersen, and Goodstein, 1995.

Chapter 8

1. Waste can be defined as cost that is incurred but failed to create use value for a target audience.

2. Milton Friedman, leader of the Chicago school of economics, and winner of Nobel Prize in Economics in 1976, had an article published in the New York Times on September 13, 1970, in which he promoted the idea that the sole purpose of a firm is to make money for its shareholders.

3. The name Mephistopheles is associated with the Faust legend of an ambitious scholar, based on the historical Johann Georg Faust. In the legend, Faust makes a deal with the Devil at the price of his soul, Mephistopheles acting as the Devil's agent.

4. John R. Boyd, "The Strategic Game of ? and ?," *Unpublished presentation* (1987), slide # 58.

5. Napoleon Hill, *Think and Grow Rich*, 42.

6. British psychologist James Reason—author of a seminal study of human error—concluded, "Although we cannot change the human condition [human fallibility] we can change the conditions under which humans work."

7. This passage is widely attributed to Abraham Lincoln, but according to the discussion in QuoteInvestigator.com, it was first said in 1684 in a popular work of apologetics titled "Traité de la Vérité de la Religion Chrétienne" by Jacques Abbadie, who was a French Protestant based in Germany, England, and Ireland. He said, ". . . *ont pû tromper quelques hommes, ou les tromper tous dans certains lieux & en certains tems, mais non pas tous les hommes, dans tous les lieux & dans tous les siécles.*" This also appeared without attribution in September 9, 1885, in *The Syracuse Daily Standard* (Syracuse, New York), "Prohibitionists in Arms: The Third Party Declare War to the Knife on Democrats and Republicans," page 4, column 4.

8. Robert M. Pirsig, *Zen and the Art of Motorcycle Maintenance*, chapter 19.

9. Ibid.

10. Robert M. Pirsig, *Zen and the Art of Motorcycle Maintenance*, chapter 20.

Chapter 9

1. Clotaire Rapaille, a French marketing consultant and the CEO and founder of Archetype Discoveries Worldwide, has published 17 books with topics ranging from psychology, marketing, sociology, and cultural anthropology.

2. Peter L. Jakab, *The Published Writings of Wilbur and Orville Wright*, (Smithsonian Institution, 2016), 17.

3. Ibid., 136.

4. Physicist James Clerk Maxwell defined a governor as a part of a machine by means of which the velocity of the machine is kept nearly uniform, notwithstanding variations in the driving power or the resistance.

5. James Reason, *Managing the Risks of Organizational Accidents*, (Aldershot, England: Ashgate Publishing Limited, 1997), 71.

6. Ibid., 70.

7. This confirms the importance of business governance in determining business performance. How we develop the value chain's capability and capacity of realizing its mission depends on an executive's ability to apply the missing link in the value chain.

8. James Reason, *Managing the Risks of Organizational Accidents*, (Aldershot, England: Ashgate Publishing Limited, 1997), 10.

9. W.A. Wagenaar and J. Groeneweg, "Accidents at Sea," 587–598.

10. Robert M. Pirsig, *Zen and the Art of Motorcycle Maintenance*, chapter 6.

11. Synthesis either resolves the conflict between thesis and antithesis or forms the final stage in the development of a new theory or system or the adjustment of existing ones.

12. From *Wikipedia*: The human condition is defined as "The characteristics, key events, and situations, which compose the essentials of human existence, such as birth, growth, emotionality, aspiration, conflict, and mortality." This is a very broad topic, which has been and continues to be pondered and analyzed from many perspectives, including those of religion, philosophy, history, art, literature, sociology, psychology, and biology. As a literary term, "the human condition" is typically used in the context of ambiguous subjects such as the meaning of life or moral concerns.

13. That is, the biblical "Do unto others as you would have them do unto you" (Matt. 7:12).

14. From *Wikipedia*: Viktor Emil Frankl was an Austrian neurologist and psychiatrist as well as a Holocaust survivor. His bestselling book *Man's Search for Meaning* chronicles his experiences as a concentration camp inmate, which led him to discover the importance of finding meaning in all forms of existence, even the most brutal ones, and thus a reason to continue living.

15. Thornton Niven Wilder was an American playwright and novelist.

16. John R. Boyd and Ginger Gholston Richards, *Patterns of Conflict*, edited by Chester W. Richards and Franklin C. Spinney (Defense and the National Interest, 2007), slide #149.

17. Chuck Spinney, *The M & M Strategy*.

18. John R. Boyd, "The Strategic Game of? and ?," *Unpublished presentation* (1987), slide #35.

19. Ibid., slide #49.

20. Ibid., slide #44.

21. People on the other side of the argument such as employees, trade unions, vendors, suppliers, clients, authorities, etc. Ibid.

22. John R. Boyd, "The Strategic Game of? and ?," *Unpublished presentation* (1987), slide #59.

23. From: *A Guide to Writing an Executive Development Plan*.

24. Peter L. Jakab, *The Published Writings of Wilbur and Orville Wright*, 153.

25. Matthew 7:12; see also Luke 6:31.

26. Robert Coram, Chapter 28 in *Boyd: The Fighter Pilot Who Changed the Art of War* (Little, Brown, 2002), 380.

27. Ibid., Chapter 13, 194.

Chapter 10

1. W. Edwards Deming, *The New Economics for Industry, Government, Education*, 103.

2. John R. Boyd and Ginger Gholston Richards, *Patterns of Conflict*, edited by Chester W. Richards and and Franklin C. Spinney (Defense and the National Interest, 2007), slide #139.

3. Ibid., slide #141.

4. Ibid., slide #144.

5. This is particularly true for countries where unionization is low and labor laws are rather lax, such as the United States of America.

6. See Chapter 9, "'Motherhood' Position."

7. John R. Boyd, "Organic Design for Command and Control," *A discourse on winning and losing* (1987), slide #37.

8. S. Berman and P. Korsten, "Capitalizing on Complexity, Global Chief Executive Officer Study," *IBM Institute for Business Value*, (Somers, New York, 2010).

9. See Chapter 9, figure 9.14, under the section "Basic Stick-and-Rudder Skills."

10. From Joseph Campbell's *The Hero with a Thousand Faces* Copyright © Joseph Campbell Foundation (jcf.org) 2008. P. 18. Used with permission.

INDEX

Page numbers followed by *f* indicate figures.

Abbadie, Jacques, 354*n*7
Ackoff, Russell:
  on education, 319
  on growth *vs.* development, 149
  on information, knowledge, and
    understanding, 153
Acute conditions/problems, 169
Aeronautics metaphor for business
  governance, 117–118, 276–283
Affirming the consequent, 135
Agility:
  defined, 226–227
  merits of, 305
Aha-erlebnis, 172, 177
Aircraft, gold plating and, 175–176
Alice in Wonderland (Carroll), 260
Amazon, 243
Amoral behavior, 298–299
Analysis:
  limitations of, 185
  synthesis *vs.*, 286, 286*f*
  (*See also* Deductive logic)
Analytic knife, 208–211
  and classic understanding of a
    system, 285
  effectiveness, 209–210, 209*f*
  and making money, 211
A–N–C axiom, 277
Aristotle, 149
Artificial horizon, 117–118
The Art of War (Sun Tzu), 78
Authenticity and creativity, 313–318
  and critical thinking, 319–320
  cultivating intellectual infrastructure,
    316–318
  development from within, 315–316,
    315*f*
  freedom and, 314–316

Authentic solutions (business gremlin),
  9, 120–125
  characteristics, 42
  creating, 123, 123*f,* 338–339
  discovery of root causes, 122–123,
    123*f*
  entering the twilight state, 123–124
  poor decision-making processes and,
    124–125
  principles that explain cause-and-
    effect relationships, 122–123
  recognizing our dominant mental
    programming, 121
Automation, 96
  degrees of, 234
  drawbacks of, 225–226
  human-centered, 235–236
  human factors in, 235–237
  and human-machine interface,
    233–234
  innovating, 234
Autopilot, 17
Aviation metaphor for business
  governance, 117–118, 276–283

Bainbridge, Lisanne, 97–98
"Being in the zone," 171
Benchmark:
  for diagnosing systemic problems,
    243–244
  for measuring vehicle's success, 242
Best practices, 109
  analysis and, 185
  as fallacies, 39, 134–136
  tampering and, 223–224
  (*See also* Gold plating)
"Be" *vs.* "do," 54–56
Bhagavad Gita, 143

Bigger, Higher, Faster, Farther
    Syndrome, 87
Bigger-picture perspective, 172–176
    business governance, 183–184
    and business system environment,
        185–186
    creating a common point of
        departure, 176–186
    destination, 182–183, 239–267
    form of ownership, 184–185
    high price of gold plating, 174–176
    journey, 179–180, 189–203
    scale preferences, 173–174
    vehicle, 180–182, 205–237
Biological organizations, human-made
    organizations vs., 115
Black Knight Syndrome, 90–91, 97,
    310, 333
Booz Hamilton, 51
Boyd, John R.:
    being versus doing, 54
    on "Bigger, Higher, Faster, Farther
        Syndrome," 87
    on breakdowns in moral behavior, 301
    on commander's intent, 324–325
    on consequences of moral-mental-
        physical conflict, 300–301
    on determining the nature of a
        system, 10
    on education, 316
    and F-15 jet engine design, 177–178
    on Fingerspitzengefühl, 131, 317
    on friction, 60
    on gold plating, 88, 175
    on handling change, 17, 60–61, 198,
        316
    on importance of employees to
        bottom-line results, 167
    on "incestuous amplification," 114, 317
    on interaction, 217–218
    on leadership, 263
    leadership defined by, 215
    on machines vs. people, 98
    on mismatch between mental image
        and reality, 52, 63
    on morality, 140
    on national goal, 322
    on occupational competence, 17
    on overspecialization in education, 44
    on pursuing a unified vision, 55–56
    on skilled leadership, 336
    on strategy, 257
    on success, 321–322
    "To Be or to Do" speech, 3–4, 340
    on unifying vision, 55–56
    on varieties of interaction, 300
    on vehicles, 287–288
    on vision rooted in human nature, 323
Boyd: The Fighter Pilot Who Changed the
    Art of War (Coram), 59
Brand identity:
    as cooperative venture, 34
    differentiation, 251f
    as integral part of use value, 244–256
    money vs. quality, 254–255
    and obvious choice supplier, 86
    as part of template for charting
        itinerary, 259–261
    quality as destination's highest value,
        249–254, 249f–251f
Branson, Sir Richard, 225
Braun, Wernher von, 129
Brickhill, Paul, 269
Bridge words, 272, 273f
Briggs, Katharine Cook, 64
Brown, Paul, 90
Buddhism, 150–151, 153
Bühler, Karl, 172
Burlingham, Bo, 85–86
Business as usual, change vs., 17
Business design, need for, 155–157
Business governance, 21f
    authenticity and creativity, 313–318
    basic stick-and-rudder skills, 276–283
    and bigger-picture perspective,
        183–184
    CEO effectiveness, 335–338
    chief executive and, 333–338
    chief executives and, 305–306
    creativity and, 51
    defined, 302
    executive development policy,
        302–313
    form of ownership, 184–185
    how to understand the vehicle, 283–
        296, 284f
    incongruent leadership behavior,
        334–335
    providing stability, 274–276
    responding to events from
        environment, 296–302
    structure as key to, 271–274, 273f, 274f
    working on the business, 271–276
Business gremlins, 59–125

authentic solutions, 120–125
committing to the core business
purpose, 74–77
defined, 71
everything is created twice, 115–120
as excuses, 73
form follows function, 78–83
interaction *vs.* isolation, 106–115
means and ends, 84–92
mental images and perception of
reality, 61–67
and twilight state, 71–73
wholeness *vs.* separateness, 94–106
Business mechanics:
big-picture perspective, 172–176,
178–179, 179*f*
effect of CEO's failure to understand,
46
as methodology, 9–10
stewardship/craftsmanship and, 164
Business processes, organizational
hierarchy *vs.*, 34–35
Business schools:
curriculum's failure to address
systemic problems, 240
and dominant mental programming,
74
and executive development, 302
lack of interest in business
governance, 50
and value chain analysis, 43
Business systems:
as comparable to mechanical
machine, 95
conditions for evolution, 111
interaction with environment,
110–111
monetary beneficiaries of, 166
(*See also* Vehicle)

Campbell, Joseph:
on aftermath of hero's journey, 146
and hero's journey, 11, 141
on master of two worlds, 157
on mystagogue, 148
on perspective, 174
on those who reject the call to the
journey, 142
on wasteland, 154
Capability:
capacity *vs.*, 221*f*, 247, 352*n*17
defined, 252

operation efficiency *vs.*, 310
quality-orientation and, 254
vehicle, 311–313, 311*f*
of vehicle, 252–253
Capability-limiting performance, 219
Capacity:
capability *vs.*, 221*f*, 247, 352*n*17
defined, 219
"Capitalizing on Complexity" (IBM
report), 10, 48–49, 294
Carroll, Lewis, 260
Cause-and-effect relationships:
character and nature of systems,
79–80
and committing to core business
purpose, 74–75, 75*f*
entering the twilight state, 71–73
input–process–output model, 80–82
knowing why, 68–70, 69*f*
principles explaining, 67–73, 78–82,
85–89, 128–132, 130*f*
"why" questions, 326
CEO dilemma, 46–47, 47*f*, 62, 141,
269, 304, 337
CEOs:
business governance and leadership,
333–338
called to adventure, 338–339
commander's intent, 321–333
dangers of rejecting underlying
principles of cause and effect/
means and ends, 328–329
defying the Peter Principle, 52–56
effectiveness, 45–46
growth *vs.* development of value
chain, 53*f*
heroic, 141–147
importance of commander's intent,
324–325
making a difference, 53–54, 53*f*
missing link in the value chain,
329–333
no on-the-job learning, 50–52
as operators skilled in business
governance, 305–306
role of, 319–340
survival skills, 49–50
taking control of the business, 48
"to Be" *vs.* "to Do," 54–56
ultimate authority, 45–46, 46*f*
"why" and "how" questions, 326–328,
326*f*

Certain to Win (Richards), 323–324
C.H.A.F.P.I.L.O.T.™ test, 99–102,
    99*f*, 102*f*
Change:
    about, 1
    business as usual *vs.*, 17
    in context of systemic problems, 25
Change management, 36–40
    allocating resources to implement
        change, 36–37
    appointing/supporting a project
        manager, 37–38
    dedicated project organization, 38*f*
    identifying root causes, 39
    identifying the problem owner, 37
    problem definition checklist, 41–42
    project management *vs.*, 38
    trusting the problem-solving process,
        39–40, 40*f*
Character:
    defined, 65–66
    influence on perception, 64–66, 65*f*
Chief executives (*see* CEOs)
Churchill, Sir Winston, 299
Classic quality, 292–293
Classic understanding of a system, 284*f*,
    285–288, 286*f*, 288*f*
    constructive induction, 287–288
    destructive deduction, 287
Clausewitz, Carl von, 60
Closed circuit, 193–195
Coaching, 350*n*10
*Collapse: How Societies Choose to Fail or
    Succeed* (Diamond), 93
Commander's intent, 321–333, 337
Commodities, 193
Common-cause variation, 220–222
    defined, 220–222
    human error as, 282–283
    systemic problems and, 227
Communication:
    craftsmanship and, 168–170
    problems arising from measures
        intended to improve operational
        efficiency, 197
    and vehicles, 217
Compassion, 150
Competition, conflict and, 198–199, 199*f*
Competitive advantage, 216–217
Complexity:
    as result of evolution, 309–310, 309*f*
    and root-cause analysis, 124

routine operations and, 1
sources of, 290*f*
uniqueness of social systems, 310
Conclusion (of syllogism), 133
Conflict (*see* Friction and conflict)
Conscience, 143*f*, 144
Conscious mind, 66–67
Constructive induction, 287–288
Control variables, 22
Core business purpose, committing to,
    74–77
    entering the twilight state, 77
    principles that explain cause-and-
        effect relationships, 74–75, 75*f*
    recognizing dominant mental
        programming, 74
    utility or profit margin, 75–76, 77*f*
Corruption, defined, 301
Cost–benefit analyses, 84, 96
Cost-cutting, 105
A Course in Miracles, 131, 148, 339
Covey, Stephen, 115
Craftsmanship, 167–172
    communication and, 168–170
    for guidance when interacting with
        business environment, 218–219
    and knowing the goal of a
        methodology, 170–171
    and quality, 171–172
Creativity, 51, 52
Critical success factors:
    change management initiatives and, 41
    and decision maker's choice of means,
        327
    decision maker's responsibility to
        provide description of, 244
    defined, 29
    and itinerary outcomes, 263
    and purpose of system, 79, 98–99
The Culture Code (Rapaille), 272
Cybernetic process, 21*f*, 213, 306–307,
    306*f*

Dahl, Roald, 71
Data, in hierarchy of incremental value
    in learning, 151
Decision-making process, 165, 165*f*,
    327
Deductive logic, 286, 287
Deep domain expertise, 150
Defensible competitive advantage,
    216–217

Deming, W. Edwards:
   on change, 161
   on compartmentalization, 175
   and Constancy of Purpose, 74
   on experience without theory, 68, 320
   on explaining work in terms of
      process, 325
   on frequency of one employee causing
      unintended/unwanted results,
      28–29
   on ignorance and consequences, 4
   on intrinsic motivation, 230
   on money-centered management,
      246
   on numerical targets, 218
   on profits, 205
   on systemic nature of most problems,
      120
   on systemic nature of most results, 11,
      28, 48
   System of Profound Knowledge, 137
   on tampering, 224
   on workers' desires and goals, 322
Describing, prescribing *vs.*, 8–9
Design, and needs of members of target
      audience, 155
Destination, 182–183, 239–267
   as benchmark for diagnosing systemic
      problems, 243–244
   benchmark for measuring vehicle's
      success, 242
   brand identity as integral part of use
      value, 244–256
   charting itinerary toward, 256–264
      (*See also* Itinerary)
   defined, 182
   fork in the road as determining event,
      265–267
   and loss of direction, 265–267
   problems with treating money as
      highest value of, 245–249
   quality as highest value of, 249–254,
      249*f*–251*f*
   and risks of tampering, 246–247
   as vehicle's purpose, 241–244
Destructive deduction, 287
Determinism, 95
Development:
   and destination, 182–183
   growth *vs.*, 149, 210
Development from within, 315–316,
   315*f*

Devil's Triangle, 22, 322
Diamond, Jared, 93
Differentiation, 251*f*
Diminishing marginal utility, first law
   of, 44, 91
Discernment:
   challenging a dilemma with formal
      logic, 132–136, 133*f*, 134*f*
   and *Fingerspitzengefühl*, 130–131
   importance of personal beliefs to
      business outcomes, 131–132
   mind shift and, 128–136
   and principles for explaining cause-
      and-effect relationships, 128–132,
      130*f*
   and trade-off decisions, 162
   when best practices become fallacies,
      134–136
Dogma, 316
Drucker, Peter, 116, 121
Dysfunctional management, 212–213

Education (term), 315
Effectiveness of vehicle, 209–210, 209*f*
Effectiveness problems, defined, 27
Efficiency problems, defined, 27
Ego, 144–146
Einstein, Albert:
   on ambition and duty, 1
   on defining a problem, 41
   on insanity, 137
   on intuitive and rational minds, 162
   on levels of thinking, 5, 53, 137, 288
   on perfection of means, 88
   on quantitative measures, 167
   on staying with problems, 294
Electricity, as metaphor for exchange,
      191–198, 191*f*, 192*f*, 194*f*, 196*f*,
      199*f*, 201*f*, 202
Empirical falsification, 347*n*3, 348*n*6
Employee benefits, 278
Employees (*see* Human beings)
EMU (European Monetary Union),
   31–32
The E-Myth (Gerber), 271
Enterprise-wide problems, solving:
   crux of solving stubborn enterprise-
      wide problems, 137–141
   different levels of thinking, 138–139,
      139*f*
   mature leadership and, 139–141
      (*See also* Systemic problems)

Entropy, 111, 112*f*
  closed systems and, 113–114
  as result of friction/conflict, 111–112
  systemic problems and, 196
Environment, business-system:
  bigger-picture perspective, 185–186
  interaction with, 217–219
  as necessary context for
    understanding, 186
Environment, responding to events
    from, 296–302
  "motherhood" position, 299–302
  quality as an event, 297
  risk of amoral behavior, 298–299
  stimulation that makes us create the
    world in which we live, 299–302
Errors and violations, 280–283
  common-cause variation, 282–283
  latent conditions and, 281–282
Errors of commission, 280
Errors of omission, 280
European Monetary Union (EMU),
    31–32
Event, quality as, 265, 297
Everything is created twice (business
    gremlin), 115–120
  entering the twilight state, 118–120
  principles that explain cause-and-
    effect relationships, 117–118
  recognizing our dominant mental
    programming, 116–117
Evil, defined, 301
Evolution, complexity as result of, 309–
    310, 309*f*
Exchange:
  of cash value for use value, 190–200,
    191*f*
  electricity metaphor, 191–197, 191*f*,
    192*f*, 194*f*, 196*f*, 199*f*, 201*f*
  friction and conflict, 195–199, 196*f*,
    199*f*
  and interaction *vs.* isolation business
    gremlin, 199–200
Excuses, business gremlins as, 73
Executive development policy, 302–313
  complexity as result of evolution, 309–
    310, 309*f*
  education/organization/discipline of
    stakeholders, 312–313
  importance of vehicle control,
    304–308
  learning through osmosis, 303–304

  preconditions for success, 311–313, 311*f*
Executive underperformance, 6, 51, 266,
    267*f*, 304, 312
Extrinsic motivation, 230

Fachidiot, 150
Fallibility, value chain and, 95–96
Far from equilibrium environment,
    111–112
Feynman, Richard P., 59
Financial solutions to problems, 31 (*See
    also* Money, as sole quantifier)
Fingerspitzengefühl, 130–131, 199, 317,
    325
Firm infrastructure, defined, 19
Five forces analysis, 193
Flow, 26
Force of life, 148–155
  dark side of, 153–155, 230
  light side of, 149–153, 231
Fork in the road, 53–54, 53*f*, 265–267
Form (*see* Vehicle)
Formal logic, 132–136, 133*f*, 134*f*
Form follows function (business
    gremlin), 78–83, 206–213, 206*f*
  and "analytic knife," 208–211
  dysfunctional management, 212–213
  effect of mental programming,
    211–212
  entering the twilight state, 82–83
  intellectual curiosity, 207
  maintaining system integrity, 83
  principles that explain cause-and-
    effect relationships, 78–82
  recognizing our dominant mental
    programming, 78
Frankl, Victor, 297, 355*n*14
Franklin, Benjamin, 164
Freedom, 314–316, 315*f*
Free will, 11, 67
Freud, Sigmund, 145
Freudvoll und leidvoll (Goethe), 349*n*11
Friction and conflict, 60
  competition, 198–199, 199*f*
  entropy as result of, 111–112
  in exchange, 195–199, 196*f*, 199*f*
  as form of entropy, 200, 201*f*
  from measures intended to improve
    operational efficiency, 197
  stock buyback programs and, 256
  unintended consequences, 196–197,
    196*f*

and unit sales, 197–198
Friedman, Milton, 181, 254
Fuller, Buckminster, 161
Fuller, Timothy, 220
Function:
  misalignment with form, 78–83 (*See also* Form follows function)
  purpose *vs.*, 181
  (*See also* Journey)

Galilei, Galileo, 137
Gandhi, Mahatma, 52
Gates, Bill, 67
Gerber, Michael, 271
Goethe, Johann Wolfgang von, 347n3, 349n11
Going Solo (Dahl), 71
Gold plating:
  defined, 90
  effect on performance, 219
  high price of, 174–176
  as result of losing sight of quality as goal, 293
  and silo optimization, 87–89
  undermining operational effectiveness, 175–176
Goldsmith, Marshall, 350n10
Gossen, Hermann, 44, 91
Governance (*see* Business governance)
Gremlins (*see* Business gremlins)
Growth, development *vs.*, 149, 210
Growth share matrix, 195

Henderson, Bruce, 195
Heroic chief executive, 141–147
  call to adventure, 141–142
  fulfillment, 142–146
  journey of, 142f, 143f
  return, 146–147
Hero's journey, 11, 141–147
The Hero with a Thousand Faces (Campbell), 11, 141
HFACS (*see* Human Factors Analysis and Classification System)
Hierarchy of increasing value in content of learning, 151–153, 152f
Hierarchy of needs, 229, 299
Hierarchy of objectives, 214–217, 214f, 215f
Hill, Napoleon:
  on journey to riches, 190
  on knowledge, 43, 240

on use value and profitability, 250
Hiring process, 229–230
HMI (*see* Human–machine interface)
Honda, 200
"How" questions (means and ends), 326, 326f
Human beings:
  employees as sources of information/solutions, 230–231
  employee training needs, 236–237
  human-error phenomenon, 227–228
  human factors in automation, 235–237
  improving flexibility/speed of vehicle, 226–227
  making vehicle performance predictable, 225–227
  management theories about, 229
  personal beliefs about people, 228–231
  as problem solvers, 97–98
  specifications for job positions, 229–230
  vehicle success as dependent on, 224–231
Human-centered automation, 235–236
Human condition, defined, 355n12
Human conscience, 143f
Human energy, 110
Human error, 227–228
  and automation, 235
  as common-cause variation, 282–283
  happy employees as best prevention, 311
  and human–machine interface, 233
  skill-based errors and, 278
  slips and lapses, 278–280
  systemic problems and, 197
Human Factors Analysis and Classification System (HFACS), 278, 279f, 337
Human fallibility, 95–96
Human–machine interface (HMI), 103–104, 104f, 232–237, 232f
  automating human activity, 233–234
  compatibility mismatches, 233
  employee training needs, 236–237
  human factors in automation, 235–237
Human resources, defined, 19
H-Y War, 200

Id, 143–145
Ideology, 316
Inbound logistics, defined, 18
"Incestuous amplification," 114,
    317–318
Inductive logic, 286–288
Information:
    employees as sources of, 230–231
    in hierarchy of incremental value in
        learning, 151
Information flow, 24–26
Innovation, 200–204
    and business governance, 120
    cutting waste, 202–203
Input–process–output (IPO) model,
    20–22, 21f
    for competing business systems,
        80–82, 81f
    control variables, 22
Instinct (movie), 54–55, 314
Intellectual infrastructure:
    cultivating, 316–318
    risk of "incestuous amplification,"
        317–318
Intellectual integrity, 16, 346n3
Interaction *vs.* isolation (business
    gremlin), 106–115
    best practices, 109, 109f
    challenge to open systems, 112–113
    and competition, 199–200
    competition as manifestation of, 200
    entering the twilight state, 114–115
    need for open systems, 111–112,
        112f
    principles that explain cause-and-
        effect relationships, 110–114
    recognizing our mental programming,
        108–109
    resistance to change, 115
    risk of closed systems, 113–114
Interaction with business environment,
    217–219
Internal resistance, 196
"In the zone," 171
Intrinsic motivation, 230, 299
IPO model (*see* Input–process–output
    model)
"Ironies of Automation" (Bainbridge),
    97–98
Isolation *vs.* interaction (business
    gremlin) (*see* Interaction *vs.*
    isolation)

Itinerary:
    charting, 256–264
    development methodology, 264
    motivation for creating, 262–263
    quality of development process, 264
    quality of outcomes, 263
    and quest for "mojo," 257–258
    risk management, 264
    specifications, 261–262
    template for charting, 258–264,
        259f

Jantsch, Erich, 115
Japan, 137, 200
JIT (just-in-time) delivery, 202
Jobs, Steve, 155, 337
John Paul II (pope), 137
Journey, 189–203
    bigger-picture perspective, 179–180
    the exchange, 190–200, 191f
    function of, 189
    and innovation, 200–204, 201f
Jung, Carl, 64
Just-in-time (JIT) delivery, 202

Keirsey, David, 65
Kelly, Walt, 324
Kelvin, William Thompson, Lord, 295
Knowledge, in hierarchy of incremental
    value in learning, 151
Koch, Maréchal Ferdinand, 295
Kotler, Philip, 163, 193

Lapses, 278–280
Latent conditions, 281–282, 282f
Latent conditions/problems, 169
Law of the instrument (Maslow's
    hammer), 44–45
Lead time (time-to-market), 194–195
Learning, hierarchy of increasing value
    in content of, 152f
Learning through osmosis (*see* Osmosis,
    learning through)
Level(s) of thinking, 5, 7, 53, 120f, 137–
    139, 139f, 288, 340
Life cycle of products, 194–195
Life force (*see* Force of life)
Logic:
    challenging a dilemma with, 132–136,
        133f, 134f
    deductive *vs.* inductive, 286

Machine, 98–102, 99*f*, 102*f* (*See also*
  Human–machine interface (HMI))
Major premise, 132
Maltz, Maxwell, 66
Management by objectives (MBO),
  116, 120–121, 200
Management integration, 50–52, 50*f*,
  309*f*, 310
Marginal utility, first law of
  diminishing, 44, 91
Margins for error, economy's effect on,
  77, 90, 91, 105, 130
Market economy, 192, 192*f*
Marketing and sales, 19
Maslow, Abraham, 229, 299
Maslow's hammer (law of the
  instrument), 44–45
Master of two worlds:
  force of life, 148–155
  need for business design, 155–157
Master of Two Worlds, 146–157
Materialism, 95
Maxwell, James Clerk, 354*n*4
MBTI (Myers–Briggs Type Indicator),
  64
Mbuti Pygmies, 174
McGregor, Douglas, 229
Means and ends, 84–92
  entering the twilight state, 90–92
  gold plating silos of specialized
    knowledge, 87–89
  "how" questions, 326
  lack of secrets/silver bullets, 91–92
  obvious choice supplier, 86–87
  principles that explain cause-and-
    effect relationships, 85–89
  short-term gains, 85
  value chain integration, 89, 89*f*
Measurement of a problem, 31–33, 32*f*
Mechanical systems, 68–70
Mechanism, organism *vs.*, 24–26
Meditation, 294–295
Mental images:
  and perception of reality, 61–67
  recognizing our dominant mental
    programming, 63–64
Mental programming, 6–8
  business gremlins and, 71
  and committing to core business
    purpose, 74
  destination as business system's
    programming, 243–244

and misalignment of form and
    function, 78
  and perception of reality, 61–62
  recognizing our dominant
    programming, 63–64
Method, vehicle description based on,
  289–290, 290*f*, 291*f*
Miller, Henry, 127, 239
Mind shift, 127–157
  crux of solving stubborn enterprise-
    wide problems, 137–141
  different levels of thinking, 139*f*
  discernment and, 128–136
  and heroic chief executive, 141–147
  master of two worlds, 147–157
Minor premise, 132
Misalignment, origins of, 82
Missing link in the value chain:
  business governance as, 48, 271, 276,
    290, 329–333
  Peter Principle and, 43
  value chain integration as expression
    of, 89
Mojo, 85–86
Money, as sole quantifier:
  failing to understand variation,
    248–249
  opportunism—stewardship conflicts,
    247–248
  problems with treating money as
    highest value of destination,
    245–249
  quality *vs.*, 254–255
  and risks of tampering, 246–247
Moral compass, 166–167
Morality, 301
Morcom, Christopher, 127
"Motherhood" position, 299–302
MOTIQ (money, organization, time,
    information, quality) variables, 22
  (*See also* Prerequisites)
Motivation, intrinsic *vs.* extrinsic, 230
Myers, Isabel Briggs, 64
Myers–Briggs Type Indicator (MBTI), 64
Mythology, 146–157 (*See also* Campbell,
    Joseph)

Needs and wants, 163–164, 193
Nelson, Lloyd, 247
Network links, 96
Networks, defined, 96–97
Nodes, defined, 96–97

Noise (*see* Common-cause variation)
Nonconscious mind, 66
Norms, establishing, 27–28

Obvious choice supplier, 76, 86–87, 199, 250–251
Occupational competence, 16–17
Office of Continuous Learning and Career Management, U.S., 302–303
Offshoring, 96
Oligopolies, 76, 190–191
Open systems, 112–113, 217
Operational effectiveness:
  gold plating's undermining of, 175–176
  and operational efficiency, 197
Operational efficiency:
  decision makers' bias towards, 211–212
  effect of addressing, 31
Operations, defined, 18
Opportunism, 247–248
Organism, business as, 24–26
Organizational chart, 106–107
  translation of value chain into, 23–24
  value chain and, 18–24
Organizational facilities, 19–20 (*See also* C.H.A.F.P.I.L.O.T.™ test)
Organizational hierarchy, business processes *vs.*, 34–35
Organizational influences, 337
Organization and structure of the machine, 213–224
  hierarchy of objectives, 214–217, 214*f*, 215*f*
  influencing performance, 219–224
  interaction with one's environment, 217–219
Osmosis, learning through, 42–52
  CEO dilemma and, 46–47
  CEO effectiveness, 45–46
  diminishing marginal utility, 43–44
  executive development policy, 303–304
  and failures of business schools, 240
  and stuckness, 295
  taking control of the business, 48
Outbound logistics, defined, 18

"Painkillers" (short-term solutions), 121
Paradigm shifts, 7–8 (*See also* Fork in the road)
Patton, George, 125, 173, 271

PEC (planning–executing–controlling) cycle, 21, 21*f*, 306*f*
People (*see* Human beings)
Perception:
  and conscious mind, 66–67
  and free will, 67
  mental images and, 61–67
  mental programming and, 6–8
  and nonconscious mind, 66
  recognizing our dominant mental programming, 63–64
  temperament/character's influence on, 64–66, 65*f*
Performance, influencing, 219–224
  measuring variation, 220–223, 221*f*
  tampering with results, 223–224
Personal beliefs, importance to business outcomes, 131–132
Perspective (*see* Bigger-picture perspective)
Peter, Laurence J., 15
Peter Principle:
  and Achilles' heel of executive leadership, 16–17
  defined, 15
  defying, 52–56
  learning through osmosis, 42–52
  mind shift as antidote to (*see* Mind shift)
  at work, 15–57
Pirsig, Robert M.:
  and analytic knife, 208, 292
  on beauty, 302
  on classic understanding of a system, 285
  on differing views of quality, 164
  on peace of mind, 171
  on quality as continuing stimulus, 295
  on quality as event, 265, 297
  on quality as goal, 208, 249, 291
  on romantic understanding of a system, 284–285
  on stuckness, 294
Popper, Karl, 140, 347*n*3, 348*n*6
Porter, Michael:
  and analytic knife, 208
  on CEO dilemma, 46–47
  five forces analysis, 193
  Value Chain model, 18–19, 18*f*
Potential difference, 191–193
Practical wisdom, 149
The Practice of Management (Drucker), 116

Predatory cultivation, 27, 90–91, 211, 333, 335
Prerequisites:
  and change management initiatives, 41
  and character of business system, 79
  MOTIQ, 29
  as organization principles, 98–99
  profit margin as, 75
  and quality of itinerary development process, 264
  in scams *vs.* legitimate businesses, 212
  and transformation process, 210
  for vehicle capability, 312–313
Prescribing, describing *vs.*, 8–9
Prigogine, Ilya, 111, 115
Primary business functions, 19
Principles:
  importance of personal beliefs to business outcomes, 131–132
  in mathematics, 329
  solutions *vs.*, 9
Privately owned businesses, 185
Problem:
  defining, 28–30, 41–42
  measuring, 28, 31–33, 32*f*
  measuring severity of, 32*f*
  organizational hierarchy *vs.* business processes, 34–35
  risk of viewing from a financial perspective, 31
  root cause *vs.*, 33–34
  as structure, 272, 273*f*
  systemic (*see* Systemic problems)
  term defined, 26–27
Problem definition checklist, 41–42
Problem–Gravity chart, 39–40, 40*f*
Problem owner, identifying, 35–37, 35*f*
Problems, symptoms *vs.*, 29
Problem-solving process, trust in, 39–40
Process chart, 107
Process execution, sequence of, 215, 215*f*
Process mapping, 172–173
Process quality, 29
Process structure, 110
Procurement, defined, 19
Product life cycle, 194–195
Profit margins, 211
Profit potential, 192–193
Profits, allocation of, 255–256
Project management, change management *vs.*, 38
Project manager, 37–38

Project organization, 37, 38*f*
Proprietary processes, 20, 81–82
Publicly owned businesses, 185 (*See also* Shareholders)
Purpose (*see* Destination)
Pushing the envelope, 308

Qualitative arguments, 162
Quality:
  as an event, 265, 297
  classic, 292–293
  craftsmanship and, 171–172
  as destination's highest value, 249–254, 249*f*–251*f*
  as goal for vehicle, 208–209, 291
  goal of, 295–296
  as methodology, 106
  money *vs.*, 254–255
  romantic, 293–295, 298, 301
  and short-term earnings, 138
  and stewardship, 164
  vehicle description based on, 290–296
Quality assurance, 22
Quality improvement, 138
Quantitative arguments, 162

Racing teams/vehicles, 225, 252–253
Random variation, 220 (*See also* Common-cause variation)
Rapaille, Clotaire, 272
Reason, James:
  on human error, 98, 228, 278, 352–353*n*20
  Swiss Cheese model, 281–282, 282*f*
Recurring and persisting problems, 5–6
Reductionism, 95
Relevance, competition and, 199
Request for Proposal (RFP), 102
Responsibility, accepting, 35 (*See also* Problem owner)
Restriction of consciousness, 62–63, 63*f*
Reynolds, Sir Joshua, 319
Rice, Grantland, 79–80
Richards, Chet, 323–324
Roman Inquisition, 137
Romantic quality:
  destruction by money, 298
  morality and, 301
  understanding, 293–295
Romantic understanding of a system, 284–285, 284*f*
Routine operations, 1

Schopenhauer, Arthur, 116
Schultz, Peter, 230
Schumacher, E. F.:
    on development, 312–313
    on wisdom, 152
The Science of Getting Rich (Wattles), 75
Scientific method, 134*f*
Self, quest to discover, 142–143
Self-actualization, 229, 299
Senge, Peter, 155
Separateness, defined, 94
Service, defined, 19
Severity of a problem, measuring, 32*f*
Shakespeare, William, 1
Shappell, Scott, 278
Shareholders, 166, 184–185
Shewhart, Walter, 220
Short-term gains, 85, 116–117, 247–248, 254, 328
Silos/silo optimization, 109, 109*f* (*See also* Gold plating)
Sin, 144
Slips and lapses (skill-based errors), 278–280
Small Giants (Burlingham), 85–86
Small is Beautiful (Schumacher), 312–313
SMART (Specific, Measurable, Attainable, Realistic, and Time-related) goals, 116
Solutions:
    employees as sources of, 230–231
    principles *vs.*, 9
Southwest Airlines (SWA), 70, 216–217
Space, between component parts, 272–274, 330
SPC (statistical process control), 220
Special-cause variation, 222–224, 227
Specialization, 90–92
Specialty goods, 193
Stability, providing, 274–276
Stakeholders, 166, 312–313
Standardization, 89
Statistical process control (SPC), 220
Stevenson, Robert Louis, 189
Stewardship and craftsmanship, 161–186
    bridging the divide between needs and wants, 163–164
    conflicts with opportunism, 247–248
    defined, 165

for guidance when interacting with business environment, 218–219
    and moral compass, 166–167
    painting the bigger-picture perspective, 172–176
Stewart, Potter, 168
Stick-and-rudder skills, 279*f*, 280*f*
    aeronautics metaphor for business governance, 276–283
    errors and violations, 280–283
    slips and lapses, 278–280
Stock buyback programs, 256
Strategic direction, 29
Structure:
    of business system, 274*f*
    character and nature, 272–274
    as key to business governance, 271–274, 273*f*, 274*f*
Stuckness, 294–295
Substance:
    defined, 309
    vehicle description based on, 288–289
Success, as structure, 272, 273*f*
Summary of the Executive Core Qualifications (ECQs) and Related Leadership Competencies, 302–303
Sun Tzu, 78, 261, 324
Superego, 144
Suppliers, 202
SWA (Southwest Airlines), 70, 216–217
Swiss cheese model, 281–282, 282*f*, 325
Syllogisms, 132–133, 136, 331–332
Symptoms, problems *vs.*, 29
Synthesis:
    analysis *vs.*, 286, 286*f*
    defined, 354*n*11
    (*See also* Inductive logic)
Systemic problems:
    and cause-and-effect relationships, 326–328
    as CEOs' personal problems, 2, 49–50, 49*f*
    common-cause variation *vs.*, 227
    crux of solving stubborn enterprise-wide problems, 137–141
    factors in CEO effectiveness at handling, 61
    identifying, 26–36
    as root of dysfunction, 5–6
    stubbornness of, 2
System of Profound Knowledge, 137

Tale of the Gremlins, 71–72
Tampering:
  defined, 246
  from failing to understand variation,
    248–249
  risks of, 246–247
  when measuring performance,
    223–224
Target audience, use value and, 208,
  250, 251
Technology development, defined, 19
Temperament:
  defined, 65
  influence on perception, 64–66, 65*f*
Theory X/Theory Y, 229
Time-to-market (lead time), 194–195
"To be" *vs.* "to do," 54–56
Toffler, Alvin, 93
Tolle, Eckhart, 5
Toyota, 323–324
Trade-off decisions, 161–162
Training, 236–237
Trajectory of accident opportunity,
  281–282
Transformation process:
  control variables, 22
  and vehicle performance, 219
Tribus, Myron, 283
Turnbull, Colin, 174
Twain, Mark, 33, 34, 131
Twilight state:
  and business gremlins, 71–73
  defined, 71
  entering, 71–73
  making excuses, 73
Two-boss problem, 38

Underperformance (*see* Executive
  underperformance)
Understanding, 185–186
Understanding Variation (Wheeler), 170
Unifying vision, 55–56, 323–324
Unintended consequences:
  compatibility mismatches in HMI, 233
  dysfunctional management and, 212
  of friction and conflict, 196–197, 196*f*
  of gold plating, 88
  incidence of in stable systems, 227
  short-term fixes and, 320, 321
  as signal of need for mind shift, 331
  systemic problems and, 28, 48
  tampering and, 224, 246

Unit sales, 197–198
Universal Father, 147
Universal Mother, 147
Unsafe acts, 279*f,* 280–281, 280*f,* 282*f*
Urgency of problem, measuring, 33*f*
Use value, 190
  brand identity as integral part of,
    244–256
  and core business purpose, 75–76, 77*f*
  creating superior use value, 76, 77*f,*
    80–81
  and defensible competitive advantage,
    216
  defined, 75
  and input–process–output model, 80–82
  varying expressions of, 76
  vehicle's creation of, 208
Utility, 190
  and defensible competitive advantage,
    216
  defined, 75
  as experience of quality, 209
  and well-being, 207

Value chain:
  allocation of profits from, 255–256
  bottom-line results *vs.* capability/
    capacity, 53–54, 53*f*
  current state of, 30*f*
  embedded in value system, 156*f*
  exchange of cash value for use value,
    190–200, 191*f*
  executives as designers of, 155
  functions of, 18–19
  as input–process–output model, 20–22,
    21*f*
  lack of synthesis in business school
    study of, 43–44
  and law of Diminishing Marginal
    Utility, 43–44
  and life cycle of products, 194–195
  and obvious choice supplier, 86–87
  as organism *vs.* mechanism, 24–26
  organizational chart and, 18–24
  perfection of means within each link,
    86–87, 87*f*
  primary *vs.* support processes, 19–20
  risks of optimizing parts in isolation
    from each other, 329–333
  and substance, 309
  translation into an organizational chart,
    23–24

Value chain integration, 89, 89*f*
Value judgments, 293
Value system, 155, 156*f,* 200, 201*f,* 312
Variation:
    common-cause, 220–222, 227, 282–283
    failing to understand, 248–249
    measuring, 220–223, 221*f*
    special-cause, 222–224, 227
Vehicle, 205–237
    bigger-picture perspective and, 180–182
    business governance and, 283–296
    capability, 311–313, 311*f*
    classic understanding of a system, 284*f,* 285–288, 286*f,* 288*f*
    control, 304–308, 306*f*
    defensible competitive advantage, 216–217
    description based on method (how), 289–290, 290*f,* 291*f*
    description based on quality (why), 290–296
    description based on substance (what), 288–289
    destination as purpose of, 241–244 (*See also* Destination)
    effectiveness, 209–210, 209*f*
    form follows function, 206–213, 206*f*
    function of, 207
    how to understand, 283–296, 284*f*
    human beings as essential to success of, 224–231
    improving flexibility/speed of, 226–227
    influencing performance, 219–224
    and making money, 211
    making performance predictable, 225–227
    organization and structure of the machine, 213–224
    romantic understanding of a system, 284–285
    as structured hierarchy, 289–290
    as synthesis, 287–288, 288*f*
Violations, defined, 280
Vision:
    creating, 295
    unifying, 55–56, 323–324
Volvo Car Nederland B.V., 223

Wants and needs, 163–164, 193
Waste, cutting, 202–203
Wasteland, 154
Wattles, Wallace D., 75
What's in It for Me (WIIFM), 86
What the Bleep Do We Know!? (movie), 61
Wheeler, Donald J., 169
Wholeness, defined, 94
Wholeness *vs.* separateness, 94–106
    entering the twilight state, 105–106
    and human fallibility, 95–96
    and human–machine interface, 103–104, 104*f*
    humans as problem solvers, 97–98
    and machine organization of tasks, 98–102
    principles that explain cause-and-effect relationships, 96–104
    quality improvement, 105–106
    recognizing our dominant mental programming, 94–96
"Why" questions (cause-and-effect relationships), 153, 326–327, 326*f* (*See also* Cause-and-effect relationships)
Wiegmann, Doug, 278
WIIFM (What's in It for Me), 86
Wilde, Oscar, 139
Wilder, Thornton, 298–299
Williamson, Marianne, 68, 131, 338–339
Wisdom, 150–153
Work-breakdown structure, 214
Wright, Orville and Wilbur:
    on discovery of new principles, 310
    first successful flight, 205
    on flying skills, 307
    on intellectual curiosity, 207
    on merits of agile vehicles, 305
    on possibility of flight, 115–116, 240
    on skill and knowledge, 275–276
    understanding of instability, 226, 275

Yamaha, 200

Zen and the Art of Motorcycle Maintenance (Pirsig), 164
Ziglar, Zig, 193
Zone, being in the, 171

ABOUT THE AUTHOR

Hans Norden started his career in branch network support for the asset management division of a major Dutch bank at their Amsterdam headquarters. His responsibility was to assist field managers in solving problems, which made him better acquainted with the intricately interdependent nature of the division's business processes. Soon it became clear to him that he enjoyed the "business mechanics" of asset management more than asset management itself.

He found his calling when he was asked to join the bank's project management-consulting division, where he received his professional training in information analysis and change management. His favorite assignment is one where everyone acknowledges they have a big problem and nobody admits to having made a mistake—they are just doing their job. Such systemic challenges cause friction and conflict among different departments, especially because of their persistent nature and unfortunate tendency to linger for years.

For Hans, the biggest reward in guiding the process of solving a systemic problem is seeing the relief and happiness on the faces of those who struggled with failure, disappointment, and frustration far too long—those who were considering quitting.

When creating authentic solutions for solving unintended and unwanted consequences of systemic problems, he finds inspiration in the work by Dr. W. Edwards Deming on continual process improvement, Dr. James Reason on human error, and Colonel John R. Boyd USAF on maneuver warfare.

Hans founded his own company—Anticipated Outcome—in San Diego, California, for the purpose of offering root-cause analyses and change management services to high-level management decision makers. He delivers these services in the form of consulting, coaching, mentoring, training, and speaking engagements.

For more information, please visit:

RootCauseTheBook.com

AnticipatedOutcome.com

https://www.linkedin.com/in/hansnorden/